WOMEN IN ISLAM

WOMEN IN ISLAM

An Anthology from the Qur'ān and Ḥadīths

Translated & edited by
Nicholas Awde

HIPPOCRENE BOOKS, INC

Typeset and designed by Desert❦Hearts, London

ISBN 0-7818-1090-6

For information, address:
HIPPOCRENE BOOKS, INC.
171 Madison Avenue
New York, NY 10016
www.hippocrenebooks.com

Cataloging-in-Publication data available from the Library of Congress

Printed in the United States of America

Contents

Phonetic transcription of the Arabic alphabet used in the transliterations

ا	ā, ’	ظ	ẓ
ب	b	ع	c
ث	th	غ	gh
ج	j	ف	f
ح	ḥ	ق	q
خ	kh	ك	k
د	d	ل	l
ذ	dh, z	م	m
ر	r	ن	n
ز	z	ه	h
س	s	و	w, ū
ش	sh	ي	y, ī
ص	ṣ		
ض	ḍ	ء	’
ط	ṭ	ة	a, at

Introduction

The very first converts to Islam were the women of the Prophet Muḥammad's household, and religious writings have always preserved their status and rights as an integral part of the religion. An accessible compilation of religious references is therefore an essential point of reference for any focus on the role of women within Islam throughout the world.

This anthology contains translations of all major references to women in the Qur'ān and ḥadīths. The excerpts have, for the most part, been allowed to stand without comment. Of the several collections of ḥadīths, two are universally considered to be the most definitive and reliable—those of al-Bukhārī and Muslim. These are known as the *Ṣaḥīḥain*—the 'Two Sound Collections', meaning that each ḥadīth included has been judged to be authentic in every way, and so represents a true account of a witnessed episode in the life of the Prophet.

These narratives were transmitted by word of mouth via an unbroken chain, or *isnād*, of named and historically known individuals of trustworthy character, who ultimately heard a ḥadīth directly from someone who was present at the event or speech described. In this way, the ḥadīths have become an indispensible support for the Qur'ān and, although they are undoubtedly secondary texts, this does not diminish their relevance. Indeed, the material in this book clarifies the central position of women in the Revelation of Islam to the Prophet Muḥammad and its development by his followers.

The selections here are from al-Bukhārī's collection rather than Muslim's. Although both contain similar material, al-Bukhārī is acknowledged to be the clearer and more concise of the two, and it is his *Ṣaḥīḥ* which holds a special place in Islam as the pinnacle of all such collections.

*

Notes on the Selections

a) As with the ḥadīths, all excerpts from the Qur'ān in this anthology are new, original translations. Each selection is followed by a reference in brackets, e.g. (Q2:229) indicates Qur'ān, sūra (chapter) 2, āya (verse) 229, according to the ordering of most editions.

b) Sources for the ḥadīths are from al-Bukhārī's *Al-Jāmiᶜ al-Ṣaḥīḥ* (various editions). To aid cross-referencing, the bracketed figures following each selection refer to the most accessible English/Arabic edition, *The Translation of the Meaning of Sahih Bukhari*, edited by Muhammad Muhsin Khan (9 volumes), e.g. (5/87) indicates volume 5, page 87 of *The Translation.*

c) Although most ḥadīth selections from al-Bukhārī have case titles or interpretations appended to them, only those of particular relevance or interest have been included. Practically speaking, this does not detract from the meaning of the ḥadīths since opinions can differ over the meaning of individual ḥadīths, and many ḥadīths have several interpretations that are often accepted equally without conflict. In addition, there should be no cause for concern over verses of the Qur'ān being taken out of context; for the most part these were revealed separately and, only much later, was it agreed to arrange them into the order in which they are now found. 'Abrogating' and 'abrogated' verses (where, for any of a variety of reasons, one verse annuls or rectifies a verse that was revealed earlier) exist, but these are few in number and no consensus of opinion exists about them. This distinction is therefore ignored.

d) Classifications are for the sake of readability only; more comprehensive 'navigation' will be found via the Index. The selections themselves are not exhaustive, but few, if any, extracts of significance have been omitted[1]—in fact, there is a degree of (necessary) repetition. Where meaning has not been affected, a few ḥadīth selections are produced with sections of narrative cut from the text, and with asterisks inserted to indicate the missing material.

It may be appropriate here to note that in order to best understand the Qur'ān and Ḥadīth, "we must consider the general meaning of the word and not only the cause for which the word was revealed."[2]

Women in Islam

The Family of the Prophet

Wives

The eleven marriages of the Prophet Muḥammad were for a variety of reasons: some from personal affinity, some to widows with no one to turn to, while others were politically motivated to create or maintain alliances. He was not married to all of his wives at the same time.

They are, in chronological order: 1) In the early part of his life Muḥammad had only one wife, **Khadīja** (556–619). She was a wealthy merchant woman and he had worked as master of her caravans before marrying her around 595, when she was between 40 and 45. She died aged 65 and was the first to believe in the Prophet's Mission. 2) After her death he married a Quraish woman, **Sauda bint Zamᶜa** (596–674), in 631 when she was 35. She was the widow of Sakran, one of the Companions. 3) **ᶜĀ'isha** (614–678) was Abū Bakr's daughter. She was six when wed but the marriage was only consummated later when, in 623/624, she came of age. 4) **Ḥafṣa**, 18, was the daughter of ᶜUmar bin al-Khaṭṭāb and the widow of Khunais. She had recently returned with other Muslim exiles from Abyssinia and married Muḥammad in 625. Born in 607, her death is variously reported as being in 647/648, 661/662 or 665. 5) **Zainab bint Khuzaima** was a widow of ᶜUbaida. She was known as 'Umm al-Masākīn' or 'Mother of the Poor' on account of her generosity. Born in 595, she died soon after the marriage in 626 at the age of 31. 6) **Umm Salāma** (598/599–682/3), the widow of Abū Salāma. 7) **Zainab bint Jaḥsh**, 40, the divorced wife of the Prophet's adopted son Zaid. She died in 640/641 at the age of between 50 and 53. 8) **Juwairiyya bint Ḥārith** (605–670) was the daughter of the chief of the Mustaᶜliq tribe. 9) **Umm Ḥabība** (591–665) was the widow of ᶜUbaid and the daughter of Abū Sufyān, the leader of the Meccans who opposed Muḥammad. They were married by proxy while she was still in Abyssinia. 10) **Ṣafiyya** (628–670 or 672), married at 17 in 628, was the widow of Kinana, chief of the Jews of Khaibar. 11) **Maimūna** (602–681), the sister of ᶜAbbās and a widow, was married to Muḥammad when she was 51.

The Prophet also had at least two concubines: 1) **Raihana**, a Jew taken captive from the Quraiẓa tribe. 2) **Marya**, a Christian slave who was a gift from the ruler of Egypt.

Children

Khadīja was the only wife to bear the Prophet children — two (perhaps three) sons: **Qāṣim** and **ᶜAbdullāh** (or **Ṭāhir**), who all died in infancy; and four daughters: **Umm Kulthūm**, **Ruqayya**, **Zainab** and **Fāṭima**. They all married, but Umm Kulthūm and Ruqayya died before their father. Marya was the mother of the Prophet's son **Ibrāhim**, who died when he was two.

I
Hygiene

The case of a woman having three periods in a month

How are women who say that they are menstruating or pregnant to be held trustworthy? God has covered the topic of menstruation in the following words:

For it is not lawful for women to hide what God might have created in their wombs.

(Q2:228)

ʿAlī and Shuraiḥ say that:

If a woman brings clear proof that she has three periods a month through the witness of members of her most intimate family who have proved themselves to be good Muslims, then she is to be believed.

ʿAṭā adds:

One should also look at her previous cycles.

Ibrāhim agrees with this. ʿAṭā also says:

Menstruation can last from one day to 25 days.

Mu'tamar's father said:

I asked Ibn Sīrīn about the woman who said that she saw blood five days after her cycle had finished, and he replied: "Women know best about this sort of thing."

(1/193)

Abū 'l-ʿĀliya says:

Paradise is free from menstruation, urine and sputum.[1]

(4/304)

Umm ʿAṭiyya said:

We never counted for much any yellow or dark-coloured discharge (from our vaginas).[2]

(1/194)

ʿĀ'isha said:

We all set out to Mecca to do the *ḥājj*,[3] but before we arrived there I started menstruating. The Prophet came to me as I was weeping, and he asked: "What is the matter?"

"I am menstruating!"

He replied: "This is something which God has ordained for the daughters of Adam. Undo your hair and comb it. Then carry out all the rituals which any *ḥājj* pilgrim would usually perform—except for circumambulating the Kaʿba—until after you are clean."

ʿĀ'isha also said:

The Prophet sacrificed cows on behalf of his wives.

(1/177, 183, 187)

The Prophet said: "Menstruation is something which God has ordained for the daughters of Adam."

Some say that the first people to be sent menstruation were the Tribe of Israel, but the Prophet's explanation is the more plausible.

(1/177)

ʿĀ'isha said that Fāṭima bint Abū Ḥubaish asked the Prophet:

"I do not become clean,[4] so should I pray or not?"[5]

And the Prophet replied: "In this case it is a vein which is causing this bleeding, and not menstruation. So only when your real period begins should you stop your prayers, and when its power has gone, then wash the menstrual blood from you and pray."[6]

Ibn ʿAbbās says that the husband of such a woman is allowed to have sex with her.[7]

(1/183, 194, 196)

A woman asked the Prophet: "What do you think any one of us ought to do if blood from her period stains her garment?"

He replied: "If the garment of any one of you is stained by the blood of her period, then she should get rid of the dried blood with her fingers and fingernails, and then sprinkle the cloth with water[8] and then pray in it."

(1/183)

ʿĀ'isha said:

A woman asked the Prophet about washing to purify oneself after one's period had finished.

His reply was: "Take a cloth scented with musk and wash yourself three times with it."

The Prophet then turned his head away in embarrassment, so I had to explain to her precisely what he meant: "Wash away the traces of blood with it!"

(1/186, 187)

The Prophet was asked: "Is it required of a woman to wash her whole body if she has had a sexual emission while asleep?"

He replied: "Yes, if she notices any discharge."

He was then asked: "Oh Messenger of God, does a woman experience such sexual emissions in her sleep?"

He replied: "Yes."

(1/97)

2
Divorce

ʿĀ'isha said:

When the Prophet was ordered by God to give his wives the choice of being divorced, he began with me, and he said: "I have something to say to you, but you do not have to hurry to make your mind up until you have consulted your parents."

He knew, however, that my parents would never have ordered me to leave him. He then said: "God has said:

'O Prophet! Say to your wives: 'If you desire this worldly life and its attractions, then I shall surely provide for you and set you free in a becoming manner.' " (Q33:28)

To this I replied: "If that is so, then should I really consult my parents? For truly, my desire is for God and His Messenger and the Final Resting Place!"

And all the Prophet's wives then did what I had done and they refused to accept the option of divorce from him.

(6/291, 293)

ʿAbdullāh ibn ʿUmar said that he divorced his wife while she was still menstruating. His father mentioned this to the Prophet, who at once became angry with ʿAbdullāh, and he exclaimed: "He must allow her to return to him and then allow her to stay as his wife until she has become clean, menstruated a second time and then again become clean. If it then seems fit to him to divorce her, then let him do it while she is still clean and before he has had sexual intercourse with her.

"That is the special period of waiting as laid down by God for the procedure of divorce!"

(6/401)

Chapter of when an oppressed person exonerates his oppressor, there is no going back on this

ᶜĀ'isha said about this:

And if a woman fears that her husband shall ill-treat her or desert her, then they shall incur no sin if they both come to a fair and peaceful arrangement between themselves; and such a peaceful settlement is best, through selfishness is forever in men's souls. (Q4:128)

This is about a man who has a wife and who has no more use for her, and he wishes to divorce her irrevocably, and she therefore says to him: "I surrender all my rights up to you, provided that you do not divorce me."

And that is what this verse of the Qur'ān is about.

(3/378)

Hilāl ibn ᶜUmayya accused his wife of adultery, so he went to the Prophet and presented his version of what had happened to him.

The Prophet then said: "Truly God knows which of you two is the liar—so will one of you repent and admit that he[1] is lying?"

The woman then stood up and gave her version of what had happened.[2]

The interpretation of this is that it is the husband who initiates 'liᶜān'.[3]

(7/172)

The matter of *liᶜān* was mentioned in the Prophet's presence, and ᶜĀṣim ibn ᶜAdī made some comment about this before departing angrily.

A man from his tribe later came to him and complained that he had found another man with his wife. ᶜĀṣim replied: "I can only comment on this—I cannot judge."

So he took the man off to the Prophet, and this man told the Prophet about the man on whom he had found his wife.

Now, the husband of this woman was a pale and skinny man with lank hair, whereas the other man he claimed to have found with his wife was a brown-skinned, well-built and fleshy man with short, curly hair.

The Prophet prayed: "O God! Let a solution reveal itself!"

The wife eventually gave birth to a child who resembled the man her husband had claimed that he had found her with, so the Prophet ordered that they should start the proceedings of *liᶜān* between each other.

Ibn ᶜAbbās was asked: "Is she the woman about whom the Prophet said: 'Were I ever to stone someone to death without any clear proof, I would stone this woman to death!'?"

And to this he replied: "No, that was another Muslim woman who showed evil in her religion."

Ibn Shihāb says that:

After the case of this particular couple, it became the custom that any couple who instituted the proceedings of *liᶜān* should be divorced.

The woman mentioned above became pregnant, and the son that was born to her after the divorce was called by his mother's name. The custom on such a woman's rights of inheritance were that she could inherit from the son, and the son should inherit from her what God had chosen for him.

Sahl ibn Saᶜd al-Sāᶜidī reported:

The Prophet said: "If the woman gives birth to a fair-skinned child, then it must be considered that she has told the truth, and that her husband has lied against her. But if she gives birth to a black-eyed child with big buttocks, then it must be considered that it is her husband who has told the truth."

She subsequently gave birth *[as mentioned above]* to a child that supported the claim made against her.

(7/175-6, 181)

The Prophet heard *li'ān* proceedings between a man and his wife, and the man had refused to accept that her child was his—so the Prophet made them divorce, and gave the woman custody of the child.

(7/180)

Al-Ḥasan says:

If a man marries a *muḥarrama*[4] while not being aware of this, they should be divorced.

She is allowed to keep whatever she has been given by him as a full dowry, but she is not entitled to anything other than this.

(7/197)

And mothers who have been divorced may suckle their children for two whole years if the father wishes this term to be completed; but the father of the child must provide fair and just sustenance and clothing for them. No individual is burdened with more than he can bear, and no mother shall be treated harshly on account of her child, nor shall a father on account of his child. and this is incumbent also on the father's heir.

And should both parents decide by mutual consent and consultation to separate the mother and the child, then there shall be no sin upon them; and should you decide to put your children into the care of fostermothers, then there shall be no sin upon you, provided that you guarantee the security of the child justly and fairly.

(Q2:233)

We have enjoined on Man kindness towards his parents— for in pain did his mother bear him, and in pain did she give birth to him, and the period during which she bore him and during which he was weaned is thirty months. And then at last when he reaches full maturity and attains the age of forty years, he says: "O my Lord! Grant that I may be grateful for Your blessings which You have bestowed on me and my parents, and that I might perform

good works that are acceptable to You—and grant me also righteousness in my offspring . . ."

(Q46:15)

And let those women who are in a waiting-period[5] live in the same way as you live, according to your means, and do not harass them in order to oppress them. And should they be pregnant, then spend and provide for them until they deliver their burden; and should they suckle your children after being divorced, then provide for them fairly and justly, and consult with each other with just concern about the child. And should you come to difficulties, then give the child to another woman to be suckled on the father's behalf.

And let the man who is of ample means spend according to his means, and let he who is of restricted means spend according to what God has bestowed upon him—for God does not place any burden upon a person beyond what He has already given him. For after hardship, God grants relief.

(Q65:6-7)

Al-Zuhrī says:

God has forbidden that a divorced mother should harm her child—i.e. when she says: "I shall not suckle the child!"—for she has the most suited sustenance for that child, and will be the most gentle and kind to it, more so than anyone else. So she should not refuse to suckle such a child, in view of what God has made her husband give her of himself.

As for the husband, as regards a newborn baby, he should not harm his ex-wife through the means of their child by preventing her from suckling—using this as a means of hurting her by giving the baby to someone else to suckle. It will not, however, be held against either of them if both the father and the mother agree to have the child suckled by some other worthy and suitable woman.

Should they wish their child to be weaned by their mutual consent and consultation, then it will not be held against either of them, provided that it is done actually by their mutual consent and consultation.

(7/209)

Ma^c^qil ibn Yasār's sister was married to a man who divorced her and then kept away from her until her waiting-period was completed, and who then promptly sought her hand in marriage again. Ma^c^qil became incensed at this sleight on his honour, so he said: "This man has kept away from her when he was able to have her, and now he wants to marry her again?!"

Therefore he intervened between them, and God revealed the following:

When you divorce women and they come then to the end of their designated waiting-period, do not prevent them in any way from marrying their husbands if they have come to a fair agreement between themselves. This is a commandment to each one of you who believes in God and the Day of Judgement, and this is the purest and most righteous path for you.

(Q2:232)

The Prophet then called Ma^c^qil to see him, and he recited this verse of the Qur'ān to him. The rage left Ma^c^qil and he followed God's order.

Ibn ^c^Umar ibn al-Khaṭṭāb divorced a wife of his with the first of the Islamic divorces[6] while she was still menstruating. The Prophet ordered him to return her home and to keep her until she was clean from her menstruation and then had had another period while still with Ibn ^c^Umar, and then he should be patient with her until she had once more become clean from her period. Then, if he desired to divorce her, he had to divorce her while she was still clean, before he had sexual relations with her.

This is the waiting-period which God has ordained by which women should be divorced.

Whenever Ibn ^c^Umar was asked about this, he would declare: "If you have divorced your wife three times in succession, then she is *ḥarām*[7] until she has married another man, and then that man divorces her in his turn."

He would also add: "If only you would divorce your wives with only the first one or two of the three Islamic divorces, and not pronounce the third and final one, for the Prophet ordered me thus!"

(7/188)

And as for those who bring an accusation of adultery against their wives and have no witness but themselves, then let them bear witness four times with an oath to God that they are speaking the truth.

And on the fifth time they should say that they will invoke God's curse upon themselves should they be speaking false.

But as for the wife, punishment will be averted from her if she bears witness four times with an oath to God that her husband is speaking false.

And on the fifth time she should say that she will invoke God's curse upon herself if her husband is speaking the truth.

(Q24:6-9)

ᶜUwaimar al-Ajlānī came to ᶜĀṣim ibn ᶜAdī al-Anṣārī, and he asked him: "What is your opinion concerning a man[8] who finds another man with his wife? Should he kill him—in which case you all will have to kill the killer in retaliation—or what else should he do? O ᶜĀṣim, ask the Prophet about this for me."

ᶜĀṣim therefore went and asked the Prophet about this, but the Prophet found the question distasteful in every way, until the gravity of this reaction of his dawned upon ᶜĀṣim.

When he returned to his family, ᶜUwaimar came and asked: "O ᶜĀṣim, so what did the Prophet say to you?"

ᶜĀṣim replied: "You have never brought me any good—the Prophet was repulsed by what I asked him about!"

ᶜUwaimar thereupon exclaimed: "By God, I shall not stop until I have myself asked him about this!"

So off he went. He found the Prophet amongst a group of people and he then asked him the same as he had asked ᶜĀṣim. The Prophet's reply was: "God has made a revelation concerning you and your wife, so go and bring her back with you."

ᶜUwaimar did so, and he and his wife both carried out the procedure of *liᶜān*, and when they had finished this, ᶜUwaimar told the Prophet: "If I were to keep her now, then I would have lied against her!"

Accordingly, he divorced her irrevocably with the three oaths of divorce before the Prophet had to order him to do so. And this is the custom for those who carry out *liᶜān*.[9]

(7/134)

Chapter of the case of a man saying to his wife: "I have parted from you!", "I have sent you away!", "I discard you!", or any other such saying that is intended as one of the three oaths of divorce

It then depends on whether this is intended or not. God has said:

O you Faithful! If you marry women who are believers, and then divorce them before you have touched them, then you do not have to reckon any waiting-period for them, so make provision for them and then set them free justly and fairly.[10]

(Q33:49)

Pronouncing the words of divorce is allowed twice, and then the man and wife should either resume their marriage with all due fairness, or separate on goodly terms.

And it is not lawful for you, the husbands, to take back anything that you have given your wives unless both parties fear that they will not be able to keep within the limits as laid down by God. Thus, should you fear that they both may not be able to keep within the limits as laid down by God, then there shall be no sin upon either of them if the wife gives something up to her husband in exchange for her freedom. And these are the limits of God . . .

(Q2:229)[11]

Masrūq asked ᶜĀ'isha about the giving to a wife the option of divorce and she answered: "The Prophet did give such an option to us his wives—now do you consider that to be one of the three steps of the Islamic divorce procedure?"

To this Masrūq replied: "I pay no attention as to whether I give a wife a single option for divorce or a hundred, if she takes me as her option!"

So to give a wife the option of divorce is not considered a part of the three oaths of Islamic divorce.

(7/136)

And thus, when they come to the end of their appointed waiting-period, either keep them in marriage with due fairness or free them with due fairness. And make two just persons from amongst you be witnesses to what you have decided, and bear witness yourselves before God. And thus is commanded he who believes in God and the Day of Judgement.

(Q65:2)

ʿĀ'isha said:

The Prophet knew that my parents would not order me to part from him.

(7/137)

Chapter of pointing and gestures in divorce and other situations[12]

During the lifetime of the Prophet, a Jew attacked a serving-girl and snatched off her some silver jewellery which she was wearing and he stove her head in. Her family carried her to the Prophet as she was breathing her last, unable to speak.

He asked her: "Who has done this to you? Was it So-and-So?" And here he mentioned the name of someone other than the guilty man.

She made a gesture to say "no". The Prophet mentioned someone else—again someone other than the guilty man—and again she made a gesture to say "no".

Finally he asked: "Then was it So-and-So?" And he mentioned the name of her assailant.

The girl gestured "yes". The Prophet therefore ordered that the Jew should have his head crushed between two rocks—and so it was done.

(7/163)

O Prophet! When you divorce women, divorce them taking into account their waiting-periods, and reckon their waiting-periods accurately, and fear your Lord God!

And do not cast them from their homes, nor shall they themselves leave unless they become guilty of immoral acts. And these are the limits as laid down by God, and he who transgresses God's limits truly sins against his own self . . .

(Q65:1)

ᶜAbdullāh ibn ᶜUmar said that he had divorced his wife while she still had her period, and this happened during the Prophet's lifetime.

ᶜAbdullāh's father, ᶜUmar, asked the Prophet about this, and he was told by him: "Order your son to take back his wife and to retain her until she is clean [from her period]. Then, when she has her period again and is clean again, if he wishes, he may retain her after this, and if he wishes, he may divorce her, before he touches her. This is the waiting-period ordered by God for the woman who is to be divorced."

The above supplies the judgement:

Divorce, according to the Tradition of the Prophet and Islam, is that one should divorce one's wife when she is clean from the periods and one has not had sex with her after the periods of the waiting-period. Furthermore, there should be two witnesses for the divorce.

(7/129)

Ibn ᶜUmar said[13] that he divorced his wife while she was having her period, and her father mentioned this to the Prophet, who replied: "He should take her back!"

Ibn ᶜUmar was later asked: "Does this divorce count?"[14]

To this he replied: "Of course! What else would you think, unless the husband was an incompetent or acts like a fool?!"[15]

ᶜUmar added: "This was considered to be a step in the divorce process."

This is interpreted as: "If a woman is divorced while she still has her period, it is still considered to be a proper stage of the three stages of Islamic divorce."

(7/130)

If you have any doubts, the waiting-period for those of your women who are beyond the age of having periods and also those who do not have a period is to be three calendar months. And the waiting-period for those women who are pregnant shall be when they have delivered their burdens.

(Q65:4)

Mujāhid said:

If you do not know if they still get their period or not, then their waiting-period is three months. This is the same also for those women who have stopped menstruating and for those who have not[16] menstruated.

(7/182)

Because of a tradition that an extremely divisive incident amongst his wives which affected Muḥammad and made him in anger cut himself off from every one of them for an entire month[17] *to teach them a lesson,*[18] *God revealed in the Qur'ān:*

And for those who vow that they shall not approach their wives, there shall be a period of four months for which they must wait—and then if they go back on their vow, then God is full of forgiveness and mercy.

(Q2:226)[19]

Ibn ᶜUmar used to say about such swearing off one's wives or wife, as defined by God in the Qur'ān:

After the period[20] has been completed, one has either to retain one's wives or wife with kindness or intend divorce as God has ordered.

ᶜUmar also said:

After four months have elapsed, the husband shall be detained until he has divorced her,[21] but no divorce shall be incumbent upon him until he carries out the divorce proceedings.

This has been mentioned by ᶜUthmān, ᶜAlī, Abū 'l-Dardā', ᶜĀ'isha and twelve other Companions of the Prophet.

(7/159)

The Prophet said: "It is not lawful for a woman to ask for the divorce of her sister[22] in an attempt to have all of her cake and eat it—for she shall get only what God has allotted her."

(7/62)

And it is not lawful for you, the husbands to take back anything that you have given your wives unless both parties fear that they will not be able to keep within the limits as laid down by God. Thus, should you fear that they both may not be able to keep within the limits as laid down by God, then there shall be no sin upon either of them if the wife gives something up to her husband in exchange for her freedom.[23] And these are the limits of God . . .

(Q2:229)

ᶜUmar[24] permitted *khulaᶜ* without any legitimation. ᶜUthmān[25] permitted *khulaᶜ* with the compensation to the husband by the wife of everything belonging to her bar the ribbons in her hair.

Ṭāwūs says about the last half of the above quotation from the Qur'ān:

This concerns what God has prescribed on behalf of each one of a couple against their partner concerning their companionship and marital relationship.

He does not say the same as foolish people[26] say, i.e. that *khulaᶜ* is not legal until the woman says: "I shall not wash myself from *janāba*[27] for you!"[28]

The wife of Thābit ibn Qais[29] came to the Prophet and she said to him: "I do not mean to cast any aspersions upon the character or piety of my husband, but I must say that I hate to be un-Islamic in any way!"[30]

The Prophet asked her: "Will you give him back the fruit orchard he gave you as your dowry?"

She answered: "Yes!"

The Prophet then turned to Thābit and told him: "Accept the orchard and divorce her!"

(7/149)

And if a woman fears that her husband may ill-treat her or desert her . . .

(Q4:128)

ʿĀʾisha said about this verse:

It is about the woman who is living with her husband, but he wants no more of her and therefore wants to divorce her and to take another wife in her stead. This wife then says to her husband: "Retain me and do not divorce me—but marry someone else if you desire, and then you will be permitted to stop maintaining me and to cease your share of me."

This is found also in God's words:

. . . then they shall incur no sin if they both come to a fair and peaceful arrangement between themselves . . .

(Q4:128)

The wife of Rifāʿa al-Quraẓī came to the Prophet and told him: "Rifāʿa has irrevocably divorced me, so I then got married to ʿAbd al-Raḥmān ibn al-Zubair al-Quraẓī after this, but he has proved to be impotent.[31] He has not come near me except for a single trifling occasion—and even then he did not get anything from me, nor did I get anything from him that I desired—so may I remarry my first husband?"

The Prophet replied: "No, you may not until your marriage with your present husband has been consummated!"

(7/136, 139)

3
Widowhood & Death

Umm Salama said that a woman's husband died and the woman subsequently developed an eye infection. Her family told the Prophet about her, and they asked him whether she could use kohl[1] on her eyes, as they felt that the eye condition was serious and becoming dangerous.

He replied: "Before the coming of Islam, each one of you women, after the death of her husband, would spend the period of her mourning in her house, living and dressing in the most revolting manner. If a dog passed by, she would throw dung at it. So no, this woman should not use any kohl until her mourning period of four months and ten days is completed!"

(7/408)

Aslam's father said:

I went with ᶜUmar ibn al-Khaṭṭāb to the market, when a young woman clung onto him and cried: "O Commander of the Faithful! My husband has died and left a family of small children behind him. They do not have anything proper to eat, they had no seeds to sow, no animal to milk, and I fear that the hyenas will eat them! I am Bint Khufaf ibn Īmā al-Ghifārī, and my father was a witness to the oath of allegiance made by the people to the Prophet at Ḥiya."

ᶜUmar did not continue on his way, but instead stood there and said: "I make welcome to one who has close kinship with me!"

He then went to a broad-backed camel that was tethered in the courtyard of his house, and he placed two sacks onto it and filled them both with food, piling money and clothes on top. When he had finished, he handed over its nose-rein to her with the following words: "Take its lead—nothing of what it carries shall run out until God brings you better!"

But one man objected: "O Commander of the Faithful, you have given her too much!"

"May your mother be bereaved of you!" cried ʿUmar in reply. "By God! I watched the father of this woman and her brother besiege a fortress and then at last atttack and conquer it—and we spent the next morning setting out their rightful shares to the booty from there!"[2]

(5/339)

The Prophet passed by a woman who was weeping by the side of a grave, and he told her: "Fear God and be steadfast!"

(2/193)

Umm ʿAṭiyya said:

When the daughter of the Prophet died, he came to us and said: "Wash her three or five times, or more than that if you deem it necessary,[3] with water and lotus blossoms, and then finally put camphor on her—or anything similar. Then notify me when you have finished."[4]

So when we had finished what he had told us to do, we notified him, and he gave us his waist-wrapper and he said: "Clothe her in this."[5]

(2/194)

The Prophet said: "It is not permitted for a woman who believes in God and the Day of Judgement to be in mourning for a dead person for more than three days—except for a deceased husband—where she should mourn for four months and ten days."

(2/206)

ʿĀ'isha said:

When the news of the slaying of Zaid ibn Ḥāritha and Jaʿfar and ʿAbdullāh ibn Rawāḥa was received, the Prophet sat down looking sad while I was looking through a crack in the door, and there came a man who greeted him and proceeded to tell him about the weeping of Jaʿfar's womenfolk.

The Prophet ordered him to stop them doing this, so the man went to do as he said.

He came back, however, saying that he had told them to stop, but they had refused to obey him. So for a second time the Prophet ordered that he should stop them weeping and wailing. The man went off, and again came back saying: "They will not listen to me at all!"

The Prophet replied: "May those women be forever shamed!"

ʿĀ'isha then said to the man: "May God abase you! For by God, you could not stop them from weeping—nor did you stop them from disquieting the Prophet!"

Umm ʿAṭiyya said:

At the time of the homage of all the people to the Prophet, he received our undertaking not to bewail the dead, but only five women ever fulfilled this undertaking, and they were Umm Sulaim, Umm al-ʿAlā, Ibnat Abū Sabra (the wife of Muʿādh) and two other women.[6]

(2/221)

We were present at the funeral of the daughter of the Prophet, and he was sitting by the grave. I saw his eyes filled with tears, and he asked: "Is there amongst you a man who did not have sex last night?"

Abū Ṭalḥa said that he had not, so the Prophet told him: "Then get down into her grave!"

So he did, and he buried her.[7]

(2/238)

When one is lost in the ranks in battle, his wife should wait for one whole year (before remarrying)

Now, Ibn Masᶜūd (bought) a slave girl[8] and looked for her owner for a year and did not find him as he was missing in action. So he began to give a dirhem here and a dirhem there away in charity, saying: "To Thee, O God, is this money on behalf of So-and-So (the slave girl's owner)! And if he should return, then I shall pay him his full due for the slave girl!"

Ibn Masᶜūd adds about this: "You should all do this in the case of anything you may happen to find."

Al-Zuhrī said about the case of a prisoner, the place of whose captivity is known: "His wife should not marry, nor should his property and possessions be split up. should news of him cease, then his case becomes that of one missing in action henceforth."

All of these interpretations are based on a ḥadīth in which the Prophet was asked about the case of apparently ownerless animals and the like, which are found.

When asked about:

—a sheep, he replied that one should take it, or else the wolves will;

—a camel, he replied that one should leave it, since it is perfectly capable of taking care of itself until its true owner eventually turns up;

—any lost inanimate thing (e.g. something found by chance such as money): "Try your best to find out whose it is. If you cannot, then advertise its existence for a complete year, and if its rightful owner has not come by then, then it is all yours."

(7/161)

And the end of the waiting-period for those women who are pregnant shall be when they have delivered their burdens. (Q65:4)

Umm Salama, wife of the Prophet, said that a woman from the tribe of Aslam, called Subaiᶜa, had her husband die while she was pregnant, and Abū al-Sanābil ibn Baᶜkak proposed to her, but she refused to marry him.

Umm Salama agreed with her, saying: "Of course it would not be right for you to marry him until you have completed the required waiting-periods!"

So the woman tarried a while for ten days after,[9] and then she went to the Prophet and he said: "You should get married!"

(7/182)

Umm ᶜAṭiyya said:

We were forbidden to mourn the dead for more than three days—except for a husband who had passed away, in which case we had to mourn four months and ten days, not being allowed to put kohl on our eyes, wear perfume or dyed clothing, except clothing that is dyed with stripes.[10]

And when any one of us washed to purify herself after her period had finished, she was allowed to put on just a dab of perfume.

And we were forbidden at that particular time to follow in funeral processions.

(1/185)

The Prophet said: "The person who takes up the responsibility of looking after the widow[11] and the destitute is like the fighter who struggles in God's Cause, or like one who fasts all day and prays all night!"

(8/23)

Umm ᶜAṭiyya said:

We were forbidden to follow the funeral processions, but this was not enforced upon us.

(2/206)

Truly the Prophet has no part with the man and woman who slap their faces, shave their heads and rend their clothes in times of mourning or great distress.

(2/215, 216)

4
The Day of Judgement

The Prophet said: "Among the signs of the Final Hour of the End of the World are the following:

"Knowledge shall dwindle and ignorance[1] shall appear; fornication shall appear also, and women will abound in number and men will decrease in number, until there shall be one man[2] for every fifty women."

(1/68)

The Prophet said: "The Final Hour shall not be until the buttocks of the women of the tribe of Daus shake around Dhū 'l-Khalaṣa!"

Dhū 'l-Khalaṣa was a tyrant whom the Daus used to worship in the days before Islam.[3]

(9/178)

The Prophet said: "God shall say on the Day of Judgement: 'O Adam!'

"And Adam shall reply: 'At Your Command, O Lord—and all good is in Your hands!'

"God shall then say: 'Produce the envoys of Hell!'

"Then Adam will ask: 'Who are the envoys of Hell?'

"God will reply: 'Of every thousand they are 999, and amongst them the young shall go grey, and every pregnant woman shall miscarry, and you shall see people as if they are drunk, though they are not drunk, but still God's wrath will be great!' "

The Prophet was then asked: "O Prophet—which of us will be that one person who is not one of them?"

He answered: "Be heartened! For that one person will be one of you, and the rest of the thousand will be from the people of Gog and Magog!"

(4/362)

5
Heaven & Hell

Abū Dharr said:

I once went to see the Prophet Muḥammad, but he was asleep. He was dressed in white clothing. I came back after he had woken up, and he said to me: "There is no slave (of God) who recites 'There is no god but God!' and then dies with this belief who does not enter Paradise!"

"Even though he had committed unlawful sexual intercourse and had stolen?" I asked.

"Yes—even if he had done those things!"

Twice more I asked him the same thing, and twice more he returned the same answer.

Abū Dharr says that this means that if one repents and regrets one's past actions and recites 'There is no god but God!' at the time of one's death, then that person shall be forgiven.

(7/481)

The Prophet said: "The first group to enter Paradise will have the brilliance of the appearance of the full moon at night.[1] There they shall not spit out sputum, blow their noses or relieve their bowels. Their eating and drinking vessels shall be of gold, and their combs of gold and silver, and their fireplaces shall burn aloes-wood, and they shall sweat musk.

"For each one of them there shall be two wives,[2] who will be so beautiful that you will be able to see the bone-marrow of their shins because of the translucency of their flesh.[3]

"There will be no hatred or dissent, their hearts will be as one and they shall all praise God morning and night."

(4/307)

Chapter of the houris (or 'maidens of Paradise') and their description.

Upon looking at them, one's sight is dazzled, for they have intensely black pupils[4] *coupled with intensely white whites of their eyes.*[5]

The Prophet said: "A single afternoon sortie, or a single morning sortie, in the Cause of God[6] is better than the world and all that it contains. And the space that could be covered by the bow or whip of any one of you who does so is better than the world and all that it contains.

"And were a woman from the people of Paradise to appear to the people of earth, she would surely illuminate all that is between heaven and earth, and she would fill it with sweet scent—and the turban on her head is better than the world and all that is in it!"

(4/41)

The Prophet said: "Hell was revealed to me, and I perceived that the majority of its occupants are women who are ungrateful."[7]

He was asked: "Are they ungrateful to God?"

"They are ungrateful to their husbands," he replied. "And they are ungrateful for any kindness shown them—and if you have been kind to any one of them for a time and then she sees something that she does not like in you, she will then say, 'I have never received *anything* from you!' "

(1/29)

The Prophet prayed the solar-eclipse prayer, and then he declared:

"Hell came near me until I was forced to cry, 'O Lord! Am I to be one of its inhabitants?!' "

And then he went on to say that he had seen a woman being tortured by being torn to pieces by a cat.

Upon asking about this, he was told: "She neither fed it nor gave it water to drink when she imprisoned it, nor did she let it go to eat the creeping things[8] of the world!"

(3/323)

6
Justice & the Law

Chapter of mistakes and/or forgetfulness in manumitting slaves, divorcing one's wife, and similar situations

Manumission of slaves should be only for the sake of God. The Prophet said: "For each individual is what that individual intended."

But there is no lawful intent in the case of one who is forgetful or who has made a mistake. The Prophet said: "On behalf of my community, God has permitted, for me, that what their hearts whisper shall pass unpunished—so long as they do not do or speak it."

He also said: "Deeds are judged by the intention, and one must consider that an individual intends what he intends. And so whoever's *hijra*[1] is to God and His Apostles, then his *hijra* is to God and His Apostles. And whoever's *hijra* is to the world in order to have it all, or to a woman in order to marry her, then his *hijra* is to what he intends."

(3/424)

O you of the Faith! Whenever you make an agreed-upon debit or credit transaction, put it in writing . . . And summon two men of your number to be witnesses. If you cannot find two men, then take one man and two women of your number whose witness will be accepted, so that should one of them[2] make a mistake, the other will be able to remind her. These witnesses are not to refuse to give their evidence no matter when they are called upon to do so.

(Q2:282)

Abū Saᶜīd al-Khuḍrī heard the Prophet say: "Is not the witness of one woman like half the witness of a man?"

"Certainly," replied his listeners.[3]

He continued: "And that is on account of the deficiency of her reason."

(3/502)

Chapter of the case when a woman is forced to commit unlawful sexual intercourse against her will—there shall be no punishment meted out to her, in accordance with God's words:

Do not, in order to gain transient temporal pleasures of the world, force your slave girls into prostitution should they wish to marry. And should anyone force them into this, then to these girls who have been so forced,[4] God will truly prove to be full of forgiveness and grace!

(Q24:33)

Ṣafiyya bint Abū ᶜUbaid said that one of the male slaves belonging to the state authorities attempted to have sexual relations with a female slave who had come as a part of the state's official share of the war booty. The female slave was unwilling, so he deflowered her by force.

ᶜUmar had him whipped according to the fixed penalty, and then he banished him, but he did not have the female slave whipped on the grounds that the male slave had forced her against her will.

Concerning the case where a slave girl is deflowered[5] by a freeman, al-Zuhrī says: "A judge should make that man pay the equivalent value of a virgin slave girl, and he should be whipped. But in the case of a non-virgin slave girl, there is to be no fine, in accordance with the judgement of the leaders of Islam, but the man must receive the legal punishment."[6]

(9/66)

The Prophet declared: "Unlawful is the shedding of the blood of any Muslim person who has testified that there is no god but God and that I am His Apostle—unless it be one of the following cases:

"A life for a life.

"A previously married woman[7] who has committed unlawful sexual intercourse.

"One who quits his religion and abandons the Community."

(9/10)

Chapter of when a man abducts a slave girl and then claims that she has since died

In this case the man is obliged to pay the dead slave girl's value. If her rightful owner then finds her alive, then she belongs to him still, and whatever has been given as her value to him must be returned and is not to be considered as a binding transaction.

Some say that the slave girl should belong to the abductor if the original owner has accepted something that is the equivalent to her value. There exists a form of deceit in this type of case, when one man desires the slave girl of another man, and he does not buy her off him but adbucts her and then pretends that she is dead so that her real owner accepts something that is equivalent to her value. In this way, the slave girl of another is rendered legal for the abductor.

The Prophet said: "The property of each of you is hallowed for the rest. Any one of you who betrays this code shall have a banner on the Day of Judgement by which he shall be recognized!"

(9/78)

Samura ibn Jundub accepted as lawful the testimony of a woman whose face was veiled.

(3/500)

Al-Ḥakam and Ḥammād say that if a hirer of asses drives an ass upon which is seated a woman, and that woman subsequently falls off it, then no claim may be made against the hirer.

(9/36)

Al-Nadr's daughter slapped a serving-girl and broke her front tooth, so the serving-girl's family went and complained to the Prophet who ordered that a retaliatory penalty be imposed on Al-Nadr's daughter.[8]

(9/21)

Chapter of the foetus of a woman

Two women from the Hudhail tribe had a fight with each other which resulted in one of them hitting the other with a stone, causing the latter to miscarry.

The Prophet, when this case was brought before him for judgement, ruled that blood-wit[9] of the best male or female slave should be paid to the injured party by the attacker (or her paternal relatives).[10]

Chapter of the witness of one who falsely accuses someone else of unlawful sexual intercourse, and the thief, and the adulterer

God says:

Those who accuse chaste women of having commited adultery, yet cannot find four witnesses[11] to the act, shall be given eighty lashes. Furthermore, do not ever again accept them as witnesses, for they have proved themselves to be thoroughly unsound of mind.

However, those who repent and make contrition after making such a false accusation will be exempted from this last commandment—for truly God is full of forgiveness and grace.

(Q24:4-5)

ᶜUmar ordered Abū Bakra, Shibl ibn Maᶜbad and Nāfiᶜ to be whipped for falsely accusing al-Mughīra of having committed unlawful sexual intercourse, and he then urged them to return to God and to repent.

ᶜUmar said: "Whoever repents in this way will then have his future testimony accepted."

This is supported by ᶜAbdullāh ibn ᶜUtba and nine other learned men.

Abū al-Zinād said: "The way how it is with us here in Medina is that if someone who has made a false accusation of unlawful sexual intercourse retracts his word and then seeks the forgiveness of his Lord God, then his testimony after that will be accepted in a court of law."

Al-Shaᶜbī and Qatāda said: "If such a man proves himself to be a liar, then he should be whipped[12] and after this his testimony may be accepted."

Al-Thaurī said: "If a slave is whipped[13] and then given his freedom, then his testimony is to be considered lawful. If anyone, in fact, is punished in this way by being lashed and is then made a judge over any matter, then his judgement is lawful and binding."

Someone else added: "The testimony of one who has made a false accusation of unlawful sexual intercourse is not lawful, even if he does repent." He then goes on to say, however, that "marriage is not lawful unless there are two witnesses. If one gets married with two witnesses who have both been punished legally for making such false accusations, the marriage is regarded as legal—but if one should marry with two witnesses who are slaves, it is not lawful."

This man allows legally the witness of someone who has been legally punished for making false accusations of unlawful sexual intercourse, as well as that of the male slave and that of the female slave, concerning the first sign of the new moon of Ramaḍān.

How is the repentance of such a false accuser to be known?

Well, the Prophet banished the adulterer for a year, and he forbade the people to talk to Kaᶜb ibn Mālik and his two companions for fifty days.

ᶜUrwa ibn al-Zubair said that a woman stole something during the raid of the Conquest of Mecca, and she was brought before the Prophet who ordered her hand to be cut off.

ᶜĀ'isha narrates: "Her repentance after that was good, and she got married, and she would later come to me, and I would pass on any request she had to the Prophet."

Zaid ibn Khālid said that the Prophet, judging the case of someone who had committed unlawful sexual intercourse, ordered that he should be given a full unstinted one hundred lashes and then be banished for a whole year.

(3/495)

In the case of giving evidence about a woman who is behind a screen,[14] al-Zuhrī says that if you know[15] her, then testify, but if you do not know her, then do not testify.

(9/205)

The Prophet ordered one hundred lashes and banishment for one year for a person who had committed unlawful sexual intercourse and was not married.

*

ᶜUmar ibn al-Khaṭṭāb also banished such offenders, and this tradition is still continued.

(8/544)

ᶜUmar said:

I was afraid that in the future it would come to the point when the people will say: "We do not find reference to Stoning[16] in the Book of God!" and so they will go astray in abandoning a divine ordinance from God which He has revealed to us.

Well, stoning is indeed legally and obligatorily to be imposed upon anyone who has committed unlawful sexual intercourse and is married—when clear evidence is furnished, or if there is a pregnancy or confession. Is it not the case that the Prophet stoned to death, and we did likewise after his death?

(8/537)

In the case of the male thief and the female thief, cut off the hands and feet of either in return for what they have committed. Let this be a deterrent from God, for God is almighty and wise.

However, should one of these repent of the sin they have committed and make contrition, then truly God shall accept his contrition, for God is full of forgiveness and grace.

(Q5:38-9)

For what level of theft should a hand be cut off?

ᶜAlī used to cut off hands at the wrist.

Qatāda says, concerning the case of a woman who had stolen something and who had her left hand cut off instead of her right hand:[17] "It should be left like that."[18]

(8/513)

When Māᶜiz ibn Mālik came before the Prophet because he had committed unlawful sexual intercourse, he was asked by the Prophet: "Perhaps you only kissed her, or felt her,[19] or looked at her?"

"No, O Prophet," Māᶜiz replied.

"Did you have sexual intercourse her?" the Prophet then asked bluntly without any euphemism.

At that, the Prophet ordered that he should be stoned to death.

(8/534)

Al-Ḥasan says:

If someone has unlawful sexual intercourse with his sister, then the legal penalty for him is the same as that given the ordinary committer of unlawful sexual intercourse.

(8/526)

The Prophet said: "If a noble person from amongst the Israelites were to steal, they would pursue the matter no further, but if a lowly person stole, then they would cut off that person's hand.

"Even if it were Fāṭima, my daughter, who had stolen, I would cut off her hand!"

(5/58)

ʿUmar said:

The Jews brought the Prophet a man and a woman of their number who had committed unlawful sexual intercourse. He ordered that they should both be stoned to death in a place by the mosque near where the funerals were held.

(2/231)

7
Modesty & Clothing

ᶜĀ'isha wore yellow clothes when she was a pilgrim to the hallowed ground of Mecca, and she said: "A woman who goes on pilgrimage to the hallowed ground of Mecca should not veil herself with a *lithām*[1] nor with a *burquᶜ*.[2] And she is not to wear any garment that is scented."

She saw no harm in wearing ornaments, dark coloured clothes or women's shoes.

Ibrāhīm notes that he sees no harm in a woman changing such clothes while in the purified state of being a pilgrim.[3]

(2/358)

Order the men of the Faithful to lower their gaze and guard their chastity—for this will keep them pure. Truly God knows all that they do.

Tell also the women of the Faithful to lower their gaze, and they should guard their chastity, and they should not display any of their charms publicly save what is decently observed, and they must draw their veils over their bosoms; and they not should display any of their charms to anyone except their husbands, or their fathers, or their husbands' fathers, or their sons, or their husbands' sons,[4] or their brothers or their brothers' sons, or their sisters' sons, or their womenfolk, or those whom they possess with their right hand,[5] or those male servants who feel sexual desire no longer, or children too young to be aware of the nakedness of women. And women should not move their legs in

such a way when they walk as to attract attention to the charms they have concealed.[6]

(Q24:30-1)

^{c}Ā'isha said, when this last verse was revealed: "The women of the first emigrants[7] to Medina took their waist-cloths and tore them up to make yashmaks out of them."

(6/267)

^{c}Abdullāh said:

God has cursed[8] women who tattoo and women who get themselves tattooed, women who depilate themselves,[9] and those women who make gaps between their teeth to make themselves look attractive—for they are adulteresses of what God has created!

Now this reached the ears of a woman from the clan of Asad, called Umm Ya^{c}qūb, and so she came to ^{c}Abdullāh and said to him in challenge: "It has reached my ears that you have cursed these types of women."

"And why should I not curse those whom God has cursed and who are cursed in the Qur'ān?" retorted ^{c}Abdullāh.

"Well, *I* have read all that is in betwen the two covers of the Qur'ān,[10] and I have not found any reference to what you claim," replied Umm Ya^{c}qūb.

"Well," ^{c}Abdullāh said, "if you have read the Qur'ān, then you should have found it—for you did not read: **Therefore receive with gratitude that which the Messenger[11] may bestow upon you, and do not seek to have what he withholds from you . . .** ?"[12]

"Yes . . ."

"And so it is that God has forbidden these things!" declared ^{c}Abdullāh.

"Well, I see *your* wife doing them!" countered Umm Ya^{c}qūb.

"Go and watch her then!" came the reply.

So Umm Ya^{c}qūb went of and watched ^{c}Abdullāh's wife, but she saw nothing that could support her case, and ^{c}Abdullāh then declared: "If my wife were like that and did any of these things, I would not sleep with her!"[13]

(3/379)

Ibn ᶜAbbās said:

ᶜAṭā ibn Abū Rabāḥ asked me: "Shall I not show you a woman from the people of Paradise?"

I replied: "Yes, please."

"Well, there was this black woman,"[14] ᶜAṭā began, "who came to the Prophet and said to him: 'I am an epileptic, and whenever I have a fit, I unintentionally expose myself[15]—so please invoke God's Name on my behalf!'

"'If you are willing,' replied the Prophet, 'you can be patient with your lot and Paradise shall be yours—on the other hand, if you are also willing, I shall invoke God's Name that He should restore you to health.'

"'I shall be patient,' was the woman's reply—but suddenly she changed her mind and she again asked: 'I unintentionally expose myself, so please invoke God's Name to help me not do this again!'

"So the Prophet invoked God's Name for her."

(7/376)

Saᶜīd ibn Abū al-Ḥasan says:

The women of the ᶜAjam[16] expose their breasts[17] and their heads.

He was told, concerning this:

Avert your sight from them—for God says:

Order the men of the Faithful to lower their gaze and guard their chastity . . . (Q24:30)[18]

And then He says:

Tell also the women of the Faithful to lower their gaze, and they should not publicly show any of their charms apart from what may be seen with modesty . . . (Q24:31)

"Lowering their gaze" means that they should not look at what has been forbidden.

Al-Zuhrī says, concerning a female who has not (yet) had her first menstrual period: "It is not proper to look with desire at any such female—even if she is a small child."

We are told that ᶜAṭā disapproved of looking at female slaves for sale in Mecca, unless he wanted to buy one.

(8/161)

Asmā' said a woman asked the Prophet: "O Prophet! My daughter has measles[19] and all of her hair has fallen out. I want to marry her to someone, so may I give her false hair to make her more presentable?"

"God has cursed[20] all those who put false hair on others, and also those who have it put on!" was the Prophet's reply.

(7/536)

ᶜĀ'isha said that one of the Anṣārī women gave her daughter away in marriage but the hair on her daughter's head had begun to gradually fall out. So the mother went off to the Prophet and told him about this, and she said: "Indeed her husband has ordered me to give her false hair!"

And the Prophet replied: "No, do not—for those women who use false hair are accursed!"[21]

(7/101)

ᶜĀ'isha said:

The Prophet gave me a yellow-striped suit of clothes and I put it on—but then I saw anger in his face, so I split it up amongst my fellow-wives.[22]

(7/213)

Umm Khālid said:

A large pile of garments was brought to the Prophet and amongst them was a black cloak.

"Who do you think we should clothe in this cloak?" the Prophet asked, and on receiving no answer, he ordered: "Bring Umm Khālid to me!"

I was accordingly brought to him, and he dressed me in the cloak with his own hand, and when he had finished, he said twice to me: "May you live long enough to wear out many such cloaks!"

He then began to look at the embroidery on the cloak, and pointing at me he exclaimed: "O Umm Khālid, that is indeed beautiful!"

(7/491)

ʿĀ'isha said:

The Prophet used to perform the dawn prayer while with him were some of the believing women wrapped up in their woollen body-cloths—and then they would return to their homes, and no one would recognize them.[23]

(1/225)

ʿUmar ibn al-Khaṭṭāb said:

God and I were in agreement over the Verse of the Veil—I said to the Prophet: "If only you would order your wives to veil themselves, for they are spoken to by wicked men as well as those with honourable intentions!"

And so the Verse of the Veil was revealed.

(1/240, 242)

Muʿāwiya ibn Abū Sufyān, in the year of his pilgrimage to Mecca, was speaking from the pulpit, and he grabbed a lock of false hair that was in the hand of one of his bodyguards and he declared: "O people of Medina! Where are your wisemen? I have heard the Prophet forbid the like of this (false hair), and he said that this led to the destruction of the Israelites when their women adopted this custom of false hair!"

(4/449)

8
Marriage

The polytheists were of two groups in their relationship towards the Prophet and the Believers.

There were the polytheists who were the warmongers, against whom the Prophet fought, and who fought against the Prophet. And then there were the polytheists who had a pact with the Prophet and they did not fight him nor he them.

Whenever a woman from the warmongers emigrated to the Muslims, she was not sought in marriage until she had had her period and become clean. When she had become clean, she would be allowed to be married. If her husband had emigrated before she had married, she would be returned to him. If any slave, male or female, belonging to the warmongers emigrated to the Muslims, then they would be considered free, and they would receive the same rights as those given the other emigrants to the Muslim camp.

Any slave, male or female, belonging to the polytheists having a pact with the Muslims, who emigrated to the Muslims would not be returned, but instead the value of their prices would be returned.

(7/156)

Chapter of when a polytheist or Christian woman becomes a Muslim while she is still married to a 'dhimmī'[1] or someone at war with the Muslims—what happens?

Ibn ᶜAbbās said that if a Christian woman becomes a Muslim shortly before her husband does, then she is *ḥarām*[2] for him.

Ibrāhim al-Sā'igh said that ᶜAṭā was asked about the case of a woman of the pact-polytheists who had become a Muslim, and then her husband became a Muslim during her waiting-period[3]—would that woman still be that man's legal wife? His reply was no, unless she wishes to undertake a new marriage and dowry.

Mujāhid said that if the husband of such a woman becomes a Muslim during her waiting period, then he has to remarry her if he wants her to remain his wife.[4]

God says:

O you of the Faithful! Whenever women who believe abandon the kingdom of evil and come to you, examine them—although it is only God who knows fully of their faith. Then if you have confirmed that they are true believers, do not return them to those who refute the Truth, for they have ceased to be lawful for them. You shall, however, give back to the refuters of the Truth all that they have spent as dowries on their wives, and after thus returning the dowries you shall be committing no sin if you then marry their women. And as for your own wives who are unbelievers, seek back what you have spent on them as dowries likewise.

(Q60:10)

Al-Ḥasan and Qatāda say, concerning a Magian[5] husband and wife who had converted to Islam, that their existing marriage still stands for them, since they have both converted together at the same time. But should one of them convert alone and the other refuses to do likewise, then the wife is considered divorced and the husband has no rights over her.

Ibn Juraij said:

I asked ᶜAṭā: "If a woman came from the polytheists to the Muslims, should her husband be compensated for losing her according to the words of God: **You shall, however, give back to the refuters of the Truth all that they have spent as dowries on their wives . . .**?"[6]

He answered: "No. That refers only to the polytheists who have officially made a pact with the Prophet."

Mujāhid says that all of this concerns a peace settlement between the Prophet and the Quraish.[7]

(7/157)

Do not marry polytheistic women until they have become true believers. For a woman who is a true believer is better than a woman who is a polytheist, even should you find the latter greatly pleasing. Furthermore, do not permit your women to marry polytheistic men until they have become true believers. For a man who is a true believer is better than a man who is a polytheist, even should you find the latter greatly pleasing . . .

(Q2:221)

Whenever ᶜUmar was asked about the marrying of a Christian or Jewish woman, he replied: "Truly, God has made polytheistic women unlawful for true believers, and I do not know anything worse in polytheism than for a woman to say 'Our Lord is Jesus', though he was merely just one of God's servants!"

(7/155)

Jābir ibn ᶜAbdullāh said:

My father died and left behind him seven or nine daughters, so I married a woman who had already been married. The Prophet then asked me: "Have you got married, Jābir?"

I replied: "Yes."

He then asked: "A virgin or a woman who has already been married?"[8]

I replied: "Well, it is a woman who has already been married."

The Prophet then asked: "Then why not a young virgin with whom you could play, and she with you, and you could laugh and joke with her, and she with you?"

I explained to him: "My father ᶜAbdullāh has died and left his daughters, and I would hate to bring home a wife just like them, so I married a woman who would be able to look after them and bring them up properly."

The Prophet exclaimed: "May God bless you for that!"[9]

(7/213)

The Prophet banned:

—Town-dwellers selling things on behalf of nomads.

—Rigging prices through pre-arranged outbidding.

—Unfair undercutting of prices.

—Making overtures of marriage to the fiancée of one's brother.[10]

—A woman's seeking the divorce of her sister in order to drive her away.[11]

(3/197)

ᶜĀ'isha said that the slave girl Barīra was manumitted and given the option of being divorced from her husband, who was still a slave.

The interpretation of this is that the selling of a female who is already married to another slave does not mean that she has to be divorced.

Ibn ᶜAbbās said:

Barīra's husband was a black slave called Mughīth, and it is as if I see him now walking around behind Barīra, weeping with his tears flowing down his beard. And the Prophet remarked to me: "Do you not, ᶜAbbās, marvel at the love Mughīth has for Barīra?—And at the hate Barīra has for Mughīth?"

He then said to Barīra: "Why can you not go back to him?"

She replied: "Are you ordering me, O Prophet?"

"I am only pleading on his behalf," said the Prophet.

"Then I have no need of him," came the reply.

(7/152, 153, 154)

Chapter of the witness of female and male slaves

Anas says that the witness of a slave is lawful provided that he is an upright person.

Shuraiḥ and Zurāra ibn Abū Awfā also consider this lawful.

Ibn Sīrīn says that such a slave's witness is lawful except in the case of a slave for[12] his master.

Al-Ḥasan and Ibrāhim consider this lawful in petty affairs.

Shuraiḥ said: "Each one of you is from the offspring of male and female slaves."

ᶜUqba ibn al-Ḥārith married Umm Yaḥyā bint Abū Ihāb. But a black female slave then came and declared: "I suckled the both of you!"

So ᶜUqba went to the Prophet and he told him what the slave had said, whereupon the Prophet exclaimed: "So how can you both stay married after this has been said?!"

And he forbade Umm Yaḥyā to him.

(3/502, 503)

Chapter of the terms of the dowry in the marriage/ wedding contract

ᶜUmar said that the details of the rights are contained in the conditions of the contract—and you get only the terms to which you have agreed.

*

The Prophet said that the most lawful of terms which you should fulfil is that by which you regard your wives' private parts as lawful.

(3/553)

ᶜĀ'isha said:

The Prophet married me when I was a girl of six years of age, and my family then took me away to Medina and we stayed there[13] amongst the clan of the al-Ḥārith ibn Khazraj.

I then fell seriously ill and all my hair fell out, but it later all grew back properly again. Then my mother, Umm Rūmān came to me while I was playing around on a seesaw with some friends of mine. She called me, so I went to her, not knowing what she wanted of me.

She took me by the hand and stood me at the gate of the house. When I had recovered my breath from playing, she took some water and washed my face and hair with it. She then made me go into the house, and there I saw some women of the Anṣār, who all spoke words of best wishes, blessings and luck to me.

My mother placed me in their hands, and they proceeded then to prepare me for what lay in store for me. After this, I was surprised to see the Prophet arrive in the late morning, and the women put me in his hands.

I was at that time a girl of nine years of age.

(5/152)

Khaula bint Ḥakīm was one of those women who came to offer themselves up to the Prophet,[14] and ᶜĀ'isha commented: "Should not a woman feel ashamed to bestow herself upon a man?"

But when the following verses were revealed:

Lest you become anxious . . .

be aware that you may put off any of them you desire, and you may take unto you any of them you desire, and there shall be no sin upon you if you seek out any one you have previously stayed away from—for thus it will be more likely that their eyes shall be cheered at your sight, and they shall not grieve and they may all be happy at whatever you give each of them . . .

(Q33:50-1)

ᶜĀ'isha said: "O Prophet—your Lord always hastens towards your desire!"

(7/35)

The Prophet put an end to *shighār*.[15]

(7/34)

ᶜAlī ibn Abū Ṭālib said that the Prophet banned the temporary marriage[16] of women on the day of the victory in battle at Khaibar,[17] and he also banned eating the flesh of domestic donkeys.[18]

(5/372)

O mankind! Know your sustainer, who has created you from a single living entity, and from this has created its mate, and from the two issued many men and women. Know God, whose name you utter in oaths in your dealings with one another, and kinship ties. Truly, God watches always over you!

Thus, give the orphans what is rightfully theirs, and do not give them things of yours that are bad in place of things that are good which are really theirs, and do not use up what is theirs along with what is yours, for this is truly a heinous sin.

And should you fear that you may not be able to treat the orphans fairly, then you should take a wife from those other women who are lawful for you: one, two, three or four. But should you fear that you may not be able to treat all of them fairly and equally, then you should marry only one such woman—or one of those women whom your right hand possesses. All of this will help you from straying from the straight path of righteousness.

Also, grant women their bridewealth as if it were a gift; and should they give you any of it back of their own free will, then you should accept it and enjoy it completely.

Also do not hand over to your wards anything with which God has entrusted you for their upkeep if they are weak of judgement, but do not cease to feed them and clothe them from it, and be kind in your speech with them.

Also, test the orphans who are your wards till the day they are of marriageable age, and, should you find them to be mature mentally, give them then what is rightfully theirs, and do not seek to use this up by needless spending, trying to spend it before they come of age. In fact, he who is wealthy should never touch the property of his ward, but he who is poor may take what he fairly needs. When you give them what is rightfully theirs, ensure that there are witnesses for them present, though there is no greater witness than God.

Men have a right to a portion of what their parents and relatives leave when they die, and women have a right to a portion of what their parents and relatives leave when they die, and this is

a God-ordained portion, be it small or large.

(Q4:1-7)

ᶜUrwa ibn al-Zubair asked ᶜĀ'isha about the third verse above [which begins: **And should you fear that . . .**] and she gave the following explanation: "This is all about a female orphan who is in the custody of her guardian who is attracted by her beauty and wealth. But he wants to marry her for a dowry far less than befits a woman of her standing. In this way, such guardians have been forbidden to marry such females unless they pay them the full dowry they deserve. If the former do not agree, then they are to marry someone else instead.

"Some time after this was revealed by God, the Prophet was asked to make a relevant legal decision, and God then revealed the following: **And they will ask you to explain the laws about women to them, so say: 'God Himself explains the laws concerning them!' For He speaks by means of what is transmitted to you through this Scripture concerning orphan women who are your wards to whom you do not give what is righfully theirs, on account of you wanting to marry them yourselves; and concerning defenceless children; and concerning your duty to treat orphans fairly and equally. And know that God is aware of every good you do.**

(Q4:127)

"God has explained in this verse that the female orphan, if she has beauty and wealth, is desired by guardians to marry without giving her her due dowry. If she was deemed unattractive due to a lack in wealth and beauty, they would abandon her and seek the hand of some other woman."[19]

ᶜUrwa ibn al-Zubair said that since in the second case they would abandon her when they found her to be unattractive, they should not be allowed to marry her if (as in the first case) they find her to be attractive unless they pay her the complete required dowry and give her all her due rights.

(4/19)

The Prophet attacked Khaibar and killed all the defenders and took the women and children captive. Ṣafiyya was amongst them, and she was first given to Daḥya al-Kabī as part of his share of the booty.

However, she was soon transferred to the Prophet's share of the booty, and he made her manumission her dowry when he married her.

*

The Prophet took Ṣafiyya as a captive, and then he manumitted her and married her.

"What did he give her as her dowry?" Anas was asked by Thābit.

"He gave her herself as her dowry," came the reply.

(5/362)[20]

The Islamic tradition according to the Prophet is that when you marry a virgin (having already married an already-married woman), you should stay with her for seven days[21] (and then give both of them equal turns of your time).

When you marry a woman who has already been married (having already a virgin[22] as a wife), then you should stay with her for three days (and then give them equal turns of your time).[23]

(7/105)

A woman asked the Prophet: "I have a co-wife.[24] Is there any harm in me claiming that I have received from my husband something that he really has not given me in order to spite my co-wife?"

The Prophet replied: "The person who boasts of riches which he has not been given is like the person who wears two garments of falsehood!"

(7/109)

Saᶜīd ibn Jubair was asked by Ibn ᶜAbbās: "Are you married?"

To which he replied: "No."

Ibn ᶜAbbās then said: "Then get married—for the best in all this community is the one most in wives!"[25]

(7/5)

Which women are lawful for marriage, and which are prohibited?[26]

God says:

Do not marry women whom your fathers had once married (although what is done is done), for this is an evil and an abomination.

You are forbidden your mothers, your daughters, your sisters, your paternal and maternal aunts, a brother's daughter, a sister's daughters, your milk-mothers, your milk-sisters, your wives' mothers, your step-daughters (your foster-children) with whose mothers you have consummated marriage (but if you have not consummated your marriage with their mothers, then there is no sin in marrying their daughter), and your natural sons' wives, and you are forbidden to marry two sisters at the same time. But what is done is done, for truly God is full of forgiveness and grace.[27]

And you are forbidden also all married women except for those whom your right hand possesses.[28] **This is God's commandment to you.**

All other women are permitted for you to court and offer them from what you own, so that you may marry them in honesty with no fornication. And give a fair dowry to those you wish to marry, and no sin shall be held against you if you both subsequently agree, of your own free will to change the amount of this dowry. Truly God is all-knowing and wise.

As regards those of you who find yourselves not able to marry women believers from those whom your right hands possess,[29] **God knows what faith you have, and each of you is an issue of the other. So marry such women with the consent of their kinsfolk and grant them fair dowries, for these are women who present themselves for an honest marriage—and not for fornication or**

illicit affairs. Should such women become married and ever be guilty of immoral conduct, they shall then suffer half the penalty to which married women who are free are liable.

This commandment to marry slave girls is for those of your number who are afraid that they would commit evil otherwise.[30] But it is good for you to be patient and persevere rather than have recourse to such a marriage. Truly God is full of forgiveness and grace.

God wishes to make you aware of all of this and thus to guide you along the paths of righteousness of the lives of those who preceded you, and to bestow upon you His mercy, but those who pursue their lusts wish you only to stray far from the path of righteousness.

God wishes to lighten your load, for Man was created weak.

(Q4:22-8)

Anas says that the term 'married women' means those women who are not slaves, and who have husbands, and he adds that they are *ḥarām* ('forbidden')—excepting, of course, those women to whom you are already married. He sees no harm in a man taking his female slave away from his male slave.[31]

Do not marry polytheist women until they have become true believers . . .

(Q2:221)

Ibn ʿAbbās says that any more than four wives is not permitted[32]—just as it is not permitted to marry one's mother or one's daughter or one's sister. He also says that there are seven types of women forbidden on the paternal side and seven on the maternal side,[33] and he then quotes the Qur'ān [*see Q4:23, p. 60*].

ʿAbdullāh ibn Jaʿfar married ʿAlī's daughter and previous wife[34] both at the same time and Ibn Sīrīn said that there was no harm in this.

Al-Ḥasan at first disapproved, but he later agreed to it.

Al-Ḥasan ibn al-Ḥasan ibn ʿAlī married two of his paternal uncle's daughters on the same night, Jābir ibn Zaid disapproved of this in account of the rivalry and loss of relations it would cause between the two girls.

But this is not a situation to be considered as unlawful, since God says:

All other women are permitted for you . . .

(Q4:24; *see p. 61*)

Other cases upon which various commentators have passed judgement are:

—Unlawful sexual intercourse with one's wife's sister does not render one's wife *ḥarām.*

—If one has a homosexual affair with a boy (and this also includes sodomizing him) then one should not marry the boy's mother.

—There is uncertainty over whether sexual relations (full or otherwise) with one's mother-in-law render one's wife (i.e. her daughter) *ḥarām* or not.

(7/28)

The Prophet forbade, at the time of the Battle of Khaibar, the eating of domestic donkey meat and temporary marriage.[35]

*

Jābir ibn ᶜAbdullāh and Salama ibn al-Akwaᶜ said:

We were in the army when the Prophet came to us and said: "I have given you my permission to do the temporary marriage—so go off and do it!"

Salama ibn al-Akwaᶜ's father said that the Prophet said: "Whenever a man and a woman are agreed to do a temporary marriage, their ensuing relationship should be for three nights. Should they then wish to continue with it, they may—and if they wish to mutually part, then they may."

It is not known whether this was directed specifically at those spoken to by the Prophet at the time, or at people in general.

Abū ᶜAbdullāh (al-Bukhārī) says that ᶜAlī has made it clear that the Prophet said: "It (temporary marriage) is no longer allowed."[36]

(7/36)

Marry also the single women of your number as well as those

male and female slaves who are suitable for marriage. Should any whom you wish to marry be poor, do not let this hinder your judgement, for God will give them from His bounty, for truly He is infinitely merciful and all-knowing.

As for those who are unable to marry, then they should live chastely till the time when God grants them the means.

Should any of those whom your right hand possesses desire a deed for their manumission, then write it out for them if you see that they are deserving. And give them also what would rightfully be theirs of the wealth which God has given you.

Do not, in order to gain transient temporal pleasures of the world, force your slave girls into prostitution should they wish to marry. And should anyone force them into this, then to these girls who have been so forced, God will truly prove to be full of forgiveness and grace!

(Q24:32-3)

A woman came to the Prophet saying that she had come to give herself up in marriage to him. To this he replied: "I have no need of (any more) women!"

A man then said: "Marry her to me!"

The Prophet turned to him and said: "First give her a dowry of clothes."

The man replied: "I do not have the wherewithal!"

"Give her anything then—even if it is just a ring of iron!"[37]

The man again made his excuses to the Prophet.

Now this man had no cloak, but he did have a waist-wrapper, and he made as if he was going to rip it in two to give half of it as a dowry for the woman's hand in marriage.

Upon seeing this, the Prophet exclaimed: "What on earth are you doing with that waist-wrapper of yours? If *you* wore it, there would be nothing of it to cover *her* body with, and if *she* wore it, there would be nothing for *you* to wear!"

The man sat down and did not say anything for a long time, and then he got up and left.

The Prophet sent someone to call him back, and he asked him: "Look, what do you know of the Qur'ān?"

"I know such-and-such and such-and-such chapters of it," replied the man.

The Prophet then asked: "But do you know them by heart?"

"Yes," said the man.

"Then I hereby marry you to her on the basis of what you know of the Qur'ān!"[38]

(6/502-4, 7/15)

^{c}Abd al-Raḥmān ibn Auf went to the Prophet and restored the oath of friendship between himself and Sa^{c}d ibn al-Rabī^{c}a al-Anṣārī

Now Sa^{c}d had two wives, so he proposed to ^{c}Abd al-Raḥmān that he should give him half of his wives and half of his property and possessions.

^{c}Abd al-Raḥmān replied: "May God bless you for your wives and property and possessions! Show me the way to the market!"

He was shown, and he went off to the market and he bought a little yoghurt and a little ghee to celebrate with. The Prophet saw him a few days later with greasy yellow stains on his clothing, so he asked him: "What has happened, ^{c}Abd al-Raḥmān?"

"I have taken an Anṣārī wife," he replied.

"What dowry did you send her?"

"Five dirhems' weight of gold."

"Well, you should also give her a feast—even if all that you have is one sheep," said the Prophet.

(7/7)

The Prophet said:

"A woman is married for four things:

"For her possessions and wealth.

"For her noble descent.[39]

"For her beauty.

"For her sense of true religion.

"But gain the one with the sense of true religion!"

(7/18)

ᶜAbdullāh said:

We used to go on raids with the Prophet, and we went without women, so we complained to the Prophet: "We might as well get ourselves castrated!"

He forbade this suggestion, but then gave us licence for the temporary marriage of women (from our captives and so on). He then recited to us:

O you of the Faithful! Do not deprive yourselves of the good things in life that have been made lawful for you by God! But take care not to overstep the boundary between what is right and what is wrong, for truly God loves not those who do wrong.

(Q5:87)[40]

Abū Huraira said:

I asked the Prophet: "I am a young man, and I fear for my soul lest I am tempted into committing the hideous sin of unlawful sex. But I cannot find any means with which to marry a woman[41]—so what should I do?"

The Prophet fell silent and did not speak to me, so I repeated my question, and again he did not speak to me.

After I had asked him a third time, he at last replied: "O Abū Huraira, the pen has dried on what is written for you. So go off and seek to be castrated, or do not!"

(7/6-9)

The Prophet asked for permission from Abū Bakr for the hand in marriage of his daughter, ᶜĀ'isha, and Abū Bakr replied: "But you are my brother!"[42]

The Prophet said: "You are my brother in the religion of God and the Qur'ān, but she is *ḥalāl*[43] to me!"

(7/12)

The Prophet said: "One should not be married to both a woman and her paternal aunt, nor a woman and her maternal aunt."[44]

(7/34)

If you have any doubts, the waiting-period for those of your women who are beyond the age of having periods and also those who do not have a period is to be three calendar months . . .

(Q65:4)

God has determined that the waiting-period for pre-pubescent girls is three months.

ᶜĀ'isha said that she was married to the Prophet when she was six years old and the marriage was consummated when she was nine years old. She further said that she stayed with him for nine years.[45]

(7/49)

Then you should take a wife from those other women who are lawful for you . . .

(Q4:3)

Three men came together to the houses of the Prophet's wives, asking about how the Prophet worshipped, and when they were told how, it was almost as if they held hatred for this. They said: "How on earth are we ever to compare with the Prophet? He has already had all of his sins forgiven him—even the ones he has not yet committed!"

One of them then said: "Well, as for me, I am going to pray every night forever!"

Another said: "I shall fast forever and never break my fast!"

The third and last declared: "I shall withdraw from women and never marry!"

Later, the Prophet came to them and said: "Are you those who said such-and-such things?"

After they had replied in the affirmative, he went on: "Well, by God, I swear that I am more God-fearing and pious than all three of you—but I fast, and then break it; I pray, and then sleep; and I marry women. So whoever turns away from my Tradition, then that person is not for me!"

(7/1)

Al-Qama said:

I was with ᶜAbdullāh when ᶜUthmān met him at Minā and he said: "O ᶜAbd al-Raḥmān,[46] I have something personal to speak to you about!"

So they went off somewhere private and ᶜUthmān said to ᶜAbd al-Raḥmān: "Would you like us to marry you off to a virgin who will make you remember the way you used to be?"

ᶜAbd al-Raḥmān thought and realized that he in fact had no such inclination for this.

He then motioned to me to join them, and he called out to me by name.

I came attentively towards them as he was saying: "If this indeed is the case what you suggest, then let me point out to you that the Prophet told us, 'O young men! Whoever amongst you is able to provide a home, then let him take a wife, for he will be best able to lower his eyes modestly[47] and the best to preserve his chastity;[48] and he who is not able to provide a home, then let him fast, for it shall then be a situation of *wijā'*[49] for him.'"[50]

(6/3)

When you divorce women and they then come to the end of their designated waiting-period, do not prevent them in any way from marrying other men if they have come to a fair agreement between themselves . . .

(Q2:232)

Maᶜqil ibn Yasār said that this verse was revealed about him:

I married off a sister of mine to a man who then divorced her. But after her waiting-period had passed, he came back asking to marry her again.

I said to him: "I gave you her in marriage, and I made it all easy for you and was generous to you[51]—and then you go and divorce her. *Then* you come asking to get married to her again! No, by God, she will never return to you!"

Now the ex-husband was not a bad man, and in fact his ex-wife did want to go back to him, so God revealed the above verse to the

Prophet and I then said: "Now I shall do what he wants, O Prophet!"

And so Maᶜqil gave his sister to the man in marriage.

(7/46)

The Prophet saw some women and children coming back from a wedding, and he got up with feeling for them, and he exclaimed: "By God, you are the most loved of people to me!"[52]

(7/77)

The chapter of he who said: There is no marriage unless it is with a woman's guardian's permission, according to the saying of God:

When you divorce women and they then come to the end of their designated waiting-period, do not prevent them in any way from marrying other men if they have come to a fair agreement between themselves . . .

(Q2:232)

And this concerns women who have already been married as well as virgins. God has also said:

Do not marry polytheist women until they have become true believers . . .

(Q2:221)

and also:

Marry too the single women of your number . . .

(Q24:32)

Now, ᶜĀ'isha, the wife of the Prophet, said that marriage in the Days of Ignorance before the coming of Islam was of four kinds:

1) Similar to the marriage of today, the man asked another man for the hand in marriage of that man's ward[53] or daughter, and he then gave her a dowry and married her.

2) The husband said to his wife[54] when she had finished her period and was clean: "Send for So-and-So and seek sex from him!" He (the husband) would then keep himself from his wife

and would not touch her at all until it was clear that she had become pregnant by the other man from whom she had sought sex. When it was clear that she was in fact pregnant, her real husband could then have sexual intercourse with her if she desired. He did all of this only out of a desire for offspring of noble blood.[55]

3) A group of men, no more than ten, got together and went to visit a woman, and each one of them would have sexual intercourse with her. When she became pregnant and bore a child, she would send for all these men, some time afterwards. Not one of them could refuse to go to her, and when she had them all gathered round her, she would say to them: "You are all aware of what you did. I have borne a child, and it is *your* child, O So-and-So!" and here she would name whoever she wished to name. The child would therefore be linked to him, and he would not be able to refuse or deny it.

4) A multitude of people would have sexual intercourse with a woman, and she would not refuse any who came to her. Such women were the prostitutes who used to attach banners to their doors as a sign for whoever wished to visit them.[56] If one of these women became pregnant and had a child, all the men who had had sexual intercourse with her would gather where she was and they would summon the physiognomists,[57] and they would then link her child to the man they decided was the father. The woman would allow her child to be linked with the man and to be called his son, and the man had to accept it.

When Muḥammad was sent with the Truth, he abolished the marriage of the Days of Ignorance before Islam—all forms of it, except for the marriage of the people as it stands today.

(7/44)

The Prophet is quoted as saying: "If any one of you is invited to a wedding feast, then he should go to it."

Abū Huraira is also quoted as saying: "The worst food is the food of a wedding-feast to which only the rich are invited and the poor are left out. He who ignores an invitation to a wedding-feast ignores[58] God and His Prophet."

(7/74-6)

Abū ᶜUsaid al-Sāᶜidī got married and invited the Prophet to the wedding, and no one else but his bride prepared and served the food and refreshments for the Prophet and his Companions.

(7/79, 80)

The Prophet said: "The widow[59] should not be married until she has been consulted. Nor should the virgin be married until her permission has been sought."

He was then asked: "And how is one to know what signifies her permission? A virgin is always shy."

He answered: "Her consent is always her silence."[60]

(7/51)

ᶜĀ'isha said that she was conducting a woman to her husband-to-be, who was one of the Anṣār, and the Prophet asked her: "ᶜĀ'isha, has not any of you provided any entertainment for the wedding? For truly, entertainment will excite wonder in the Anṣārīs!"

(7/67)

The Prophet said: "Do not be suspicious, for suspicion is the most lying of speech. Do not spy, do not listen to gossip, do not engage in mutual enmity, but be brothers.

"Furthermore, do not seek the hand in marriage of a woman already betrothed to one's Muslim brother until after you know whether he is going to marry her or leave her."

(7/56)

ʿUmar has said that the details of the rights in marriage are in the conditions of the marriage contract (verbal or otherwise): "The most important conditions you should all legally observe in a marriage contract are those by which you are empowered to consider the private parts as lawful."

(7/61)

Khansā' bint Khidām al-Anṣāriyya said that her father married her to someone when she was a woman who had already been married. She did not like this state of affairs, so she went to the Prophet and he revoked the marriage contract for her.[61]

(7/52)

9
Prayer

The Prophet was very late in starting the night-prayer, so ᶜUmar went to find him and he said: "The night-prayer, O Prophet! The women and children are fast asleep!"

The Prophet came out with head dripping, having just done his ritual ablutions for the prayer, and he exclaimed: "Were it not too hard on my community, I would order them all to pray at this hour!"

(9/260)

The Prophet said: "A woman who starts her period should stop praying."[1]

A woman asked ᶜĀ'isha: "When a woman has finished her menstrual period and is able once again to pray, should she make up for the prayers she has missed during her period?"

ᶜĀ'isha replied: "Are you a heretic? Whenever we had our periods, when we were with the Prophet, he never once ordered us to do that!"[2]

(1/191)

The people[3] used to pray with the Prophet with their waist-wrappers knotted up round their necks on account of their smallness,[4] and the women were told: "Do not raise your heads until the men have straightened up from prostrating to a sitting position!"[5]

(2/171)

Women do not have to pray on Friday, the Muslim day of communal prayer, and therefore they do not have to perform full ritual ablutions before the prayer,[6] as all males do.

(2/2)

ᶜĀ'isha was told the things that make any prayer void—a dog, a donkey, a woman—if any of them should walk in front of one who is praying.

She exclaimed: "Are you trying to make us the equals of dogs and donkeys?!"

And she continued: "I remember that I would lie on my bed and then the Prophet would come and place himself in the middle of the bed and start praying with me before him. But as I did not like to be in front of him and in his way, I would quietly move myself away."[7]

(1/289, 291)

Maimūna, one of the Prophet's wives, said that she did not pray when she was having her period. She used to spread herself out by where the Prophet prayed on a palm-leaf mat, and whenever he prostrated, some of his clothes would touch her.

(1/197)[8]

ᶜĀ'isha said:

The Prophet used to pray while I was stretched out asleep on his bed, with my legs in the direction of the direction in which he prayed. And whenever he prostrated in prayer, he would touch me with his hand, so I would pull in my legs, and when he stood up as a part of the prayer ritual, I would stretch them out again.

There was no form of lighting, by the way, in those days.

Also, whenever the Prophet wanted to pray any extra private prayers, he would wake me up and I would pray with him.

(1/294)

ʿĀ'isha said:

One of the wives of the Prophet went into a spiritual retreat of prayer with him while she had bleeding which was not her period together with a yellow discharge—and she put a brass bowl under her to collect the blood.[9]

(1/184, 185)

The Prophet said: "If a man sits between the arms and the legs of a woman,[10] and penetration occurs, then washing the whole body is obligatory."[11]

(1/174)

10
Religion

Abū al-Zinād said:

The traditions and aspects of duty[1] on many occasions go against public opinion; but Muslims will find no other way except to follow these traditions and aspects of duty. Among these is that the menstruating woman[2] should make up for any time that she has missed on account of her having had her period during a period of fasting—and *not* to make up for any prayers she may miss for the same reason.

*

The Prophet said: "Is it not that when a woman has her period, she neither prays nor fasts? *That* is the shortcoming in her religion."

(3/88)

Ibn ʿAbbās said:

Men would come to Medina to join the Muslim community, and if their wives gave birth to a boy, and their mares foaled, they would say: "This is a good religion!"

But if their wives did not give birth or their mares did not foal, they would say: "This is an evil religion!"

(6/238)

Jābir ʿAbdullāh said:

The Prophet arose and began to pray in the mosque. When he had finished, he then gave the official Friday sermon to the people there. When he had finished this duty, he left and went to the women and preached to them, all the while leaning on the arm of Bilāl. In the meantime, Bilāl had laid out his cloak, and the women were putting alms in the form of jewellery and other such things into it.

I asked al-ᶜAṭā: "Do you consider it a duty for the Muslim leader now to go to the women and to preach to them after he has finished in the mosque?"

He replied: "This is a duty for all Muslim leaders—and why should they not do so?"

(2/42)

The pilgrimage shall be made during the months which are appointed for it.[3] Furthermore, whosoever makes the pilgrimage during these months is to abstain from lewd words and from evil conduct and from all dispute while he is a pilgrim. God knows of any good you may do.

(Q2/197)

Muḥammad said: "Whoever performs the *ḥājj* to the Kaᶜba in Mecca, and does not have sex nor commits any other lewd deed, he shall return as pure as the day his mother gave birth to him!"

(2/347, 3/29)

ᶜĀ'isha, Mother of the Faithful, said to the Prophet: "We see the *ḥājj* as the best of deeds!"

He replied: "For you women the best jihād is the reverent *ḥājj*!"

And she added:

From that moment on, after hearing him say this, I have never neglected the *ḥājj*!

(2/347, 3/49)

A man from the tribe of Juhaina came to the Prophet and said: "My mother vowed to do the *ḥājj*, but she died before she was able to, so should I carry out this pilgrimage on her behalf?"

The Prophet replied: "Yes—perform the *ḥājj* on her behalf!—For if you had seen that there was any other debt on your mother would you have paid it?

"In this way all should repay any debt to God they may have, for God is more entitled than any other to repayment!"[4]

(3/46)

A man came to the Prophet and he said to him: "My mother has died! And she had to do a month's fasting—so should I myself fulfil this obligation on her behalf?"

"Yes," replied the Prophet. "God's debt is the one to be repaid above all others!"

(3/99)

Al-Faḍl was riding behind the Prophet on the same beast on the Prophet's final pilgrimage to Mecca. And they had halted for the Prophet to deliver formal legal opinions and decisions for some people.

A beautiful woman from the tribe of Khathᶜam then approached him seeking a formal legal opinion, and al-Faḍl began to gaze at her, for her beauty astonished him, and she began to gaze at him, for al-Faḍl was a good-looking man . . .[5]

But the Prophet physically made him look the other way by turning his face with his hand.

The woman then said: "O Prophet, my father has come at last to do God's pilgrimage, but he is too old to sit properly on his mount, so my I fulfil this obligation of his and do the pilgrimage on his behalf?"

"Yes," replied the Prophet.

(3/37-8, 8/162)[6]

II
Sex, Unlawful Sex & Chastity

ʿAmr ibn Maimūn said:

During the days before the coming of Islam, I saw a female monkey, and other monkeys had ganged up against her and were stoning her because she had committed unlawful sexual intercourse—and so I too joined them in stoning her.[1]

(5/119)

A man came to the mosque and he called the Prophet and said: "O Prophet! I have committed unlawful sexual intercourse!"

The Prophet ignored him. But when the man had made the same confession four separate times, he at last turned to him and demanded: "Are you insane?!"

"No," answered the man.

"Then take him away and stone him to death!" ordered the Prophet.[2]

(9/211)

Ḥammād says that if one confesses to unlawful sexual intercourse once, then that person must be stoned to death.

But al-Ḥakam says that this should only be after he has confessed four separate times.

(9/213)

Sa^c^d ibn ^c^Ubāda said: "Were I to see a man with my wife, I would strike him with a sword—and I do not mean with the flat of it!"

Now this reached the Prophet's ears, and he commented: "You all wonder at the *ghaira*[3] of Sa^c^d! Well, by God, *I* have more *ghaira* than him, and God has more *ghaira* than I do! God's *ghaira* has made Him outlaw immoral deeds,[4] whether they be private or public . . ."

(9/368, 378)

^c^Umar asked,[5] while with him were ^c^Alī, ^c^Abd al-Raḥmān and ^c^Uthmān, about a woman who was making a complaint to him but who could not speak Arabic:[6] "What is this woman saying?"

^c^Abd al-Raḥmān explained: "She is telling you about her master[7] who has had unlawful sexual intercourse with her."[8]

(9/232)[9]

^c^Abdullāh said:

I asked the Prophet: "Which sin is the greatest in God's eyes?"

"For you to ascribe equals to God, in spite of the fact that it is He alone who created you, and He alone," replied the Prophet.

"Truly, that is a great sin," I said. "And then what?"

"That you should kill your son[10] for fear that he will share your food," came the reply.

"And then what?" I continued.

"That you should commit unlawful sexual intercourse with your neighbour's wife."

(6/6)

When the order to fast during Ramaḍān was revealed by God, the people were not allowed to have sexual intercourse with their wives during the whole period of Ramaḍān. But some men betrayed themselves by failing to observe this rule, so God revealed the following:

It is lawful for you to enter upon your wives in the nights

before each day's fast: they are like a garment for you, and you are like a garment for them. God knows that you would deprive yourself of this right,[11] thus he turns to you in mercy and lifts this hardship from you. Hence you are free to lie skin to skin with them and to take of that which God has decreed for you, and also to eat and to drink until you are able to see the white streak of dawn against the dark of night. Then begin again your fast till nightfall. Be sure not to lie skin to skin with them just before you go to retreats of prayer in the mosques . . .

(Q2/187)[12] (6/27)

Hilāl ibn ᶜUmayya accused his wife before the Prophet of having had unlawful sexual intercourse with Sharīk ibn Saḥmā.

And the Prophet said: "Produce clear proof, otherwise the legal penalty will be on *your* back!"

To this Hilāl replied: "O Prophet! If any one of us sees another man on his wife, does he go on and ask for clear proof?"

The Prophet thought and then declared again: "Clear proof must be given, or else the legal penalty shall be on your back!"

He then went on to talk about *liᶜān*.[13]

(3/518)

Chapter of 'If people seek a reconciliation of wrongdoing then that reconciliation is not to be accepted'

A Bedouin came to the Prophet and said: "O Prophet! Pass judgement on us according to God's Book!"

His adversary then stood up and said: "He has spoken true—pass judgement on us according to God's Book!"

The Bedouin then went on to explain: "My son was a labourer hired by this man, and he had unlawful sexual intercourse with this man's wife. I was then told: 'Your son has to be stoned to death!' So I ransomed my son's life from this penalty with one hundred sheep and one slave-born girl. I then consulted the wisemen about this situation, and they replied: 'Your son should only be given a hundred lashes and be banished for a year!' "

The Prophet said: "I certainly shall pass judgement between you according to God's Book. As for the slave-born girl and the sheep, they should be returned to you. As for your son, he should be whipped one hundred times and banished for one year."

He then turned and said: "And as for you, Unais—go in the morning to the wife of this man and stone her to death."[14]

So Unais went the next morning to her and stoned her to death.[15]

(3/535)

Chapter of sexual caressing for the fasting man

ʿĀ'isha said:

A woman's private parts are not permitted to such a man.

She also said:

The Prophet used to kiss and caress while he was fasting, and he had more control than any of you over his sexual member!

Jābir ibn Zaid said:

If one looks at a woman and then experiences a discharge,[16] one can still complete one's fast.

(3/82)

Chapter of kissing for the fasting man

ʿĀ'isha said:

The Prophet used to kiss some of his wives while he was fasting.

And then she laughed.

*

Zainab heard her mother, Umm Salama, say:

While I was with the Prophet in bed, I suddenly got my period, so I slipped away and put on my menstruation attire.[17]

He then asked me: "What is the matter with you? Do you have your period?"

I replied "Yes," and then I slipped back into bed with him.

She and the Prophet used to wash together from one container and he used to kiss her—while he was fasting.

(3/82, 83)

Chapter of the selling of an adulterous slave

If one wishes, one can return such a slave to his original owner on account of his unlawful sexual intercourse.

*

The Prophet said:

"If a female slave commits unlawful sexual intercourse, and clear proof of her crime is furnished, then her owner should whip her but should not afterwards blame her further.

"And then, if she commits unlawful sexual intercourse again, her master should whip her, but should not afterwards blame her further.

"If she should commit unlawful sexual intercourse a third time, her master should then sell her, even if it is for just a piece of rope/halter of hair."[18]

*

The Prophet was asked about a female slave who commits unlawful sexual intercourse and has not been married before, and his reply was: "If she does this, then whip her. And if she does it for a second time, whip her again. If she commits unlawful sexual intercourse for a third time, sell her, even if it is just for a piece of rope/halter of hair."

Ibn Shihāb said:

I do not know any further than that about what happens if she does it a fourth or fifth time.[19]

(3/203)

The Prophet said: "If any one of you has sexual relations with his wife and says first: 'In the name of God! O God—ward Satan from us, and ward Satan from any child you may bless us with!'[20] and if they then have a child, then Satan will not be able to harm that child, nor be able to have any power over it."[21]

(1/105, 4/323)

We went out with the Prophet to raid the al-Mustaᶜliq tribe, and we captured some of their women.

We longed for our own women, and our celibacy was too much for us. We wanted to have *coitus interruptus* with the women we had captured, and so we asked the Prophet about this.

"You should not do that!"[22] he said. "For whatever is destined to exist, will exist!"

(3/432)

And all food was once lawful for the Tribe of Israel except for what Israel forbade itself before the Torah was revealed. Say: "Then bring the Torah and study it—if you are people of Truth!"

(Q3:93)

Those to whom We have vouchsafed Our Revelation in the past know it as well as they know their own children . . .

(Q2:176)

The Jews came to the Prophet and told him that a man of their number and a woman had committed unlawful sexual intercourse.

The Prophet asked them: "What do you find in the Torah about the matter of stoning?"

They replied: "Nothing—it only says that we should dishonour them publicly and whip them."

ᶜAbdullāh ibn Salām then spoke up: "You lie! Stoning to death *is* in the Torah!"

So they were brought a scroll of the Torah, and it was unrolled, then someone placed his hand over the verse of stoning to death and read out aloud[23] the verses that come before and after it. ᶜAbdullāh ibn Salām then told him: "Raise your hand!"

So the man raised his hand, and lo!, there was the Verse of

Stoning to Death. The people said: "Spoken true, O Muḥammad! The Verse of Stoning to Death is in it!"

And so the Prophet ordered that the both of them should be stoned to death—and they were. And ᶜAbdullāh said: "I saw the man fall on the woman and shield her from the stones."[24]

(4/432)

The Prophet said: "Should a husband call his wife to his bed and she refuses, so causing him to spend the night in anger against her, then the angels shall curse her till morning."[25]

(4/302)

Chapter of: Can one travel with a slave girl before she has had a period and become clean from it (and thus one knows that she is not pregnant)?[26]

Al-Ḥasan sees no harm in kissing her or caressing her.

Ibn ᶜUmar said:

If a slave-born female who is suitable for having sexual intercourse with is given away or sold or freed, then the new owner should abstain from having sexual intercourse with her until she has had one menstrual period and is then clean from it, and thus the new master knows that she is not pregnant—but there is no need of this if she is a virgin.

ᶜAṭā said:

There is no harm in one having sex with one's slave girl if she has arrived already pregnant by someone else—but to the exclusion of her vagina.

And God has said (in a list enumerating those who are not filled with self-pity):

. . . And those who guard their chastity.

Except with their wives and those whom their right hands possess . . .

(Q70:29-30)

*

The Prophet went off to Khaibar, and after God granted him victory over the city's defences, he was informed of the beauty of Ṣafiyya bint Ḥuyai ibn Akṭab, whose husband had been killed while she was still a bride.

So the Prophet therefore chose her especially for himself, and he took her with him until we came to Sadd al-Rauḥā. By this time she had had her period and was clean, thus showing that she was not pregnant, and the Prophet then had sexual intercourse with her, and made a meal of dates mixed with butter and curd on a small leather-cloth, and he said: "Call those who are around you!"

Thus was the Prophet's banquet to celebrate his wedding with Ṣafiyya. We then went back to Medina, and I saw the Prophet wrapping Ṣafiyya up in his woollen cloak behind him, and he had squatted by his camel and put forward a knee to make a foothold for Ṣafiyya to ride the camel.

(3/239)

The Prophet said: "Whoever can guarantee the chastity of what is between his jaws for me, as well as what is between his legs,[27] then I shall guarantee Paradise for him."

(8/320)

The Jews used to say that if one has sexual intercourse with a woman from the rear, then the resulting child will turn out to be squint-eyed. God therefore revealed:

Your wives are tilth for you—so go then to your tilth as you desire,[28] but first providing some good act for your souls. And fear God and remain aware that you shall meet Him in the Next World.[29]

(Q2:223) (6/38)

12
Status & Rights

Sentence to eighty lashes those who bring accusations of adultery against chaste women and who then cannot produce four witnesses to support them; and forever after this refuse their testimony, for they have proved themselves to be thoroughly unsound of mind.

And exempt from this last commandment only those who repent and make contrition after making such a false accusation—for truly God is full of forgiveness and grace.

(Q24:4-5)

And truly those who make false accusations, without repentance, against women of unblemished reputation who have been unmindful yet stayed true to the Faith, shall be cast from the grace of God both in this world and the next. And a terrible doom awaits them.

Upon the Final Day when their very own tongues, hands and feet will become witnesses against them for all the deeds that they performed!

(Q24:23-4)

The Prophet declared: "Avoid the seven greatest sins!"

"What are they?" the people asked him.

He replied: "They are: polytheism, witchcraft, killing someone rendered inviolate by God unless it be by right, usury, unlawful spending of the estate of an orphan, desertion in the face of the enemy, and falsely accusing[1] unmindful[2] Muslim women of unblemished reputation."

(8/559-60, 4/23)

Abū Hāzim said that Sahl told him: "We were very happy on Fridays!"

"Why is that?" asked Abū Hāzim.

"Well, we used to know an old woman who would get supplies every Friday from Buḍāᶜa,[3] and then she would drop beetroots into a pot, cover them with pearl-barley and cook it all. After we had finished the Friday prayer, we would leave the mosque and greet her as we passed and she would offer us portions of the food she had just cooked.

"And so we were very content on account of this. We never used to have a siesta or eat anything until after the Friday prayer had been completed."[4]

(8/174)

When Suhail ibn ᶜAmr agreed to the terms of Ḥudaibiya,[5] among the terms of the pact he imposed on the Prophet were the following:

"There should not come to you (Muslims) any person from us even if that person is of your religion, and if anyone does, then that person shall be returned by you to us, and you shall not intervene between us and such a person."

The faithful, however, were extremely unwilling to agree to this, and they were very unhappy about it.

But Suhail would agree to these terms only, so the Prophet had it written down this way with him. He then handed over Abū Jandal[6] to his father Suhail.

After this no man came to the Prophet from Suhail's people except that they were returned, during the period covered by the pact—even if that man were a Muslim.

Believing women came as emigrants as well, and Umm Kulthūm bint ᶜUqba ibn Abū Muᶜiṭ was one of those who went out to join the Prophet at that time while she was still a young girl. Her family came to the Prophet and asked him to return her to them, but he did not do this, following what God had revealed about these women—*(Q60:10—see p. 52)*.

When ᶜUmar heard this verse, he irrevocably divorced both of his wives, Qarība bint Abū ᶜUmayya and the daughter of Jarwal al-Khuzāᶜī. Muᶜāwiya married Qarība, and Ṣafwān ibn ᶜUmayya [or Abū Jahm] married the other.

(3/547, 570, 572)

A man came to the Prophet and asked him: "Who is most entitled to the best of my companionship?"

"Your mother," came the reply.

"And then who?"

"Your mother," repeated the Prophet.

"And then who?"

"Your mother," said the Prophet for the third time.

"And then who?" persisted the man.

"Your father."

(8/2)

The Prophet declared: "Among the greatest of sins is for a man to curse his parents."

He was then asked: "And how does a man curse his parents?"

"One man grossly abuses the father of another, who, in his turn, grossly abuses the former's father and also his mother," replied the Prophet.

(8/3)

ᶜUmar said:

I said to the Prophet:

"O Prophet, both pious and impious people come to visit you, so I wish that you would order the Mothers of the Faithful[7] to wear the veil in front of them!"[8]

And so God revealed the Verse of the Veil.[9]

Now, news of the Prophet rebuking some of his wives reached me, so I went to see them, and I told them that they should cease this rebellious behaviour, otherwise God would replace them for the Prophet with better wives, and they were.

But when I visited one of the wives, she said to me: "Do you honestly think, ᶜUmar, that you know better than the Prophet?"

God therefore revealed the following verse:

O wives of Muḥammad! Should he divorce any of you, it may be that God will replace you with better wives than you; and no matter whether they are women who have already been married or virgins, they will be women who give themselves up to God, who are true believers, who obey His every will, who repent in His Name, who worship only Him, and who forever have recourse to Him.

(Q66:5) (6/11)

Chapter of a woman being allowed to treat a man with 'ruqya'[10]

ᶜĀ'isha said:

The Prophet used to blow with a little spittle into his hands, rub them over his face whenever he was ill and then recite the last two chapters of the Qur'ān.[11]

When he was too ill, however, I myself would blow with a little spittle into his hands, recite the chapters, and rub his hands over him on account of their blessings.

(7/433)

The Prophet was asked: "Who of all your people is most loved by you?"

He replied: "ᶜĀ'isha."

"Then who?"

"Her father."[12]

"Who then?"

"ᶜUmar ibn al-Khaṭṭāb,"[13] and the Prophet then went on to count off the names of other men.

(5/9)

ʿĀ'isha said:

I used to be jealous of those women who came to offer themselves up to the Prophet (in marriage),[14] and I would say: "Should a woman offer herself up like this?"

Then, after God revealed the following:

You may put off any of them you desire, and you may take unto you any of them you desire, and there shall be no blame upon you if you seek out any one you have previously stayed away from—for thus it will be more likely that their eyes shall be cheered at your sight, and they shall not grieve and they may all be happy at whatever you give each of them . . . (Q33:51)

I told the Prophet: "Your Lord is seen hastening to do your will only!"

(3/294)

The Prophet stayed with Ṣafiyya bint Ḥuyai for three continuous days on the Khaibar way until he had consummated his marriage with her. Ṣafiyya was amongst those on whom the veil was imposed.

*

During the Prophet's and Ṣafiyya's wedding feast, some of the Muslims asked: "Will she be one of the Mothers of the Faithful[15]—or just a concubine of his?"

Others replied: "If he veils her, then she is one of the Mothers of the Faithful, but if he does not then she has become a concubine for him."

When it was time to saddle up and depart, the Prophet made a place for Ṣafiyya to ride behind him, and he spread the veil.[16]

(5/370)

ʿĀ'isha said:

I used to wash together with the Prophet from the same bowl when both of us were in the state of major impurity after sex.

He used to order me to put on a waist-cloth and then he would make love to me[17] while I was still menstruating.

This was true of the other wives as well.

She added:

Not one of you men has the control over your sexual desire[18] as he did!

(1/180)

The Prophet went out once to offer the pre-dawn prayer at the place of prayer, and he passed by a group of women and he said: "O group of women! Give alms, for I have been shown that you women form the majority of the inhabitants of Hell."

And they asked: "Why is this, O Prophet?"

He replied: "You are always cursing and being ungrateful to your husbands, and I have never met anyone with such a lack in their intelligence and religion. A single one of you would make even the most resolute of men go out of his mind!"

They said: "What lack is there in our religion and intelligence, O Muḥammad?"

He replied: "Is not the testimony of a woman equal to half the testimony of a man?"

They replied: "Certainly."

"Then this is the lack in your intelligence. And is it not that when a woman is menstruating, she is neither to pray nor fast?"

They replied: "Certainly."

"Then this is what lack a woman has in her religion."

(1/181)

When the news reached the Prophet Muḥammad that the people of Persia had put the daughter of Kisrā[19] to reign over them, he said: "No people will ever be successful if they have entrusted the governing of their affairs to a woman!"[20]

(5/508)

The Prophet said: "Allow the women to go at night to the mosques."

*

One of the wives of ᶜUmar used to do the dawn prayer and the evening prayer amongst the congregation in the mosque. She was asked by a man: "Why do you women come out when you know that ᶜUmar does not like you doing this, for he is a jealous and possessive husband?"

She replied: "What is preventing him from stopping me?"

The man said: "The words of the Messenger of God prevents him: 'Do not prevent the female servants of God from the mosques of God!' "

(2/10)

ᶜAmmār said:

I saw the Prophet in the company of five slaves, two women and Abū Bakr.[21]

(5/8)

Umm Hānī', daughter of Abū Ṭālib, said:

I went to the Prophet in the year of his Victory at Mecca, and I found him washing, with his daughter Fāṭima screening him.

I greeted him and he asked: "Who is it?"

I answered: "It is I, Umm Hānī', daughter of Abū Ṭālib."

And he replied: "Welcome, Umm Hānī'!"

After he had washed, he prayed for a while, wrapped in a single garment. I waited for him to finish and then I said to him: "My brother ᶜAlī has declared that he is going to kill someone in my protection—So-and-So, son of Hubaira!"

He replied: "Then I also have protected the one you have protected, O Umm Hānī'!"[22]

(4/263)

The Prophet said: "There are three things that could be of evil omen: a woman, a horse and a dwelling-place."

Truly, some from among your wives and children are enemies to yourselves—so beware them . . . !

(Q64:14) (4/74, 75)

The Prophet was asked by ᶜĀ'isha and his other wives about their participation in the *jihād*, the holy war, and he said: "The best *jihād* for you is the *ḥājj*!"[23]

(4/83)

The Prophet said: "If any one of your women seeks permission to go to the mosque, then you are not to stop her."

(1/459)

ᶜĀ'isha said:

The Prophet would lie back in my lap while I was having my period, and then he would recite the Qur'ān.

(1/179)

Whenever the Prophet had finished the public prayer, the women would get up and leave, while he would stay on a little before he himself left, and all the men would therefore do likewise.

This staying on of his was in order to allow the women to go before any of the men could.

(1/443)

Umm Salama said:

While I was with the Prophet, lying under a cloak, I suddenly got my period. I therefore slipped out and put on my menstruation attire.[24]

The Prophet asked me: "Are you bleeding?"

I replied: "Yes I am."

The he called me and I lay with him under a coverlet.

(1/179)

The Messenger of God said: "There are three types of people who shall be doubly rewarded in Heaven. The first are those from the Peoples of the Book[25] who have believed in their particular Prophet and then believe in the Prophet Muḥammad. The second is a slave who discharges his duties fully to God and to his master. The third is the man who owns a female slave and who teaches her good breeding and manners, and educates and trains her in the best possible ways and then frees her, and then takes her for his wife—to such a man indeed is a doubled reward!"

(1/78)

ᶜUrwa was asked by another man: "Can a menstruating woman serve me? Can a woman come near me while she is in a state of major ritual impurity?"[26]

ᶜUrwa replied: "That is all quite simple! Any one of them can serve me—or anyone else—without any risk of doing wrong."

He also said:

ᶜĀ'isha told me: "I used to comb the head of the Prophet while I had my period."

She also said: "I would wash his hair while I was menstruating."

(1/178, 180)

Chapter of the one who has said to his wife: "You are ḥarām[27] for me!"

Al-Ḥasan says that the meaning of this will depend on the intention. Learned sources have said that if the divorce formula is pronounced thrice, and thus irrevocably, then the wife has become *ḥarām* for her husband. Thus they call this '*ḥarām* due to divorce and separation'. This is not, however, like the case of one who makes food *ḥarām*, because the term *ḥarām* cannot here be applied to *ḥalāl*[28] food, whereas a divorced woman can be, and is, called *ḥarām*.[29]

It is said, concerning irrevocable divorce, that the woman involved is not *ḥalāl* for her husband until after she has been married to another man.

O My Prophet! Why, just to please any of your wives, have you forbidden to yourself the doing of something which God has rendered lawful for you?

(Q66:1)

Ibn ᶜAbbās was heard to say: "There is nothing significant in a man calling his wife *ḥarām*."

And it is added: "You all have a good model in the Prophet."

(7/138, 140)

The Prophet said: "Treat women with kindness, for woman has been created from a rib, and truly the most curved part of a rib is the upper part, and should you attempt to straighten it, you will break it—but if you leave it as it is, it will remain curved (and intact). So treat women with kindness!"

(4/346)

ᶜĀ'isha said:

My foster-paternal uncle came and asked for permission to come in and see me. I refused this until I had asked the Prophet about it.

When he came, I asked him and he replied: "He is your uncle, so give him permission to visit you."

I replied: "O Prophet, it was a woman who suckled me—not a man!"

He answered: "He is indeed your uncle, so let him enter your home!"

ᶜĀ'isha said that this was after the veil had been imposed on us women. She also adds that whatever is declared lawful and unlawful for blood-relations applies equally also to foster-relations.

(7/120)

A woman should not fast while her husband is with her,[30] unless it is with his consent.

And she should not give permission for anyone to enter his house unless it is with his permission, and half of whatever she spends of his estate[31] without his order shall be restituted to him.

(7/92, 94)

Pledging arms as security

The Prophet demanded: "Who will deal with Kaᶜb ibn al-Ishrāf for me? For this man has harmed God and His Apostle!"

Muḥammad ibn Maslama volunteered: "I will!"

And so he went off to Kaᶜb, and he said to him: "We want an interest-free loan from you of a camel-load or two."

Kaᶜb replied: "Then give us your women[32] as security for the loan!"

Muḥammad and his men protested: "How can we give you our women as security when *you* are the most attractive of Arabs?"[33]

"Then give us your sons as security," Kaᶜb suggested.

"How can we give you our sons when we know that every one of them will be given a bad name and reviled[34] for having been used as security for a measly camel-load or two. That would be a disgrace for us. But what we *will* do is to give our weapons as security."[35]

Muḥammad ibn Maslama thereupon promised Kaᶜb that he would come back later to see him—which he did, and he and his men killed Kaᶜb. Then they returned and reported this to the Prophet.

(3/415)

The Prophet said to ᶜAbdullāh: "Have I not been told that you fast all day and pray all night?"

ᶜAbdullāh replied: "Certainly, O Prophet!"

"Well do not do that," the Prophet told him. "Fast and also break your fast, pray but also sleep—for truly your body[36] has a right over you, and your eye[37] has a right over you, and your wife has a right over you."[38]

(7/97)

ʿĀ'isha said:

The Prophet used to caress me while I had my period, and when he was in spiritual retreat for prayer, he would stick his head out from the mosque to me, and I would wash and comb his hair for him.

(3/136, 137)

Spiritual retreat for prayer of women

ʿĀ'isha said:

The Prophet used to go into spiritual retreat for prayer during the last ten days of Ramaḍān, and I would pitch a tent for him. He would pray the morning-prayer and then enter the tent.

Ḥafṣa asked ʿĀ'isha for permission to pitch her own tent there, and when this was granted, she pitched the tent, and when Zainab, the daughter of Jaḥsh, saw this, she too pitched her tent there.

When the Prophet got up in the morning, he saw the tents, and he demanded: "What is this?"

When it was explained to him, he told his wives: "Do you honestly mean to say that you think that this is a sign of piety?"

He therefore abandoned his spiritual retreat for that month and did it instead during the last ten days of the next month.[39]

(3/138)

Men and not women are to carry the coffin

The Prophet said: "When the body is in its coffin and the men carry it upon their shoulders, if it contains a pious person, it will say 'Forward with me!', and if does not, it will say 'Woe unto me! Where are you taking me?' and all shall hear its voice except for human beings. Were people to hear its voice, they would be smitten unconscious by it!"

(2/225)

Chapter of the circumambulation of the Kaʿba by women along with the men

ʿAṭā said:

When Ibn Hishām forbade women to perform the circumambulation of the Kaʿba with the men, I said to him: "How can you prevent the women from doing this when the wives of the Prophet used to circumambulate the Kaʿba along with the men?"

"Was this after the Veiling or before?"

"Ah! By my life! I know that this happened *after* the Veiling!"

"How did they mix with the men?"

"They did not mix with the men."

*

ʿĀ'isha used to circumambulate the Kaʿba to one side of the men and she did not mix with them. A woman said to her: "Come, Mother of the Faithful! Let us kiss or touch the Black Stone!"

ʿĀ'isha replied: "Go yourself!" And she refused to go.

*

The wives of the Prophet used to go out disguised (*or* incognito) during the night and circumambulate the Kaʿba along with the men.

But whenever they wanted to enter the Kaʿba, they would stand until they could enter, after the men had come out.

*

ʿUbaid ibn ʿUmair and ʿAṭā used to visit ʿĀ'isha while she was at Jawf Thabīr, and ʿAṭā was asked: "What was her veil?"

He answered: "She was living in a Turkish leather circular tent and was wearing a covering-veil[40] which was the only thing between us and her, and I saw that she was wearing a red-dyed shift."

(2/399)

^{c}Ā'isha said that she wanted to buy the slave girl Barīra, and to give her her freedom, but her owners wanted to do this only on the condition that they retained her patronage.[41]

^{c}Ā'isha mentioned this to the Prophet and he said to her: "Buy her—such patronage belongs only to the one who frees the slave."

She continues:

Later on, the Prophet was brought some meat, and I told him: "This is what was donated as charity to Barīra."

And he replied: "It is charity for her, but for us it is a gift."

(2/332)[42]

The Prophet imposed the giving of the *zakāt al-fiṭr*[43] of a certain weight of dates, or a weight of barley, upon every slave and freeman, male and female, young and old, of the Muslims. He ordered that this should be paid before the people went out to the main prayer of the festival at the end of Ramaḍān.

(2/339)

The Prophet said: "Not one of you should say to a slave 'Feed your lord!' or 'Aid your lord in his ablutions!' or 'Give your lord something to drink!'

"But let him say 'my master!' or 'my patron!'

"And not one of you should say 'my slave!' or 'my female slave!' but let him say 'my boy!' or 'my girl!' or 'my youth!'."

Marry also those who are single of your number as well as those male and female slaves who are suitable for marriage.

(Q24:32) (3/437)

. . . Then the Prophet went away, and when he got home, Zainab, Ibn Mas^{c}ūd's wife, came seeking permission to see him, and he was told; "O Prophet, it is Zainab to see you!"

And he asked: "*Which* Zainab?"

"The wife of Ibn Mas[c]ūd," came back the reply.

"Fine, let her enter," the Prophet then said, and she was allowed to enter.

"You ordered today that people should give alms," she told the Prophet, "and I have some pieces of jewellery and I wanted to give them away as charity, but Ibn Mas[c]ūd my husband has declared that he and his children have a greater right than anyone else to be the recipients of the jewellery if it is given away as charity!"

The Prophet replied: "Ibn Mas[c]ūd is perfectly correct—your husband and your children have more right than anyone else to be the recipients of your giving the jewellery as charity!"

(2/213)

The reaching of puberty of any female is when menstruation begins, as in the words of God *(Q65:4—see p. 24)*.[44]

Al-Ḥasan ibn Ṣaliḥ said:

I knew of a neighbour of ours who became a grandmother when she was twenty-one years old.

(8/110, 148)

Chapter of the Prophet's statement that: "Possessions and wealth are like sweet green vegetables!"

God's words about this are:

Attractive to men is the love of the pleasurable things of life: women, children, heaped-up treasures of gold and silver, horses of pedigree, cattle and well-tilled land. For such are the things to be enjoyed in this world, though with God is the best of goals[45]

(Q3:14)

ʿUmar said:

O God, we cannot but be happy with that which you have made alluring for us—and I ask of you that I may spend of these things in a befitting manner!

(8/298)

Al-Maᶜrūr ibn Suwaid said:

I saw Abū Dharr al-Ghifārī wearing a complete suit of clothes, and his serving-boy was *also* wearing a complete suit of clothes!

So we asked him about this and he answered: "I grossly abused a man, who then complained to the Prophet, who asked me: 'Did you revile him by using his mother's name?

" 'Truly,' he went on, 'your brothers are your servants whom God has placed in your hands. So anyone who has his brother in his hands should then feed him from that which he himself eats, and clothe him from that which he himself wears, and he should not overburden them. If you all would do this, then give them such aid!' "

(3/434)

The Prophet said: "Shall I tell you about the inhabitants of Paradise?—They are every one of the weakest of the weak . . .

"And shall I tell you about the inhabitants of Hell?—They are every one of the arrogant and haughty wicked!"

Anas ibn Malik adds, with reference to the above:

Any one of the female slaves belonging to the inhabitants of Medina could take the Prophet by the hand and take him to wherever she wished to go.

(8/62)

A woman came to the Prophet and offered herself up to him,[46] saying: "Do you have any desire for me?"

At this Anas' daughter said: "The woman has no shame!"

"She is better than you," the Prophet told her, "for she has offered herself up to the Prophet of God!"[47]

(8/91)

Abū Qatāda said:

The Prophet came out to where we were with ᶜUmāma bint

Abū 'l-ᶜĀṣ, one of his granddaughters, on his shoulder. He then began to pray, and each time he bowed down in prayer, he would first put Umāma down, and then when he straightened up again, he would put her back up on his shoulders.

(8/18)

The Prophet said: "Not one of you should beat your wife as hard as you beat your slave, for you might have sex with her at the end of the day."

(7/98, 100)[48]

13
Travel

The Prophet said: "A woman should not travel a three-day journey[1] unless she is with a *maḥram.*"[2]

He also said: "It is not permitted for a woman who believes in God and the Day of Judgement to travel on a journey of a day and a night if no respectable female chaperones are with her."

(2/109)

The Prophet said: "No woman should travel except with a *maḥram*, and no man may visit her unless in the presence of a *maḥram.*"

A man said to the Prophet: "I wish to go out with the army of So-and-So, but my wife wants to go on the *ḥājj*!"

The Prophet replied: "Then go with her!"

(3/50)

The Prophet said: "If any one of you has been away for a long time, then he should not come to his family at night-time."[3]

*

The Prophet said: "Tarry until you enter at night,[4] I mean the evening, so that the woman with dishevelled hair may comb it, and the woman whose husband has been absent may shave off her pubic hair."[5]

(7/123, 125, 126)[6]

14
Inheritance

Jābir said:

The Prophet and Abū Bakr came on foot to visit me while I was sick amongst the tribe of Salama, and they found me unconscious, so the Prophet called for some water, did ablutions with it and then sprinkled the rest over me. I came to, and I asked: "What do you order me to do with my estate, O Prophet, if I die?"

As a result, the following was revealed by God:

As for the inheritance of your children, God directs you to do the following: The male shall have a portion equal to that of what two females receive. If there are two or more females and no sons, they shall have two thirds of the inheritance; and if all there is is one daughter, then her share shall be one half.

Parents shall receive a sixth share each of what is left if the deceased has died with chidlren; but if there is no child and the parents are the only heirs, then the mother shall receive a third. If the deceased left brothers and sisters, then the mother shall receive a sixth.

These are to be paid after all debts and bequests have been settled and paid.

You yourselves do not know whether your parents or children are more deserving of your benefit—thus God has settled and fixed these shares for you, for God is all-knowing and wise.

You shall have half of what your wives leave behind when they die, provided that they have left no children; but if there is a child, you shall receive one quarter.

This is to be paid after all debts and bequests have been settled and paid.

If a man or a woman dies without direct heirs, but leaves behind a brother or sister, then the two of them shall each receive a sixth of what the deceased has left behind; but if there are more than two siblings, they shall all share one third.

This is to be paid after all debts and bequests have been settled and paid. And this should be done so that no one's interests are prejudiced.

Thus God commands, for God is all-knowing and forbearing.

(Q4:11-2)

The Prophet has said that no self-respecting Muslim should go for even two days without making a will (provided, of course, that he has something to leave).

(4/1)

Muḥammad said: "My heirs receive not a dinar or dirhem from my estate. Everything I have I leave to charity—after maintenance for my wives and provision for my workers has been taken into account."

(4/29)

Saʿd said:

The Prophet came to where we lived to visit me when I was ill. The illness I was suffering from had worsened during the Prophet's last pilgrimage to Mecca, and I said to him: "The illness has worsened to the stage at which you now see me. I am a man of property, but I have no one to inherit it except a daughter, so may I give two thirds of my estate away as charity?"

The Prophet replied: "No."

"A half, then," I asked.

"No," he repeated.

"A third?"

"Even a third would be too much," the Prophet answered. "The reason is that to leave your heirs wealthy is better by far than to abandon them destitute, having to hold out their hands to beg from people. However, anything that you spend that would incur God's pleasure will bring you a reward, even if you put what you have spent into the mouth of your wife."

(7/388)

15
Family & Care

^{c}Alī sought the hand in marriage of Bint Abū Jahl. Fāṭima[1] heard about this, so she went to the Prophet and she said to him: "Your people assert that you are not angry for the sake of your daughters in view of the fact that ^{c}Alī is going to marry Bint Abū Jahl!"

The Prophet stood up at this, and after he had recited the creed of the Islamic belief, he said: "Having recited this creed, I may now begin to speak my mind . . . Well, I have married one of my daughters to Abū 'l-^{c}Āṣ ibn al-Rabī^{c}, and he has always been honest and frank with me. But it is true that Fāṭima is a part of me and I would hate to see her wronged. So by God! Should it be that the daughter of the Prophet and the daughter of an enemy of God be the wives of the same man?!"

And so ^{c}Alī broke off the engagement.

(5/56)

The Prophet said: "Each of you is a guardian, and each one of you is responsible for what is in your care.

"An imam is guardian and responsible for those in his care.

"A man is guardian to his family and responsible for all in his care.

"A woman is guardian to the house of her husband and responsible for all in her care.

"A servant is guardian to the property of his lord and responsible for what is in his care."

And it is thought that he also said: "A man is guardian to the property of his father and he is also responsible for what is in his father's care.

"And each one of you is guardian and responsible for what is in your care."

(2/8)

Umm Ḥabība, wife of the Prophet, said:

I said to the Prophet: "Marry my sister, the daughter of Abū Sufyān!"

"Would you like that?" he asked.

"Yes," I replied. "I am not your only wife, and I would like the person who shares with me in the best of things to be my sister."

"That is not lawful for me," the Prophet replied.

"O Prophet!" I exlaimed. "But by God! We have heard that you are to marry Durra bint Abū Salama!"

He asked: "The daughter of Umm Salama?"

I replied: "Yes."

"By God!" the Prophet replied. "Even if she were not my stepdaughter close to my bosom, she would not be lawful for me, for she is the daughter of my foster-brother, Abū Salama—Thuwaiba suckled the two of us—and thus you should not offer your daughters or sisters to me!"

Thuwaiba was a slave girl freed by Abū Lahab.[2]

(7/217)

The Prophet said: "Fāṭima is a part of me, so whoever angers her, angers me!"

(5/50)

ʿĀ'isha said:

ʿUtba made an agreement of custody with his brother Saʿd, saying: "The slave girl Zamʿa's son is mine, so be his guardian should anything happen to me!"

After the capture of Mecca by the Muslims during which ᶜUtba died, Saᶜd took the child and said: "This is my brother's son, entrusted to me by him!"

On hearing this, ᶜAbd ibn Zamᶜa, a son of Zamᶜa's and her master, stood up and countered: "But this is *my* brother—and the son of my father's slave girl. This child was born on my father's bed!"

So they took their complaint before the Prophet and Saᶜd told him: "O Prophet, this is my brother's son, entrusted to me by him!"

ᶜAbd ibn Zamᶜa then repeated his claim: "This is my brother—and the son of my father's slave girl. This child was born on my father's bed!"

"He is yours, ᶜAbd ibn Zamᶜa!" declared the Prophet. "A child belongs to the bed, and to the adulterer belong stones!"

He then told Sauda bint Zamᶜa[3] to veil herself in the presence of the child, because he saw a resemblance in the child to ᶜUtba, and the boy never saw Sauda's face till the day he died.

(8/489)[4]

Asmā', daughter of Abū Bakr, said:

My mother came to me when she was still a heathen, and this was at the time of the treaty between the Quraish and the Prophet to return all such refugees back to the Quraish. She had brought her father with her. I consulted the Prophet for his opinion regarding this, and I asked: "My mother has come humbly seeking my favour, so should I treat her with friendship and favourably?"

The Prophet replied: "Yes—receive her with friendship and favourably!"

(4/272)

The Prophet said: "When a Muslim spends something on his family in anticipation of God's reward in the Hereafter, he has done a charitable act on his own behalf."[5]

The Prophet also said: "The person who looks after the helpless and the poor[6] is like one who fights in God's Cause—or like one who prays all night and fasts all day."

(7/201, 203)

The Prophet never entered the house of anyone[7] in Medina apart from the house of Umm Sulaim. And when he was asked about this, he said: "I have pity for her, as her brother was killed at my side."

(4/69)

ᶜUthmān absented himself from the Battle of Badr because he was married to a daughter of the Prophet and she was ill. And the Prophet said to him: "Truly, you shall receive the same reward and share of the booty as any man present at the Battle of Badr!"

(4/233)

Al-Aswad ibn Yazīd said:

I asked ᶜĀ'isha: "What did the Prophet use to do about the house?"

She answered: "He would do chores for his family,[8] and then, whenever he heard the call for prayer, he would go out to pray."

(7/211)

Hind bint ᶜUtba came and said to the Prophet: "My husband, Abū Sufyān, is a miser—so do I commit any crime in feeding our family from what he himself owns?"

The Prophet replied: "No—provided that it is done sensibly and with consideration, and you take only what you actually need."

The Prophet said that if a woman[9] has spent of anything belonging to her husband without his order, then the husband is entitled to be recompensed with half the amount spent by her.[10]

(7/208, 212)

16
Property, Possessions & Wealth

The possessions and property of the clan of al-Naḍīr were amongst the booty which God had caused the Prophet to gain—the like of which the Muslims had never gained before, whether they fought using horse cavalry or camels.

All this booty therefore was to be the Prophet's and his alone. He gave his wives[1] the share he was accustomed to give of any booty that he received, and then he put the rest of it into acquiring weapons and oxen to be military equipment and supplies for fighting in God's Cause.

(6/379)

Anas said that certain men of his tribe used to give the Prophet palm-trees up to the time when he conquered Quraiẓa and al-Naḍīr. His people then ordered him to go to the Prophet and to request him to return what they had previously given him—or at least a part of it. But the Prophet had given all the palm-trees to Umm Aiman, so she came and put her gown on Anas' neck and she said: "No! By the One True God, Muḥammad shall not give you back the palm-trees, for he gave them to *me*!"

The Prophet kept on pleading: "But you will get such-and-such in return!"

But she persisted, always replying: "No, by God!"

Finally the Prophet gave her what Anas reckoned to be ten times the worth of the palm-trees in return for her handing them back.

(5/307)

Chapter of the earnings of prostitutes and female slaves (hired out by their masters for sex)

Ibrāhim totally disapproved of the wages of the professional female-wailer/mourner and the songstress.

*

God has said:

Do not, in order to gain transient temporal pleasures of the world, force your slave girls into prostitution should they wish to marry.

And should anyone force them into this, then to these girls who have been so forced, God will truly prove to be full of forgiveness and grace!

(Q24:33)

*

The Prophet banned the price of a dog, the dowry of a prostitute, and the fees of a fortune-teller.

*

The Prophet banned the earnings of slave girls (hired out by their masters for sex).

(3/266)

The Prophet made a deal with the people of Khaibar to use some land of theirs in return for one half of all fruit and vegetables produced from it.

He used to give his wives a hundred camel-loads of its produce—eighty camel-loads of dates, and twenty of barley.

When [c]Umar was Caliph, he divided Khaibar up and gave the wives of the late Prophet the choice of him giving them a share of the water and the land, or to carry on as in the past. Some of them took the choice of the land, others took the choice of the produce.

ᶜĀ'isha chose the land.

(3/301)

The Prophet cursed:
The woman who tattoos.
The woman who gets herself tattooed.
The person who takes loans with interest.
The person who gives loans with interest.
He prohibited:
The price of a dog.
The earnings of the prostitute.[2]
And he cursed too those who make pictures.

(7/197)

Chapter of a (free) gift from a woman to someone other than her husband—and of her manumitting slaves while she has a husband

This is allowed if she is not incompetent; but if she is incompetent, then it is not allowed.

God has said:

Also, do not hand over to your wards anything with which God has entrusted you for their upkeep if they are weak of judgement,[3] but do not cease to feed them and clothe them from it, and be kind in your speech with them.

(Q4:5)

Asmā' said that she asked the Prophet: "I have no possessions or property except that which al-Zubair, my husband, has bestowed on me. Can I give any of it as alms?"

"Give any of it as alms," came his reply, "And do not be miserly with it—else God will be miserly with you!"

*

Quraib, who was under the patronage and protection of Ibn ᶜAbbās, said that Maimūna bint al-Ḥārith told him that she manumitted a slave-born female without first getting the Prophet's permission. But when the day of her turn to have the Prophet stay with her came round, she asked him: "Are you aware that I have manumitted my slave-born female?"

"Have you really?" he replied.

She answered: "Yes."

The Prophet then said: "Were you instead to have given her to one of your maternal uncles, you would have gained a much greater reward!"[4]

*

ᶜĀ'isha said:

Whenever the Prophet went out on a journey, he would first draw lots amongst his wives—and the one whose lot came out would be taken by him on the journey."

He would also allot for each one of his wives a set day and night to be spent with him. Sauda bint Zamᶜa, however, gave her allotted day and night to ᶜĀ'isha in the wish to fulfil the Prophet's desires by doing this.

(3/461)

ᶜĀ'isha said that the Prophet would give something in return for any gift he himself received.

(3/458)

Chapter of the (free) gift of a man to his wife, and the woman to her husband

Ibrāhim says that this is allowed.

God says that neither should demand such a present back.

During an illness, the Prophet asked his wives' permission[5] to be nursed in ᶜĀ'isha's house, and he said: "The one who takes back[6] a free present he has given is like a dog that swallows its own vomit!"[7]

Al-Zuhrī mentions the case of one who says to his wife "Give me some of your dowry" or "All of it!" and then he shortly afterwards irrevocably divorces her, and so she tries to get back what she has given him.

Al-Zuhrī says that he should pay her back if he has been deceitful with her, but, on the other hand, if she had given him freely and willingly with no deceit on the husband's part, then the gift stands, and the man is permitted to keep it, for God has said:

. . . And should they give you any of it back of their own free will, then you should accept it and enjoy it completely.

(Q4:4) (3/459)

Al-Nuʿmān ibn Bashīr said:

My mother asked my father for a portion of his estate to be a gift for me. He thought about it and then gave it to me, and my mother said: "I shall not be satisfied until this has been witnessed by the Prophet!"

So my father took me by the hand, as I was then just a lad, and he led me to the Prophet and he told him: "This boy's mother, Bint Rawāḥa, has asked me for a portion of my estate to be a gift for him."

"Do you have any other son but this one?" the Prophet asked.

"Yes," replied my father.

"Then do not make me a witness for any injustice!"

(3/497)

Chapter of borrowing by the bride at the time of her wedding

Aiman said that he went to see ʿĀ'isha at her house, and he found her wearing a shift of striped stuff worth five dirhems,[8] and she said to him: "Raise your sight to my serving girl, and look at her! for she is too proud to wear such a dress as I am wearing—even in the house! Although, during the lifetime of the Prophet, I was the only woman to possess such a shift, and there was no woman wanting to dress up in Medina[9] who did not hesitate to ask me to borrow it!"

(3/480)

17
Social Conduct

ʿĀʾisha said:

I perfumed the Prophet with my own hands before he went into the state of ritual consecration for the pilgrimage to Mecca and I used the best perfume I could find.

(7/527, 531)

ʿĀʾisha said:

I used to comb the hair of the Prophet while I was menstruating.

(7/529)

Umm ʿAṭiyya said:

We were ordered to come out on the day of a religious festival, and this included bringing out with us even the pubescent girls and older virgins from their private apartments,[1] and also the menstruating women—and they would all stand behind the men of the congregation and prayed and lauded with them, hoping for the blessings of that day and for its purifying grace.

Ḥafṣa added to this ḥadīth*:*

But Umm ʿAṭiyya may very well have said: ". . . The pubescent girls and older virgins in seclusion were allowed to go to the place of prayer, but the menstruating women were kept away."[2]

(2/47, 48, 52)

Chapter of what is lawful for a man and a woman to be alone together, provided it is in public

An Anṣārī woman came to the Prophet and he went off with her alone to one side and said: "By God! You, the Anṣāris, are the most beloved of people to me!"

(7/118)

Ḥafṣa bint Sīrīn said:

We always forbade our girls to go out on the days of the religious festivals. There then came a woman who stayed at the fortress of the Khalaf tribe.

I went to see her, and she said that her husband's sister had gone out raiding with the Prophet on twelve separate occasions, and her sister had been with him on six of those raids and she had said: "We used to nurse the sick and treat the wounded."

And once she asked the Prophet: "O Messenger of God, is there harm for any one of us women if she does not go out on a religious festival because she does not have a proper veil?"

And the Prophet had answered: "A friend of hers should veil her with her own veil! All women should bear witness to good deeds and the call to prayer of the Faithful!"

Ḥafṣa added:

And when Umm ᶜAṭiyya arrived, I went and asked her: "Have you heard about such a thing?"

She replied reverently: "Yes. The Prophet said, 'Let the pubescent girls and the older virgins in seclusion and the menstruating women come out for the religious festival—(but he bars the menstruating women from the place of prayer)—for all women should bear witness to good deeds and the call to prayer of the Faithful!'."

I asked her then: "Are the menstruating women included in this last part of what he said?"

And she replied: "Of course they are!"

(2/51)

Sauda bint Zam^{c}a went out one night, and ^{c}Umar saw her and recognized her.

He said: "It's you, by God, O Sauda—you cannot hide from us!"

So she returned to the Prophet and told him what had happened while he was in his private apartment having his supper (and in his hand was a bone stripped from its flesh).

There suddenly came a revelation upon him, and then it ended, and he was saying: "God has granted you permission for you to go out to anwer your calls of nature!"

(7/120)

^{c}Umar said:

We used to guard ourselves against chatting and taking our leisure with our wives during the Prophet's lifetime, dreading that something might be revealed from God concerning this practice. But when the Prophet passed away, we resumed chatting to our wives and taking our leisure with them.

(7/81)

The Prophet said: "A woman should not look at or touch another woman to describe her to her husband in such a way as if he was actually looking at her."

(7/121)

The Prophet said: "O Muslim women! A woman should not look scornfully at all at anything that her neighbour gives her—even if it is a sheep's foot."

(8/28)

The Prophet said: "You shall not visit women!"

A man from the Anṣār then asked: "O Prophet, but what then do you say about the male in-laws of a woman?"

The reply came: "The male in-laws are death!"[3]

(7/117)

The Prophet cursed effeminate men and masculine women.[4]

He furthermore said: "Expel them from your homes!"

He expelled one such man, and so did ᶜUmar—and the names of neither of these men are revealed by the narrators.

(8/545)

A man came to the Prophet and said: "O Prophet! I have been overcome by the strain of fatigue and hunger!"

On hearing this, the Prophet sent to his wives for something for the man to eat, but they had nothing to give,[5] so he asked: "Is there no man who will take this man as a guest and look after him for tonight? God shall surely have mercy on such a man!"

There then stood up a man from the Anṣār and he said: "I will take this man, O Prophet!"

And so he took the man home with him. When he got there, he quietly told his wife: "We have a guest of the Prophet to stay with us, so spare him nothing!"

But she replied: "By God! I have nothing but the children's food!"

"Then prepare the meal" said her husband. "Light your lamp, and when the children want their supper, put them to bed instead. Then pull yourself together and put out the light, and we too shall go hungry and pull in our belts for the night!"

So the wife prepared the meal, lit her lamp, put the children to bed, stood as if she were adjusting the lamp and then put it out. She and her husband then proceeded to look as if they were eating, while in reality the guest was eating all the food there was in the house, and the couple spent the night hungry.

The next morning, the guest went to the Prophet and told him what had happened and he replied: "God has laughed at what happened last night—or else he has marvelled at this couple's deed!"

(6/382, 5/90)

18
Mothers & Children

Abū Ṭalḥa had a son who was sick, and when he was out one day, his son died. On his return, Abū Ṭalḥa asked his wife, Umm Sulaim: "How is my son doing?"

"He has never been quieter," came the reply.

Umm Sulaim then brought him his supper, and after he had eaten it he went to bed with her and had sexual intercourse with her.

After he had finished, his wife said: "Bury the child."

In the morning Abū Ṭalḥa got up and went to the Prophet and told him about this.

"Did you and your wife make love last night?" the Prophet asked him.

"Yes," Abū Ṭalḥa replied.

"O God!" the Prophet then invoked. "Cast your blessings on these two people for the night they have just had together!"

Nine months after this, Abū Ṭalḥa's wife gave birth to a boy whom the Prophet held in great favour.

(7/273)

ʿĀ'isha said:

A woman with two girls[1] came to me and asked me for alms, but all I had was a single date. Nevertheless I gave it to her, and she divided it out between the girls, and then they rose and left.

When the Prophet came, I told him about this, and he said: "Whoever takes the slightest share of responsibility for these girls and is good towards them, they shall then be a screen for him from the fires of Hell!"

(8/17)

Samura ibn Jundub said:

I prayed behind the Prophet over a woman who had died in childbirth and he stood over the middle of her body.

(2/233)

A woman had died in childbirth and the Prophet prayed over her and stood over the middle of her body.

(1/197)

Chapter of the killing of children in war

It was reported that a woman had been found killed during a series of raids led by the Prophet, and the Prophet declared that he disapproved of the killing of women and children.

*

Chapter of the killing of women in war

A woman was found killed during a series of raids led by the Prophet. So the Prophet forbade the killing of women and children.

(4/159-60)[2]

The Prophet was heard to say at the pulpit: "Truly, the tribe of Hishām ibn al-Mughīra have sought permission to marry their daughter to ᶜAlī ibn Abū Ṭālib—but I do not give permission, and nor shall I unless ᶜAlī divorces my daughter to whom he is already married and then he can marry their daughter.

"For truly my daughter is a part of me and whoever disturbs her disturbs me, and whatever causes harm to her causes harm to me!"[3]

(7/115)

The Prophet said: "Each time I begin my prayers,[4] I have the intention of spending a long time doing them.

"But should I ever hear the cries of a baby, I shorten my prayers to prevent the baby's crying from making its mother over-angry."

(1/381, 382)

Asmā' bint Abū Bakr said:

In the days before Islam, I saw Zaid ibn ᶜAmr ibn Nufail[5] standing with his back against the Kaᶜba, crying: "O you people of the Quraish! By God—not one of you follows the religion of Abraham save I!"

He used to revivify[6] baby girls who had been buried alive, and would say to any man who wanted to kill his daughter: "Do not kill her!—I shall provide for her!"

Thus he would take the daughter, and when she had grown up well, Zaid would say to her father: "If you wish, I shall deliver her up to you, but if you want me to continue to provide for her, then I will!"

(5/108)

A group of women were talking to the Prophet, and they asked: "The men take up all your time to the exclusion of us—so could you set aside a day for us so that just we can see you?"

He agreed, and he promised them a day on which he would regularly meet them and give them sermons and commandments.

It was on such a day that he said to them: "Any woman of you who has had three children die in infancy shall be shielded from the fires of Hell."

A woman asked: "And what if she has had only two children who have died?"

"They shall also shield their mother from the fires of Hell!" came the reply.

(1/80)

The Prophet said: "God has forbidden you to be disobedient to mothers and to bury daughters alive."

(3/348)

The Prophet said, upon the death of his son Ibrāhim: "There is a wet-nurse for him in Paradise!"

(8/139)

ʿĀ'isha said:

I used to play with dolls in the Prophet's presence. Friends of mine would also play with me, but whenever he came in they would rush off in all directions and hide from him. He would then round them up and send them all back to play with me again.

(8/95)

Captive women and children were brought before the Prophet. Amongst them was a woman who was milking her breasts in order to feed the children. When she found one of them, she would pick it up and hold it to her bosom and suckle it.

The Prophet asked us: "Would you say that this woman would throw a child of hers into the fire?"

We answered: "No—even though she is undoubtedly able to do that!"

He then went on to say: "God is more merciful to His servants than even this woman is to that child!"

(8/19)

19
General

The Prophet of God, Solomon (Sulaimān), had 60 wives, and one day he declared: "I shall go and sleep with each one of my wives tonight—and each wife of mine shall conceive and then give birth to a male child who will grow to be a knight to fight in the Cause of God!"

And so he went and slept with each of his wives, but not one of them gave birth except for one—and she gave birth to a half-child, a deformed boy.

The Prophet Muḥammad explained: "Were Solomon to have said 'God Willing!' then each one of his wives would have conceived and given birth to a knight who would fight in the Cause of God."

(9/420)

Umm Sulaim used to spread out a leather-cloth and the Prophet would take his siesta on it while she was still there. While he slept, she would collect his sweat and some of his hair, put them together in a glass bottle and mix them in with perfume.

When Anas ibn Malik knew that he was soon to die, he requested Umm Sulaim to allow some of this compound perfume to be mixed in with the aromatics to be used to embalm him, and it was done so.

(8/198)

Lo! There are those who cover up their hearts so that they might hide from Him. Truly, even when they cover themselves with their garments. He knows all that they conceal and all that they reveal, for He knows all that is in the hearts of men!

(Q11:5)

Muḥammad ibn ᶜAbād ibn Jaᶜfar said that he heard Ibn ᶜAbbās reciting this verse from the Qur'ān, and that he asked him about it, and Ibn ᶜAbbās replied: "It was revealed concerning a people who used to conceal themselves whenever they went to answer the call of nature while in a deserted place open to the sky, and also whenever they had sexual intercourse with their wives in a deserted place open to the sky."

(6/166)

ᶜĀ'isha said:

The Prophet said: "When a woman gives in charity food from her house which is not spoiled and which does not waste her husband's property and possessions, there shall be a reward for her as great as that which she has given away.

"Her husband, moreover, shall receive the reward for what he has earned for the household, and the shopkeeper who supplied her with the food shall be rewarded likewise.

"And not one of them shall diminish the reward of the others."

(2/290)

God knows what every female bears in her womb, and how soon or how late the issue will be born, for with Him all things are created with a purpose.

(Q13:8)

The Prophet said: "The keys to the Unknown are five in number, which no one knows save God:

"No one knows what will happen tomorrow save God;

"No one knows how early a child will be born save God.

"No one knows when the rain will fall save God.
"No one knows the place of one's death.
"And no one knows when the Last Day will come save God."

(6/182)

ʿĀ'isha said:

The Prophet ordered me and everyone else to have *ruqya*[1] done as a protection from the Evil Eye."

*

Umm Salama said that the Prophet saw a slave girl in his house with black spots[2] on her face, so he ordered: "Have *ruqya* done for her, for with her is an Evil Eye!"[3]

(7/426)

It is claimed that there are five things in the *fiṭra*:[4]

1. Circumcision.
2. Shaving the pubic hair.[5]
3. Plucking the armpit.[6]
4. Cutting fingernails (and toenails).
5. Cutting the moustache.[7]

(7/515)[8]

The Prophet said: "O Community of Muḥammad—there is no one who is more jealous and possessive than God if a slave,[9] male or female, commits unlawful sexual intercourse—and, O Community of Muḥammad, were you to know what I know, you would laugh less and weep more!"

(7/110)

Muḥammad had been delayed by some business of tribal arbitration elsewhere, and the Muslims were anxious to start praying, but they had no one to lead them in prayer as the Prophet was absent, so Abū Bakr was asked to stand in for him, which he did.

In the middle of the prayers, however, the Prophet returned, and he made his way to the front row of the ranks of the praying men.

The congregation started clapping in mid-prayer at his arrival, causing Abū Bakr to look back. Muḥammad beckoned to him to continue and finish that section of the prayer, and then he took over for the rest of the service.

When the prayers were over, he turned and said to the congregation: "O people, what on earth has led you to start clapping during prayers when something unusual happens? Clapping is only for women. Anyone who sees something unusual during his prayer should say *'Subḥān Allāhi!'*[10]—for no one hearing him say this will turn around and be distracted."[11]

(2/173, 184)

Fāṭima complained that she was exhausted and tired out from using the handmill and grinding with it, so when she heard the news that the Prophet had been brought some captive women, she went to him, and asked him for one of them to be her servant.

But she could not find him, so instead she spoke to ᶜĀ'isha about this, and when the Prophet did come, ᶜĀ'isha told him what Fāṭima wanted.

She continued:

And then[12] he came to our house after we had gone to our beds. As we were going to get up, he ordered: "Stay where you are!"

And I could feel the coolness of his two feet on my chest, and he continued: "Shall I make you aware of something better than what the two of you have asked for?—Whenever you two take to your beds at night, you should say *'Allāhu akbar!'*[13] thirty-four times, *'Al-ḥamdu lillāhi!'*[14] thirty-three times, and *'Subḥān Allāhi!'*[15] thirty-three times. This is indeed a better thing for you both than that which you have asked for!"[16]

(4/221)

ʿĀ'isha, wife of the Prophet, said:

When the believing women emigrated to the Prophet and the Muslims, he used to test them in accordance with the words of God:

O you of the faithful! Whenever women who abandon the kingdom of evil and come to you, examine them although it is only God who knows fully of their faith . . . Then if you have confirmed that they are true believers, do not return them to those who refute the Truth, for they have ceased to be lawful for them . . .

(Q60:10)

And whichever of these believing women agreed to this condition had also then agreed to the test, and the Prophet would say, after they had agreed to this verbally: "You are now at your liberty to go, for I have accepted your homage and have made a contract with you!"

And not once, by God, did the hand of the Prophet ever touch the hand of any one of these women—he accepted instead their homage verbally. And, by God, the Prophet did not make the women swear to anything but what God had directed him to make them swear, saying to them as they swore: "I have accepted your homage verbally!"

(7/159)

ʿUmar ibn al-Khaṭṭāb asked for permission to enter the Prophet's house. Already with the Prophet were women of the Quraish who were asking for favours from him in voices louder than his own, but as soon as they heard ʿUmar's voice, they all hurriedly veiled themselves.

When ʿUmar was granted permission and he entered, he found the Prophet laughing, so he said to him quizzically: "May God keep you laughing, O Prophet, may my mother and father be sacrificed for you!"

The Prophet then explained to him: "I was amazed at the reaction of these women here with me—as soon as they heard the sound of your voice, they immediately veiled themselves!"

"They should righfully do that with you—not with me!" replied ᶜUmar.

And he then turned to the women and said to them: "O you enemies of yourselves! Do you do this kind of thing with me but not with the Prophet?"

"Well, you are harsher and rougher than the Prophet!" replied the women.

And at this the Prophet exclaimed: "So tell me about it, ᶜUmar! By He in Whose Hands is my soul, I would say that if you were travelling along a mountain road even Satan himself would take another route rather than meet you face to face!"

(8/70)

The Prophet said: "A man is not to be alone with a woman, nor is a woman to travel unless there is a *maḥram*[17] with her."

A man then stood up and said to him: "My name has been put down for a raid on such-and-such a place, but my wife has gone to do the *ḥājj* to Mecca!"

The Prophet replied: "Go and do the *ḥājj* likewise with your wife!"[18]

(4/154)

The Prophet said: "All children of Adam[19] are speared in both sides by the two fingers of Satan when they are born[20]—except for Jesus son of Mary, whom Satan tried to spear, but speared instead his midriff."[21]

(4/324)

Abū Huraira said:

A man came to the Prophet and he said: "I am ruined!"

The Prophet asked him: "Why?"

He replied: "I had sexual intercourse with my wife during Ramaḍān!"

"Then free a slave as penance," the Prophet told him.

"I have no slave," came the reply.

"Then fast for two successive months."

"I am not able to."

"Then feed sixty of the poor."

"I can find nothing to do that with."

The Prophet was then brought a pannier full of dates, and he asked: "Where is that man who has been talking?"

The man answered: "I am here!"

The Prophet then offered him the pannier of dates, saying: "Give this away as alms."

The man promptly exclaimed: "What? Give this away to those more in need than us, O Prophet?! By He who sent you with the Truth! There is no family between the two mountains of Medina more in need than us!"

The Prophet laughed aloud[22] until his canine teeth showed, and he said to the man: "Then it is yours to take!"

(7/214)

The Prophet was more shy[23] than a virgin in seclusion.

(4/492)

The Prophet was more modest than a virgin in seclusion, and whenever he saw something that he did not approve of, we would know it from his face.

(8/79)

If someone is compelled by oppressive circumstances to say "This is my (blood) sister" about his wife, there is to be no blame attached to him—for the Prophet said: "The Prophet Abraham (Ibrāhim) said about his wife Sārah, 'This is my sister'—and he really meant 'sister in God'."

(7/143)

The Prophet said: "God has divided His Mercy into one hundred portions. He has sent down to earth one single portion of it, whilst keeping the other ninety-nine with Him.

"Yet on account of that one single portion of Mercy, all of Creation has mercy for each other—so much so that the mare lifts her hooves from her foal lest she should harm it."

(8/20)

Chapter of what was said about the house of the Prophet's wives[24] *and which houses were attributed to them*

O you of the Faithful! Do not enter the houses of the Prophet unless leave is given to you . . .

(Q33:53)

ʿĀ'isha, wife of the Prophet, said:

When the Prophet was seriously ill, he sought the permission of his other wives to be nursed in my house—and this was given.[25]

*

ʿĀ'isha said:

The Prophet passed away in my house on the day of my turn to have him stay with me, and he died while he was leaning on my chest, and God joined my spittle with his (in other words, ʿAbd al-Raḥmān had brought a chewing-stick for the Prophet, but he was too weak to use it himself, so I took and chewed on it and then I cleaned his teeth with it).

*

Ṣafiyya, the wife of the Prophet, said that she came to visit the Prophet while he was in spiritual retreat for prayer in the mosque for the last ten days of Ramaḍān.

When she finally got up to go, the Prophet got up with her and accompanied her past the gate of the mosque by the door of Umm Salama's house, who was also the Prophet's wife. Two Anṣārī men passed the couple by and they greeted the Prophet and went on.

But the Prophet called after them: "You may relax, gentlemen—there is nothing amiss—she is my wife!"

And they at once answered back: "Good heavens! Of course, O Prophet! Of course!" For the fact that he had to say this to them was too momentous for them.

He then said to them: "Truly, Satan circulates in society as blood does in the body—and I was afraid that he had cast doubts and suspicion in both your hearts!"

*

ᶜAbdullāh ibn ᶜUmar said:

I went up to the top of Ḥafṣa's house, and I saw the Prophet answering the call of nature with his back to the direction of prayer and facing Syria.[26]

*

ᶜĀ'isha said:

"The Prophet used to pray the afternoon prayer[27] while the sun had not yet left the enclosure of my house."

*

The Prophet stod up to deliver a sermon, and he pointed towards the dwelling of ᶜĀ'isha, and said three times:

"*There* is sedition, from the place where the horn of Satan rises!"[28]

*

ᶜĀ'isha said:

Once, while the Prophet was at my home, I heard the sound of someone outside asking for permission to enter Ḥafṣa's house. I told the Prophet: "This man is asking for permission to enter your house."

He answered: "I think that it is So-and-So (a paternal foster-uncle of Ḥafṣa's). The divine laws concerning foster-relations are the same as those that concern blood-relations."

(4/215)

ᶜAbdullāh ibn ᶜUmar said:

The Prophet said in a sermon from the pulpit: "Kill vipers and other venomous snakes, for some of them destroy the sight and can also cause pregnant women to miscarry!"

Once, when I was chasing after a snake in order to kill it, Abū Lubāba called out to me: "Do not kill it!"

I replied: "But the Prophet has ordered the killing of snakes!"

"But after that he exempted house-snakes," came Abū Lubāba's reply.

(4/330)

The Prophet said: "Seven kinds of people shall be given shade by God on the Day when there shall be no shade but His Shade:

"1. The just leader.

"2. The youth grown up in the true worship of God.

"3. The man who regularly prays in the mosques.

"4. Two men[29] who love each other in God's name and who meet and part for His sake only.

"5. A man who is both sought and desired by a noblewoman of great beauty and he refuses, saying, 'I am a God-fearing man!'[30]

"6. A man who gives charity so discreetly than even his left hand does not know what his right hand spends.

"7. And a man who mentions the name of God in private and whose eyes flood with tears."

(1/356, 629)

Chapter of when a man voices his doubts as to whether a child is really his

A man came to the Prophet and said to him: "O Prophet, there has been born to me a black boy!"[31]

The Prophet asked in reply: "Do you have any camels?"

"Yes," replied the man.

"What are their colours?" asked the Prophet.

"They are red."

"Would there be an ash-coloured one amongst them?"

"Yes," replied the man.

"Now how do you think that came about?" the Prophet went on.

"Perhaps it is something hereditary," the man suggested.

"Well then, perhaps this *son* of yours is something hereditary!"

(7/171)

Qatāda said:

I said to Saᶜīd ibn al-Musayyab: "If a man has had a spell cast on him,[32] or is unable to have sex with his wife, would it be possible for him to have the spell broken or else to be given an amulet for curing the sick?"

Saᶜīd replied: "There is no harm in that—for by doing so, such a man wishes only to make things better, and you are not forbidden that which profits you!"

(7/442)

Chapter of abundance of women

ᶜAṭā said:

We were present, along with Ibn ᶜAbbās, at the funeral of Maimūna at Sarif, and Ibn ᶜAbbās said: "This was the wife of the Prophet, so when you raise her funeral bier, do not shake or quake her, and be gentle, for the Prophet had nine wives and would give eight of them their due night to be with him and he did not give one her due night."[33]

(7/4)[34]

ᶜĀ'isha said that the Prophet came to see her while she was in the company of another woman, and he asked her: "Who is this?"

And ᶜĀ'isha replied: "This is So-and-So."

And she then went on to tell him about this particular woman's excessive and fervent praying, at which the Prophet exclaimed with disapproval: "You should do such things within the limits of your own capacity—and no more! For God is tireless, but you mortals shall tire.

"The greatest act of devotion one can make to God is that which one makes within moderation, yet regularly!"

(1/36)

Umm Salama said that the Prophet was at her home while in the same house was an effeminate man, who said to her brother ᶜAbdullāh ibn Abū ᶜUmayya: "If God conquers Ṭā'if for you tomorrow, then I shall suggest that you take the daughter of Ghailān for yourself, for she shows you four rolls of fat when she faces you, and eight rolls when she walks away!"

And the Prophet said: "Such a man should not visit you!"[35]

(7/118)

20
Islamic Women

Abū Huraira says that Zainab was called 'Barra', which means 'pious', but people used to say: "Is she trying to make herself into a saint with that name?"

So the Prophet changed her name to 'Zainab', which means 'timid'.

(8/137)

The Prophet said: "In a dream I saw a black woman with masses of hair go out from Medina till she set down at Mahyaᶜa.[1] I interpreted this as the spreading of the plague to Mahyaᶜa."

(9/132)

Abū Maryam ᶜAbdullāh ibn Ziyād al-Asadī said:

When Ṭalḥa, al-Zubair and ᶜĀ'isha went to Baṣra,[2] ᶜAlī despatched ᶜAmmār ibn Yāsir and al-Ḥasan ibn ᶜAlī to us at Kūfa.

When they arrived, they ascended the pulpit of the mosque there, with ᶜAmmār standing a step below al-Ḥasan, and we all gathered to hear what they had to say.

I heard ᶜAmmār proclaim: "ᶜĀ'isha has gone to Baṣra—and certainly she is the wife of your (deceased) Prophet in this world and the Next—but God is now testing you in order to find out whether you obey Him or whether you obey her."

(9/171, 172)

^{c}Ā'isha said to ^{c}Abdullāh ibn al-Zubair: "Bury me with my co-wives, and do not bury me with the Prophet in the house,[3] for I would not want at all to be sanctified through this!"

*

^{c}Umar sent a request to ^{c}Ā'isha, saying: "Give me permission to be buried with my Companions."[4]

"Of course, by God!" she replied.

But whenever any other of the Companions of the Prophet had made the same request of her, she had replied: "No, by God!—I shall never make them into a soft bed for anyone!"

(9/319)

Whenever the Prophet went to Qubā', he would visit Umm Ḥaram bint Milḥān (who was married to ^{c}Ubāda ibn al-Ṣāmit), and she would prepare a meal for him.

One day he went to visit her, and after he had eaten the meal she had made, he went to sleep.

After a while he woke up laughing, and Umm Ḥaram asked: "What made you laugh?"

"I saw in my dreams some of my Community," came the reply. "They were arrayed before me as if they were champions of Islam and warriors in the cause of God, sailing across the middle of this sea, and kings upon their thrones!"

"Call upon God to make me one of them!" pleaded Umm Haram, and so he did.

The Prophet then put his head down and went to sleep again—and woke up a second time laughing.

"What made you laugh?" repeated Umm Ḥaram, to which the Prophet this time replied:

"You are among the first of them!"

Later, in the time of Mu^{c}āwiya,[5] Umm Ḥaram sailed the sea, and when she was landing, she was thrown from her mount and died.

(8/199)

ᶜAlī said that the Prophet said: "The best of the women of her time was Mary, and the best of the women of her own time was Khadīja."[6]

*

ᶜĀ'isha said:

I was not as jealous as any of the Prophet's wives as I was of Khadīja, who had died long before the Prophet married me. This was because I used to hear him mention her often, and he said that God had ordered him to tell her the good news that there was a pavilion built of jewels waiting for her in Paradise. Also, whenever he slaughtered a sheep he would send a good share of it to women who had been her close friends when she was alive.

Sometimes I would say to the Prophet: "It is as though the only woman in the world was Khadīja!"

"She was like this, and she was like that," he would reply, "and she bore me children!"

*

ᶜĀ'isha said:

Hāla bint Khuwailid, sister of Khadīja, asked the Prophet's permission to enter his house, and the way she did this reminded him of the way Khadīja used to ask. This moved him greatly, and he cried: "O God, Hāla!"

I became jealous at this, and so I asked him: "What is it that reminds you of one of the old women of the Quraish—a toothless old hag who died a long time ago, and in whose place God has given you one better!"[7]

(5/102, 4/427)

The people used to send their gifts to the Prophet when it was the day of his turn to be with ᶜĀ'isha.

Now ᶜĀ'isha said that her co-wives went in a group to Umm Salama,[8] and they said to her: "O Umm Salama, by God! The people send their gifts to the Prophet when it is ᶜĀ'isha's day with him. We too would like to receive the benefit of this, just as ᶜĀ'isha does—so could you tell the Prophet to order the people to send their gifts to him wherever he happens to be. And if he is with a wife, then it should not matter which wife!"

So Umm Salama mentioned this to the Prophet, but she then came back and reported: "The Prophet turned away from me after I told him what you told me to tell him. Furthermore, when he had turned back to me again and I repeated the demand, he just turned away again from me! But when he had turned back once more and I had mentioned it to him for the third time, he said: 'O Umm Salama, do not try to hurt me through ᶜĀ'isha—for, by God, no divine inspiration[9] comes down to me while I am under the sheets of any one of you women save her!' "

(5/78)

The Prophet was praying at the Kaᶜba in Mecca[10] when a group of Quraish came by, and one of them said: "Do you not see this hypocrite? Which of you will go to the camel that such-and-such a family has just slaughtered and take its bowels, blood and womb membranes[11] and then bring them back, and then wait until he prostrates so he can put it all over his back between his shoulders?"

The most destitute of their group was duly despatched, and he returned with all of the camel's innards and these they put on the Prophet's back when he prostrated in prayer.

As soon as this happened, he merely remained prostrate while they laughed so much that they were forced to prop each other up.

Someone went off to fetch Fāṭima—she was a slip of a girl then—and she came running. The Prophet remained prostrate until she had removed all of the offal from his back and thrown it away. She then turned on the group of Quraish, and she swore at them.

When Muḥammad had finished his prayer at last, he cursed those Quraish thrice with God's revenge, and this was said later to have come true with their deaths in the Battle of Badr.[12]

(1/295)

The Prophet said: "A prostitute[13] was forgiven her sins[14] by God when she passed by a dog that was panting at the mouth of a deep well, on the point of dying from thirst. So she pulled off her shoe, tied it fast with her yashmak and drew out some water from the well with it for the dog to drink.

"And thus God forgave her her sins."

(4/338)

The Prophet said: "Were it not for the Israelites, meat would not rot and stink, and were it not for Eve, a woman would not betray her husband."

(4/345)

When the Prophet's iron helmet was broken on his head, and his face was bleeding and his front teeth were broken, ᶜAlī went off to look for some water, and he brought some back in his shield. Fāṭima washed the Prophet with the water, and when she saw that it only made the bleeding worse, she took a piece of rush matting, burned it and then cauterized the wound with it—and the bleeding was stopped.

(4/98)

Ibn ᶜAbbās said to ᶜĀ'isha: "The Prophet married no other virgin but you."

*

ᶜĀ'isha said that she said to the Prophet: "Suppose you had alighted in a valley where there grew a bush whose fruit had already been eaten,[15] and then you found some other bushes of which nothing had been eaten. Which do you let your camel graze on?"

His reply was: "On that which had not been grazed on before."

And by this ᶜĀ'isha meant to say that the Prophet had married no virgin but her.

*

The Prophet told ᶜĀ'isha:

"I have been shown you twice in my dreams,[16] when a man comes carrying you wrapped up in a piece of silken cloth, and he says to me 'This is your wife!'—I uncover her, and there, it is you, and I say 'If this is from God, then it shall come to pass!' "[17]

(7/9)

Fāṭima came to the Prophet during his final illness, and he whispered something in her ear, at which she burst into tears. But he whispered something else to her, and she started laughing.

ᶜĀ'isha asked her afterwards what it was that the Prophet had told her, because she had never seen such joy so near to sadness as on that day, but Fāṭima said that she would not discuss it.

When the Prophet finally passed away, ᶜĀ'isha again asked Fāṭima about what the Prophet had whispered to her, and this time Fāṭima replied: "The Prophet told me that, 'Each year the Archangel Gabriel [Jibrīl] has come a single time to revise the Qur'ān with me.

" 'But he has come to do this with me twice this year, and I can interpret this only as heralding the approach of my death, and my time on this earth shall shortly expire—and I know that you shall be the first of my family to join me.'

"And so I wept bitterly, but then he added, 'But will you not be pleased to be the mistress of all the women of the folk of Paradise,[18] or of all the women of the Faithful there?'

"And so I laughed joyously!"

(4/526, 527)

Truly God chose Adam, and Noah, and the line of Abraham, and the line of ᶜImrān above all mankind—

all of one and the same descent. Truly God knows and hears all things!

Once there was a woman of the line of ᶜImrān who prayed: "O my Lord! Unto Thee do I dedicate what is in my womb to serve

in Thy Name. So accept this from me, for Thou knowest and hearest all things!"

But when she at last gave birth,[19] she said: "O my Lord! Behold—I have given birth to a female child!"—of what she would give birth to, God had known all the while; and she could have hoped for no male like this female!—"And I have named her Mary, and I offer up her and her offspring[20] for Thee to protect against Satan, the Accursed One!"

And her Lord accepted her kindly and graciously and caused her to grow up with purity and beauty, and He entrusted her into the care of Zachariah [Zakariyya].

*

And behold! The angels said: "O Mary! See—God has chosen you and made you pure—and raised you above the women of all the worlds!

"O Mary! Be devout unto your Lord in worship and bow down in prayer with those who bow down in prayer!"

*

And behold! The angels said: "O Mary! God has given you glad tidings in a Word from Him—and he shall become known as the Christ, Jesus, Son of Mary, who shall be held in great honour in this world and the Next, and who shall be amongst those nearest to God.

And he shall speak to the people as a child and as an adult, and he shall be among the righteous!"

Mary replied: "O my Lord! How can I bear a son when no man has touched me?"

The angel answered: "It is as we have spoken—God creates what He wills, and when He wills a thing to be, He but commands it, 'Be!' and it is!" (Q3:33-7, 41-2, 45-7)[21]

*

Chapter of when one said: "I have given you this slave girl to serve you according to the custom recognized by the people" —and this is lawful

Now some say that this is a loan. But if the man says "I clothe you in this garment" then that is to be considered as a gift without ties.

The Prophet said: "The Prophet Abraham[22] fled with Sārah. Sārah was given Hagar[23] and she came back and said to Abraham: 'Are you aware that God has humbled the pagan and given me a slave-born girl, Hagar, to serve me?' "

(3/484)

Ibn Kaᶜb ibn Mālik heard his father say:

We used to have some sheep which grazed at Salᶜa.

One day a slave girl of ours saw one of them dying, so she immediately smashed a stone and slaughtered the sheep with it.[24] But I told everyone: "Do not eat the sheep until we have asked the Prophet about this!"

And so we asked him about this, and he said that we should eat the sheep."

ᶜUbaidullāh said: "It amazes me that she was a slave girl yet she had the sense to slaughter that sheep!"

(3/284)

The Prophet was heard to say: "The women of the Quraish are the best of those women who ride camels—they are the most caring for their children—the most responsible of wives for their husband's property!"[25]

It is added that Mary, the daughter of ᶜImrān, never rode a camel.

(4/428, 7/212)

And God has produced for the Believers the parable of the wife of Pharaoh when she prayed: "O my Lord! Build for me near You a mansion in Paradise, and save me from Pharaoh and his works, and save me from the evil-doing people!"

And there is also the parable of Mary, the daughter of ᶜImrān, who guarded her chastity—and We then breathed Our spirit into her womb—and who testified to the Truth of the words of her

Lord and His Scriptures, and who was among the devout servants of God.

(Q66:11-2)[26]

The Prophet said: "Many men have attained perfection,[27] whereas of women only Āsiya, the wife of Pharaoh, and Mary, the daughter of ᶜImrān,[28] have attained perfection.

Furthermore, the superiority of ᶜĀ'isha over all women is like the superiority of *tharīd*[29] over all other foods!"

[See Q3:45-7, p. 142]

(4/411)

Further Reading

Appendix 1
Further selections from the Qur'ān

Divorce

And should any of you die and leave behind your widows, they shall then have a waiting-period, with no remarriage, of four months and ten days. And when they have finished this term, there shall be no sin upon you for whatever they may do with themselves in a lawful manner, truly God knows of all that you do!

And there shall be no sin upon you if you make an offer of bethrothal to one of these women, or if you keep such an offer unspoken in your hearts—for God knows that you intend to ask for their hand in marriage. Do not make any secret pledge of bethrothal with them, but speak to them honourably, and do not resolve on tying the knot of marriage before the waiting-period is over. And you should know that God is aware of what is in your hearts, so take heed of him: and know also that God is much forgiving and most-forbearing.

There shall be no sin upon you if you divorce women before you have touched them[1] or before their dowry has been settled; but even in these cases, bestow on them a suitable provision—the wealthy according to his means, and the poor according to his means—a fair and just settlement. This is a duty for those who wish to do good.

And if you divorce them before you have touched them but after having fixed a dowry for them, half of the dowry will then be for them—unless they forgo their half, or unless he in whose hands is the marriage-tie forgoes his claim to the other half. And to forgo the man's half is the more righteous of acts.

And do not forget to act with gracious generosity towards one another, for truly God sees full well all that you do!

(Q2:234-7)

And should any of you die and leave behind widows, they are to bestow to their widows the provision of one year's maintenance and the right to stay on in the dead man's house for the same period. But if they leave the house, then there shall be no sin upon you for whatever they may do with themselves in a lawful manner. And God is almighty and wise!

And as for the divorced women, they also are to be provided with a fair and just maintenance—and this is a duty for those who wish to do good.

Thus God makes clear to you His Signs to you—so that you may achieve understanding.

(Q2:240-2)

The Day of Judgement

O mankind! Fear your Lord! For truly the convulsions of the Final Hour will be a terrible thing!

On the Day when you behold it, every nursing mother shall forget the child she is suckling, and every pregnant woman shall bring forth her burden prematurely—and it will seem as if all of mankind is drunk, though they will not be drunk—but dreadful will be God's wrath!

(Q22:1-2)

Heaven & Hell

The Believers, both men and women, are protectors of one another: they command the doing of what is just and forbid the doing of what is evil, and they observe regular prayer and regular almsgiving, and they obey God and His Apostle. It is on these that God will place his Grace—for truly God is almighty and wise!

God has promised to the Believers, men and women, that they shall abide for eternity in gardens under which rivers flow and in sumptuous mansions in the gardens of everlasting bliss.[2] But the greatest bliss of all is the favour of God—that surely is the highest achievement!

(Q9:71-2)

"And on that Final Day,[3] no person shall be wronged in the least and you shall be repaid for nothing except for your past deeds.

"Truly, those who shall have Paradise shall on that Final Day find joy in all that they do—

"They and their spouses shall recline on couches in shady groves,[4]

"Every delight will be there for them and they shall have whatever they ask for.

"True peace through the words of a Lord full of Mercy!"

(Q36:54-8)

Enter Paradise joyously, you and your spouses!

(Q43:70)

It is He who has sent down His Divine Presence and Tranquility into the hearts of the Believers, so that they might grow stronger in their faith—for to God are all the forces of the heavens and the earth; and He is all-knowing and wise—

and so that He might admit all the Believers, men and women, to the gardens under which rivers flow, for them to abide there eternally, and to take from them their evils. And in the sight of God, that is the highest achievement:

and so that He might punish the hypocrites, men and women,

and the polytheists, men and women—all those who consider God with evil in their hearts. They are encompassed by evil, and the wrath of God is upon them: He has cursed them and prepared Hell for them, and how evil a destination!

(Q48:4-6)

As for the righteous, they shall be in gardens and in happiness on that Final Day,

joyous in all that their Lord has bestowed upon them, and their Lord shall have warded off from them the fiery doom.

And it will be said to them: "Eat and drink with satisfied joy on account of what deeds you have done,

while you recline on arrayed couches!"

And We shall mate them with pure companions with beautiful eyes,[5]

And as for those who believe and whose offspring follow them in belief, We shall reunite them with their offspring, and We shall not deprive them of any of the good resulting from their deeds—but every individual shall be held in pledge for his deeds.

And We shall bestow upon them whatever they desire of meat and fruit;

and there they shall hand round a cup full neither of frivolity nor of temptation to sin;

and they shall be served by youths devoted to their service,[6] like well-hidden pearls in their shells.

(Q52:17-24)

And they shall be on thrones encrusted with gems

reclining on them, face to face.

Immortal youths shall serve them[7]

with goblets and ewers and cups filled with water from clear springs

— which will not sully their minds nor make them drunk—

and with any fruit they may choose.

and with the flesh of any fowl they may desire.
And there shall be with them pure companions with beautiful eyes,[8]
like well-hidden pearls in their shells.[9]
And all this will be as a reward for the good deeds of their past life.
No frivolity will they hear there, nor any temptation to sin—
but only the call of 'Peace!', Peace!'
And as for those who have attained to righteousness, what will become of them?
They too shall be amongst lote trees bearing fruit
and acacia trees laden with flowers
and extended shade
and copiously flowing water
and abundant fruit
that grows all year round and is easy to pick.
And they shall recline on raised high thrones.
And We have created anew their spouses
and made them virgins again.[10]
comely and well-matched
for those who have attained to righteousness—
a good many from olden times.
and a good many from recent times.

(Q56:15-40)

Justice

O you who are Believers! You are commanded to use equal retribution in cases of unlawful killing—the free for the free, the slave for the slave, and the woman for the woman. But should any remission be made to the guilty person by the slain one's brother, then it should be adhered to fairly and justly, and fair compensation should be made . . .

(Q2:178)

Concerning those of your women who are guilty of immoral acts, call for four from amongst you who have witnesses against them, and if they so testify, then confine the guilty women to houses until death takes them away or until God decides upon some other way of dealing with them.[11]

And concerning those two men who are guilty of immoral acts,[12] punish them both; but should they both repent and mend their ways,[13] then leave them alone—for God is a source of recourse and mercy.

(Q4:15-6)

Modesty & Clothing

And women who have grown old, who no longer feel sexual desire, shall incur no sin if they put aside their outer garments—provided that they do not make any wanton display of their charms. But despite this, it is still better for them to be modest—and God knows and hears all things.

(Q24:60)

And those who malign the believing men and women without due cause take upon themselves the glaring sin of calumny!

O Prophet! Tell your wives and daughters, and all the other women Believers, that they should put their outer garments over their bodies when they are in public—for this is the most convenient to their being recognized in such a modest manner and not molested. And God is full of forgiveness and grace!

(Q33:58-9)

Marriage

This day all the good things in life are made lawful to you. The food of the Peoples of the Book[14] is lawful to you, and your food is lawful to them.[15] And not only are chaste women of the Believers lawful to you to marry, but so too are chaste women of the Peoples of the Book who received this revelation before your time—and give them their dowries, and take them in honest wedlock and not in fornication, or as secret lovers.[16] And should anyone reject his faith in God, then all his works shall have been for nothing, and in the Hereafter he shall be among the lost.

(Q5:5)

O Prophet! Say to your wives: "If you desire this worldly life and its attractions, then I shall surely provide for you and set you free in a becoming manner.

"But if you desire God and His Apostle and life in the Hereafter, then truly, for those who do good amongst you God has prepared a huge reward!"

O wives of the Prophet! If any of you becomes guilty of apparent immoral conduct, then her punishment will be double that of any other person—for this is an easy thing for God.

But if any one of you devoutly serves God and His Apostle, and performs good works, then We shall bestow upon her a reward twice that of any other person—and We have prepared for her a most generous sustenance.

O wives of the Prophet! You are not like any other women provided that you fear God. But do not be too gentle in your speech, lest one with a diseased heart is moved to desire you,[17] but speak kindly yet firmly.

And you should live quietly in your houses, and not flaunt your charms as they used to do in the olden times of Ignorance; and perform regular prayer and give alms regularly, and serve God and His Apostle. Truly, God wishes only to remove all abominations from you, O you members of the Prophet's household, and to purify you completely.

And make known what is recited to you in your houses

concerning the Signs of God and His wisdom—for God understands the deepest mysteries and knows them all.

Truly, for all Muslims, men and women, and all Believers, men and women, for all devout men and women, and all true men and women, and all steadfast men and women, and all humble men and women, and all men and women who give alms, and all men and women who fast, and all men and women who guard their chastity, and all men and women who are continuous in God's praise—for all of these God has prepared forgiveness for all their sins and a great reward!

And when a matter has been decided upon by God and His Apostle, it is not fit for any believing man or woman to claim any choice of their own about their decision—for the one who in this way opposes God and His Apostle has clearly gone astray wildly!

And behold, O Muḥammad! You did say to one who had received the favour of God and yourself: "Keep your wife in marriage and fear God!" And in this way you hid in your heart that which God was about to reveal—for you had fear of the people although it is God alone Whom you would fear! But when Zaid ended his marriage with her and divorced her, We married her to you so that there might be no sin in the future upon the Believers when they marry the wives of their adopted sons after the latter have formally divorced them. And thus this Commandment of God was fulfilled.[18]

(Q33:28-37)

O Prophet![19] We have made lawful to you your wives to whom you have paid their dowries, as well as those whom your right hand possesses from the war captives which God has granted you, and the daughters of your paternal uncles and aunts, and the daughters of your maternal uncles and aunts, who have migrated from Mecca to Medina with you, and any woman believer who offers herself up[20] to the Prophet should the Prophet wish to marry her.

— And this latter commandment is for you alone, O Prophet, and not for the other Believers, for We know what We have already ordained for them as regards their wives and the captives possessed by their right hands.

And lest you become too anxious . . .

be aware that you may put off any of them you desire, and you may take unto you any of them you desire, and there shall be no sin upon you if you seek out any one you have previously stayed away from—for thus it will be more likely that their eyes shall be cheered at your sight, and they shall not grieve, and they may all be happy at whatever you give to each of them—for God knows all that is within your hearts, and truly God is all-knowing and forbearing.

It is not lawful for you to marry any more women, nor to substitute them with other wives, though their beauty greatly attract you—aside from those whom your right hand already possesses[21]—and God watches over all things.

O you of the Faithful! Do not enter the houses of the Prophet until you are given permission: and when you are invited to a meal, do not go too early so that you have to wait for it to be made ready. But whenever you are invited, enter, and whenever you have finished your meal, leave, and do not linger merely to chat—for such behaviour may annoy the Prophet but he may feel shy to dismiss you, yet God is not shy to tell you what is right.

And if you ask anything of his wives that you have need of, ask them before a screen—for this will make your hearts purer and theirs.

Furthermore, it would not be right for you to annoy God's Apostle nor to marry his widows after he has passed away—for truly, that would be a terrible thing in the eyes of God.

And truly God knows full well of all that you reveal, be it secretly or openly.

There is no sin upon these women if they appear before their fathers, or their sons, or their brothers, or their brothers' sons, or their sisters' sons, or their womenfolk, or those whom their right hands possess. And fear God, O you women! For God is a witness to all things.

(Q33:50-5)

Prayer

O you of the Faithful! Do not try to pray while you are in an intoxicated state until you are in a position to comprehend what you are saying; and do not attempt to do so while you are in a state of bodily ritual impurity[22] until you have washed yourself—unless you are travelling. But if you are ill or on a journey, or have answered the call of nature, or been in sexual contact with women, and you can find no water, then take clean earth or sand and rub it lightly over your face and hands[23]—for truly God absolves sins and forgives.

(Q4:43)

O you Faithful! When you make preparations for prayer, wash your faces and your hands and arms to the elbows, rub your heads with water, and then wash your feet to the ankles. If you are in a state of major ritual impurity,[24] then you must wash your whole body. But if you are ill, or on a journey, or have answered the call of nature, or have had sexual contact with a woman, and you are unable to find any water . . .[25]

(Q5:6)

Sex, Unlawful Sex & Chastity

. . . and do not commit adultery, for lo! it is an abomination and an evil!

(Q17:32)

Status & Rights

It is He who has created you from a single being, and from it made his mate, so that he might dwell with love with her. And when he has embraced her, she conceives at first a light burden, and she bears it and when it grows heavy within her, they both pray to their Lord God, saying: "If you give us a sound child, then we vow that we shall be amongst those who are grateful!"

(Q7:189)

And whosoever performs righteous deeds, man or woman, and is a Believer, truly We shall give him a good life, and We shall give them their reward equivalent to the best of the deeds they have done!

(Q16:97)

And the corrupt women are for the corrupt men, and the corrupt men are for the corrupt women; and good women are for good men, and good men are for good women—for they are not touched by what others say, and for them is forgiveness and a noble provision.

(Q24:26)

O you of the Faithful! People should not mock other people—it may be that those who are mocked are better than those who mock! And women should not mock other women—for it may be that those who are mocked are better than those who mock! And do not defame each other or insult each other with names—for evil is the name of corruption after one has attained to True Belief, and those who do not repent are amongst those who do evil!

(Q49:11)

O you who believe! It is unlawful for you to seek to inherit from your wives against their will, and it is unlawful too to treat them oppressively in order to take away a part of their dowry which you gave them—unless it is the case that they have been guilty of immoral acts.[26]

But live with your wives fairly and justly—for should you dislike them, it may be that you dislike something in which God has created much good.

But should you wish to replace one wife with another, even if you had given a pile of treasure to the first wife, do not take a thing of it back—for would you take it by committing the grevious sin of slandering her?[27]

And how would you take it away when you have gone in to one another,[28] and the wives have taken solemn agreements from you?

(Q4:19-21)

And do not covet those things on which God has bestowed his Bounty more so than on others—for to men is the result of what they have earned, and to women is the result of what they have earned—so ask God for His bounty, for truly God is knowledgeable of all things.

(Q4:32)

Men are the ones who support women according to what God has given to the former from His bounty more so than the latter, and according to what the men spend from their possessions. Thus righteous women are those who are devout and who guard when their husbands are away what God orders them to guard. and as for those women whose ill will you fear, first admonish them and then refuse to sleep with them, and then beat them![29] And then if they obey you, then do not continue to harm them—for God is great and most high!

But should you fear a breach between a couple, appoint an

arbiter from his family and an arbiter from her family if they desire peace and reconciliation, then God will provide it for them—for truly God is all-knowing and aware!

(Q4:34-5)

And you will not be able to treat all of your wives equally and justly, even if you desire it greatly[30]—but do not lean towards one to the exclusion of another to the extent that the latter is almost in a state of being without a husband. And if you do good works and fear God, then God will be forgiving and merciful!

But if a couple separates, then God will provide wealth for each of them, for God is caring and wise!

And to God belongs all that is in the heavens and the earth!

(Q4:129-31)

Inheritance

They will ask you for your legal opinion. Say: "Thus is God's commandment concerning those who die and leave no direct heir: If a man dies and has a sister but no child, then she shall receive half the inheritance; if it is a woman who has died with no child then her brother is entitled to this inheritance. If there are two sisters, then they shall together receive two thirds of what he leaves behind; and if there are brothers and sisters, then the male shall have twice that which the females receive."

(Q4:176)

Family & Care

And God has made for you mates of your own kind, and He has made for you from your mates children and grandchildren, and has given you sustenance from all the good things of life.

(Q16:72)

God has not made a man with two hearts in one body; nor has He made your wives—whom you declare "as unlawful to you as your mothers' bodies"[31]—your mothers; nor has He made your adopted sons your sons. Such are only figures of speech invented by your mouths, whereas God speaks the Truth to you and indicates the True Path.

Call your adopted sons by their fathers' names—for this is the most just way according to God—and if you do not know their fathers' names, then call them your brothers in faith or your protected wards. But there shall be no sin upon you should you make a mistake in this matter, for it is what your hearts intend that counts; and God is merciful and forgiving.

The Prophet has more claim over those who believe than their own selves, and his wives are their mothers. Those related by blood have, according to God's commandment, have a greater claim over each other than do those who are believers in Medina and those who came from Mecca with the Prophet. Nonetheless, you should act with justice and fairness towards those who are your closest friends—and such is God's command also.

(Q33:4-6)

Children & Mothers

And We have commanded man to be good to his parents—for in pain after pain his mother bore him, and he was suckled by her for two years. Therefore thank Me and your parents, and with Me is the Final Destination![32]

(Q31:14)

General

And their Lord has answered their[33] prayers: "Truly, I shall never miss any one of the deeds you do, be you male or female: each of you is an issue of the other . . ."

(Q3:195)

He is the Originator of the heavens and the earth! And how can He have a son when there has never been a mate for Him? He has created all things and He knows all things!

(Q6:101)

Some would say that some of these cattle[34]—four kinds of either sexes—are unlawful,[35] either of the two sexes of sheep and either of the two sexes of goats. So say; "Has he forbidden the two males, or the two females, or what is contained in the wombs of the two females? Tell me what you know of this if you claim to speak true!"

And they would say the same concerning either of the two sexes of camels and cows. So say: "Has he forbidden the two males, or the two females, or what is contained in the wombs of the two females? Perhaps then you were present when God commanded you thus!" And who could do more evil than the one who invents a lie in God's Name in order to lead astray people without knowledge? Truly God guides not a people who commit evil.[36]

(Q6:143-4)

And thus God punishes the hypocrites, men and women, and those who do not believe, men and women; and thus too God grants His mercy to those who believe, men and women—for God is forgiving and merciful.

(Q33:73)

And God created you from dust, and then from a drop of sperm, and then He made you into either of the sexes. And no female conceives or gives birth without His knowledge, and no man who has a long life has that life lengthened or shortened without God's command—for all this is easy for God to do!

(Q35:11)

To God is the dominion of the heavens and the earth, and He creates what He wills, and He grants male children to whomsoever He wills.

Or else He grants both males and females, and He makes barren whomsoever He wishes—for He is omniscient and omnipotent!

(Q42:49-50)

And thus, the other gods they believe in have made goodly for most of the polytheists the killing of their children,[37] but this has brought about their destruction and it has caused confusion for them in their religion. And should God have wished it, they would not have done this, so you should keep away from them and all that they invent!

And they say that such-and-such cattle[38] and crops are taboo and should not be eaten by anyone except for those they say We wish to, as they claim, and they also say that there are cattle on which it is forbidden to put a yoke or burden, and also that there are certain types of cattle over which they do not pronounce the name of God when they slaughter them—and these are all inventions falsely attributed to God. It shall be that He will have His retribution upon them for what they have invented.

They say: "That which is in the wombs of such-and-such cattle is reserved for our men and is forbidden to our women—but should it be stillborn, then all may have a share of it." God shall have His retribution upon them for all that they falsely attribute—for He is full of wisdom and knowledge.

And lost are those who murder their children out of their folly and ignorance, and who forbid food that God has provided them with, and who thus invent against God. They have gone astray and they are not rightly guided!

(Q6:137-40)

And yet they attribute to Him offspring[39] from amongst those He has created! Truly man is devoid of all gratefulness!

Do you really say that he has taken daughters from what He has created, but bestowed upon you sons?

And whenever any one of them is brought the news of what he attributes to the Merciful God, his face darkens, and he is filled with suppressed rage.

And he says, "Am I to have a child to be reared merely to wear trinkets and jewellery?" and he finds himself in a quandry with no clear guidance.

But still they claim that the angels are all female, who are but servants created by God. Did they witness their creation? Their testimony shall be taken down and they shall be questioned!

But they say: "If it had not been the will of the most gracious God, we would not have worshipped these gods!" But of this they could have no knowledge, and all they can do is guess![40]

(Q43:15-20)

Truly God has received the statement of the woman who pleads with you concerning the case of her husband, and who makes her complaint to God. God hears the arguments of you both, for He sees and hears all things.

And should any of you divorce your wives by saying, "You are as unlawful for me as my mother's body,"[41] and who then wish to go back on what they have uttered, then they shall free one slave before the couple may touch each other again. For thus you are admonished, for God is aware of all that you do.

But the one who does not have the wherewithal to free a

slave should fast for two consecutive months before the couple may touch each other again; and if any one is unable to do this, then he should feed sixty of the needy. And this is so that you might show your faith in God and His Apostle. And these are the limits as ordained by God, and for those who disbelieve there awaits a terrible doom.

(Q58:1-4)

And should any of your wives go over to the Unbelievers, and you are afflicted in turn, then pay to those whose wives have departed the equivalent of what they had spent on their dowries, and fear God in Whom you have faith!

O Prophet! When women who believe come to you in order to vow allegiance to you, pledging that they will not worship anything other than God, that they will not steal, that they will not commit unlawful sexual intercourse, that they will not murder their children, that they will not slander and make deliberate falsehood, and that they will not disobey you in anything you say to be just, then accept their vow of allegiance and pray to God to forgive them their sins—for God is full of forgiveness and mercy!

(Q60:11-2)

Appendix 2
Women in the Qur'ān

Abū Lahab's wife is cursed along with her husband in Q111:4-5, but she is not named. She is reputed to be a wife of one of the Prophet Muḥammad's uncles, both of whom showed an undisguised hatred for Muḥammad and his cause in the very early days of Islam. Abū Lahab's wife is even said to have strewn thorns in the dark for the Prophet to step on.

Āsiya, Pharaoh's wife,[1] is used as an example of outstanding virtue in womanhood (perhaps righteousness is a better word here) in Q66:11 (p. 143) and she appears at the beginning of Q28:9 to save the Prophet Moses from death when he was abandoned in the Nile.

Eve (Hawā) is a faceless creature and is never specifically mentioned except in passing:

> **And We said: "O Adam, dwell you and your wife in the Garden . . . "** (Q2:35)

The general impression is that she was not created from Adam's rib, while it is never mentioned that she led Adam into temptation (see Q7:18-25). In fact, Q20:115-21 implies that Satan corrupted Adam directly, and it is taken for granted that the fate of his wife unquestionably follows that of his own—and as a matter of course.

Lot's wife is never named, but cursed in Q66:10[2] for betraying her husband. She has her fate spelt out for her in Q11:81 where the angels urge her husband Lot to flee Sodom before it is destroyed by God:

"O Lot! We are messengers from your Lord! Your enemies shall never catch up with you! Move on now with your family while it is still night, and let not one of you look back—but your wife shall remain; for what will befall the people of Sodom will befall her also . . . !"[3]

Mary or Maryam, the mother of Jesus (Īsā), probably has the most appearances and references in the Qur'ān—but very little personality, if any. The following extract is taken from the chapter of Maryam, considered, along with that of Joseph, to be the most beautiful and popular in the Qur'ān:[4]

And recall in the Book the story of Mary when she parted from her family and went to a place in the east,

where she secluded herself from them; and then We sent Our Spiritual Messenger to her to appear to her in the form of a man in all his respects.

She said: "Truly I seek refuge in the Merciful Lord from you! Do not approach me if you fear God"

He replied: "I am only a Messenger from your Lord, come to announce the bestowing on you of a holy son!"

She said: "How can I have a son when no man has ever touched me—nor have I been a loose woman!"[5]

He answered: "Thus will it be—your Lord says: "It is an easy thing for me, so that you might have a son whom We shall make as a Sign to Mankind and a Sign of Our mercy!"

And so the matter came to pass,

and she conceived him and then she secluded herself in a remote place,

and the pains of childbirth made her come to the trunk of a palm-tree.

She cried out: "Oh would that I had died before this happened, and would that I had become a thing forgotten!"

But then a voice called to her from under the tree: "Do not grieve! For your Lord has created a rivulet beneath you.

"And shake the trunk of the palm-tree in your direction so that it will drop fresh ripe dates upon you.

"So eat and drink and cool your eyes and be refreshed! And should you see any person, say: 'I have vowed to fast to the Merciful God, and thus I will not speak this day with anyone!' "

In time she went to her people, carrying her baby boy, and they said:

"O Mary! Truly you have brought an amazing thing!

"O sister of Ḥārūn! Your father was not an evil man, nor was your mother a loose woman!"[6]

And then she pointed to him . . .[7] (Q19:16-29)

The mother of Moses (Mūsā) appears on a few occasions, most notably at the beginning of Q28:7 onwards. There are touching scenes of her devotion to her son, who is eventually taken from her before Pharaoh's men come to slaughter him as all the other Israelite male babies.

The wife of Noah (Nūḥ) is not named, but cursed along with Lot's wife for betraying her own husband (she doubted him and traditionally is the first 'nag') in Q66:10.[8]

Potiphar's wife (ᶜAzīz's wife or 'the great man's wife')[9] is not named, and she emerges as a strangely redeemable villainess as she attempts to seduce Joseph—a victim and slave to her passions:

And when Joseph attained full manhood, We bestowed upon him knowledge and the power of judgement—for thus do We reward those who do good.

But she in whose house he was living sought to make him yield himself to her, and she bolted the doors and she said: "Now come to me!" But he answered: "God forbid! Your husband is my lord and he has been good to me! Truly, those who do wrong come to an evil end!"

And with passion she desired him, and he desired her, and he would have succumbed to this temptation had he not seen in this evidence of his Lord God—and thus We commanded so that We might turn from him all evil and abominations, for he was one of Our true servants.

So they raced each other to the door, and she grabbed his

shirt and ripped it from his back—and there suddenly they found her lord[10] at the door! She said: "What is a suitable punishment for one who has formed evil designs on the virtue of your wife? What indeed, but prison or terrible torture?"

Joseph said: "It was she who sought to make me yield myself up to her!"

But someone from her household[11] who was there made the suggestion: "If this shirt is torn from the front, then she is telling the truth and he is the liar!

But if his shirt is torn from the back, then it is she who is the liar, and he who is telling the truth!"

So when her husband saw his shirt and that it was torn from the back, he said: "Behold! This is an example of your deception, O womankind! Truly your deception is great!

"O Joseph, let this pass! And O my wife, seek forgiveness for your sin, for truly you are one of the sinners!"

Now, the women of the city said: "The wife of the great man is seeking to seduce her slave and to make him yield himself up to her! Truly he has pierced her with a violent passion—we see that she has clearly gone astray!"

But when she heard of this malicious talk of theirs, she sent for them and prepared a feast for them, and to each one of these women she gave a knife. Then she called to Joseph: "Come out and reveal yourself to them!" And when they saw him, they marvelled at his beauty and in their amazement, they cut their hands with their knives: They cried: "God preserve us! This is no ordinary man—this can only be a noble angel!"

Then she said: "Here before your eyes is the one about whom you did blame me! Indeed, I sought to make him yield himself up to me, but he resolutely saved himself without stain. But now, if he will not do whatever I bid him, he shall most assuredly be cast into prison and there find himself in the company of the vilest of people!"

And he replied: "O my Lord! More desirable to me is prison than that to which these women are inviting me—for

unless You ward their wiles from me, I shall yield to their allures and become one of the ignorant!"

And his Lord heard his prayer, and He warded their allures from him, for truly it is He who knows and hears all things!

Then it occurred to the nobleman and his household, even after they had seen the signs of his innocence, that it would be best to cast Joseph into prison for some time. (Q12:22-35)

Potiphar's wife, however, repented and admitted finally that it was she who had tempted Joseph. Popular legend has it that, having seen the error of her ways, she at last became Joseph's lover, and God remade her a virgin every night for his pleasure.

The Queen of Sheba is cool, clever and resourceful. She is summoned by Solomon (Sulaimān) to be subtly tested by him and put back onto the path to righteousness in Q27:20-44. This includes the unusual and mildly erotic verse of her baring her thigh(s) to enter what she believes to be a shimmering pool of water.

There were **two shepherdesses** whom Moses helped, who were 'quaint and shy'. His marriage to one of them is mentioned in the same chapter that refers to his mother (see above).

Appendix 3
Glossary of Names

This is a list of some of the more significant names that occur in the ḥadīths of this volume. Note that while 'bint/ibnat' means 'daughter of . . .', it is occasionally used for 'wife of . . .' All dates are AD.

ᶜAbd al-Raḥmān ibn ᶜAuf (577[?]-652)—A prominent early convert from the Quraish tribe of Mecca. He was renowned for his political and financial astuteness.

Abū 'l-ᶜĀliya—A freed slave who was a well-known, trustworthy transmitter of ḥadīths.

Abū Bakr (570-634)—The first Caliph and father of ᶜĀ'isha, wife of the Prophet. He was a merchant and reputedly the first male convert to Islam (the women of the Prophet's household being the very first). He was a close friend of Muḥammad's and was buried beside him.

Abū Bakra (d. 671)—An Abyssinian slave who was freed by the Prophet, and who subsequently became a Companion. He was notable for keeping out of politics and later became a transmitter of ḥadīths.

Abū Huraira (d. 678, aged 78)—A Companion of the Prophet. He was called Abū Huraira (lit: 'Father of the Kitten') because he used to play with a kitten when he herded his people's goats. He converted only four years before the Prophet's death. He had no property or wealth and depended on the Prophet for charity. He was a prolific narrator of ḥadīths.

Abū Ṭālib (d. 619)—Paternal uncle of Muḥammad. A man of some standing and a clan chief, he was therefore able to provide Muḥammad with protection when he needed it most during the period of his persecution by the Quraish, who feared the nascent religion. He was the father of ᶜAlī, but never himself converted to Islam.

ᶜĀ'isha (614-678)—The daughter of Abū Bakr and the third and favourite wife of Muḥammad. She was literate, noted especially for her eloquence and knowledge of poetry. While married to the Prophet, charges of adultery against her were repudiated by the revelation of Q24:10-20. She was left a childless widow at the age of 18, forbidden to remarry (as were all the Prophet's widows). She resisted becoming involved in politics until after the assassination of the third Caliph, ᶜUthmān. ᶜAlī opposed her rise and defeated her along with Ṭalḥa and al-Zubair. However, after this setback she became reconciled with ᶜAlī and the Caliphs who succeeded him, and she was permitted to live in peace in Medina. Her approval and disapproval of state and religious affairs continued to hold great sway in the Muslim state.

ᶜAlī ibn Abū Ṭālib—Cousin of the Prophet and son of Abū Ṭālib. He married the Prophet's favourite daughter, Fāṭima, and married no one else while Muḥammad lived. One of the first converts to Islam, he also became the fourth Caliph. He fought ᶜĀ'isha for the Caliphate at the Battle of the Camel (656), and was killed in 660 while still in power, albeit with drastically dwindled powers.

Anṣār/Anṣārī—'The Helpers', the citizens in Medina who supported the Prophet and his cause after his flight to the city from Mecca.

ᶜĀṣim ibn ᶜAdī al-Anṣārī (d. 745)—One of the Medina converts, he became a renowned reciter of the Qur'ān and set the standards for its final vowelling. He was also a minor transmitter of ḥadīths.

Asmā' (d. 693)—Daughter of Abū Bakr, and elder half-sister of ᶜĀ'isha. She converted early to Islam and is revered for her piety and devotion to the Prophet.

al-Bukhārī (Muḥammad ibn Ismā^{c}īl Abū ^{c}Abdullāh al-Ju^{c}fī) (810-870)—Originally from Bukhāra, he became compiler of the finest collection of ḥadīths, *Al-Jāmi^{c} al-Ṣaḥīḥ*. He is reputed to have taken 16 years to complete the work from an original pool of 600,000 ḥadīths.

Fāṭima—The favourite daughter of Muḥammad and Khadīja, whose life in particular has been woven with many legends. She was married to the Prophet's nephew, ^{c}Alī, and was the mother of the Shi^{c}i martyrs, Ḥasan and Ḥusain. She died six months after the Prophet's death.

Ḥafṣa (607-661[?])—Daughter of ^{c}Umar ibn al-Khaṭṭāb and wife of the Prophet. She was a close friend of ^{c}Ā'isha's. She stood out from the majority of the Prophet's wives in that she knew how to read and write.

Ibn Hishām (d. 833)—Author of the best known collection of ḥadīths concerning the life of Muḥammad.

Ibn Mas^{c}ūd (d. 652)—Companion of the Prophet and one of the earliest Muslims. He carried Muḥammad's sandals and picked his chewing-sticks each day for him—essentially he held the position of valet for the Prophet. He was also one of the first reciters of the Qur'ān.

Ibn Sīrīn—A renowed transmitter of ḥadīths who died in 728.

Ibn ^{c}Umar ibn al-Khaṭṭāb—The son of ^{c}Umar ibn al-Khaṭṭāb. He was one of the first true generation of Muslims, and is one of the most quoted sources for ḥadīths. Offered the Caliphate on three separate occasions, he refused each time. He died in 693, well into his eighties.

Jābir ibn Zaid (642-720)—The compiler of what is considered the first collection of ḥadīths.

Ka^{c}b ibn Mālik—An Anṣārī poet who lent Muḥammad his support.

Khadīja (556-619)—The first wife of Muḥammad. She is said to have been married twice before. A woman of property, she was considerably older than Muḥammad, although they had several children, among them Zainab, Umm Kulthūm, Fāṭima and Ruqayya. She supported and encouraged Muḥammad, and died in 619, to his immense grief. He married no other woman while she was alive.

Maimūna bint al-Ḥārith (602-681)—The last wife to be married by Muḥammad. She was a widow, and it is thought that this was a political marriage. She died at the age of 79, having survived all the other wives.

Muḥammad—The Prophet and founder of Islam, and through whom the Qur'ān was revealed. He was born into a poor family of good blood (his father ᶜAbdullāh was a merchant) in Mecca between 570 and 580, orphaned at an early age, and died in 632. His calling to Prophethood came late in life.

Muslim (ibn al-Ḥajjāj) (816-873)—Born in Nishapur, his compilation of ḥadīths is rated second only to that of al-Bukhārī. It is said that his own collection was gathered from 300,000 ḥadīths, each recorded personally.

Quraish—The dominant tribe of Mecca, who ran the city commercially and socially. They fiercely opposed Muḥammad and the rise of Islam (and then were defeated by him), rightly sensing in him and the new religion a threat to their power and influence.

Saᶜd ibn al-Rabīᶜa al-Anṣārī—He was highly trusted by the Prophet, most especially in political matters, and is considered a hero of Islam, since he died from his wounds after fighting for the faith in battle.

Saᶜd ibn ᶜUbāda (d. 636)—One of the few individuals who was fully literate in the region during the beginnings of Islam. He proved to be of invaluable assistance to the Prophet in political matters. He made a strong bid to become the Prophet's successor after his death, but ceded to Abū Bakr.

Sauda bint Zamᶜa (596-674/676[?])—The second wife of Muḥammad. She was one of the first of his household to embrace

Islam. She married the Prophet, in part, as an attempt to console him for the loss of his first wife Khadīja. Tradition holds that she swiftly lost her looks and grew fat—to the point that the Prophet wearied of her and divorced her. However, he took her back after she offered to give up the day of his turn with her in favour of ᶜĀ'isha, his favourite wife. In spite of these domestic problems, she continued to enjoy the love and respect of all.

Ṣafiyya bint Ḥuyai ibn Akhṭab (628-670[?])—A war-captive from a Jewish tribe, who so dazzled Muḥammad with her beauty that he made her his full wife, when she was 17 or 18. She was freed by him when he married her, but was regarded with great jealousy by the Prophet's other wives and insulted frequently because of her Jewishness. Undaunted, she stayed devoted to the Prophet and became a close friend of his daughter Fāṭima.

Ṭalḥa (d. 656)—One of the Companions of the Prophet and one of the earliest converts to Islam. He was one of Muḥammad's councillors and closest friends. He died at the Battle of the Camel, fighting against ᶜAlī.

ᶜUmar ibn al-Khaṭṭāb (d. 640)—The second Caliph. Like St Paul, he was at first a vociferous opponent of the Muslims but he finally converted and defended Islam with the same zeal he had used to attack it. Clearly a political genius and master statesman, as Caliph he established the foundations of the Islamic State but developed a puritanical reputation on account of his harsh judgements and rulings.

Umm Kulthūm—Daughter of the Prophet and Khadīja. ᶜUthmān married her after the death of his wife, her sister Ruqayya.

ᶜUrwa ibn al-Zubair (645-715)—A nephew of ᶜĀ'isha, he collected many ḥadīths from her as well as from other contemporaries of the Prophet.

ᶜUtba (d. 638)—A Companion of the Prophet and one of the first to adopt Islam. He founded the city of Baṣra in modern-day Iraq.

ᶜUthmān—The third Caliph and one of the first converts to Islam. He was a rich merchant married to Ruqayya, daughter of the Prophet. Opinions vary as to his effectiveness as Caliph, and he met a bloody end in 656.

Zaid bin Ḥāritha (d. 627)—A slave given to Muḥammad by his first wife Khadīja. Muḥammad freed him, adopted him as his son, and then married him to his cousin Zainab bint Jaḥsh, whom Zaid later divorced.

Zainab (d. 630)—Daughter of the Prophet, said to have been his eldest, and wife of Abū al-ᶜĀs ibn Rabīᶜ.

Zainab bint Jaḥsh (590[?]-630)—Cousin of Muḥammad. She was first married to Muḥammad's adopted son, Zaid. After the latter divorced her, Muḥammad took the decision to marry her when she was about 35. She was Muḥammad's second favourite wife after ᶜĀ'isha, whose close friend she also became.

al-Zuhrī (670-746)—A famous trasmitter of ḥadīths.

Notes

Introduction

1. The *Ḥadīth of the Lie* has not been included here on account of its length and availability elsewhere in other books as well as in popular lore.

2. Khan, vol. 6, p. 76.

1. Hygiene

1. Blood in any form is considered a contamination (as are all bodily fluids). Since it forms a part of menstruation, menstruation is considered therefore a continuous ritually impure state.

2. i.e. never considered it a part of full menses.

3. The guidelines given here for menstruating women are similar to those for the sick (see 7/18).

4. i.e. "my period has not stopped."

5. i.e. "as I usually do after my normal period stops"—a menstruating woman cannot pray.

6. i.e. "Stop praying on the days that you normally stop praying when you have your period, wash, and then start praying again on the day you usually do so."

7. A man is not permitted to have full sex with a normally menstruating woman.

8. ᶜĀ'isha adds that she should wash the stain and sprinkle the rest of the garment with water. In 1/185 she is quoted as saying that she would put some spit on the stain and scratch at it with her fingernail.

2. *Divorce*

1. Or 'she'.

2. 7/177-8 adds: a) The Prophet asked the couple three times to resolve who was lying, and, upon receiving no reply, he made the husband divorce the wife. b) The man asked: "What about the property and possessions that I gave her as her dowry?" The Prophet replied to this: "You do not have any! If you have spoken the truth about her, then she keeps the dowry as payment for your conjugal rights with her as her husband, but if you have lied against her, and accused her falsely of adultery, then certainly you have no right to claim any of it back!"

Q 2:236-7 & 241-2 (pp. 147-8) are quoted with regard to the above, the latter showing that even in *liᶜān* (see following note) a wife thus divorced receives a minimum maintenance equivalent to her dowry.

3. *Liᶜān* (لعان) is "an oath by which a husband may allege, without legal proof, adultery by his wife without becoming liable to the punishment by which (false accusation of unlawful sexual intercourse) is threatened, and deny the paternity of a child borne by the wife, is in itself not a divorce proper but has the dissolution of the marriage as a consequence" (*Shorter Encyclopaedia of Islam*—entry 'Liᶜān/Ṭalāḳ'). Women cannot accuse men, they can only deny.

4. *Muḥarrama* (محرمة)—A female who is a blood, or foster, relation and thus unlawful for a man to marry.

5. i.e. after divorce or being widowed—to see if she is pregnant.

6. Proper Islamic divorce (*ṭalāq* طلاق) involves the husband saying, over a period of time, any invocation to the effect that he wishes to divorce his wife (this may also be in writing, and can specify the precise time of divorce at any point in the future). Only after the third and final invocation is the divorce considered to be complete and irrevocable.

7. 'Ritually forbidden.'.

8. i.e. he (ᶜUwaimar) himself is that man.

9. See note 3 of this section.

10. Specified here is 'divorce after wedding/marriage' (7/143).

11. The verses that follow are: **So when he divorces her irrevocably and finally, he cannot after this remarry her until after she has taken another man to be her husband; and then, if the latter divorces her, there is no sin upon either of the two if they reunite—provided that**

they are of the opinion that they will be able to keep within the limits as laid down by God. Such are the limits of God which he makes evident to those who have knowledge!

And when you divorce women and they reach the end of their waiting-period, either keep them in marriage with all due fairness, or free them with all due fairness. But do not keep them in marriage in order to harm them or to take undue advantage—he who does so commits a sin against himself. And do not take these Signs from God lightly, but make mention of God's blessings upon you and what He has revealed to you as Scripture and Wisdom for Him to instruct you. So fear God and know that God knows all things full well. (Q2:230-1)

12. In this chapter, a number of ḥadīths are quoted concerning a wide variety of situations, each involving someone, or the Prophet, making a gesture, instead of words, in reply to some crucial question. This is an important subject from a legal point of view, and by analogy the general interpretations have been applied to divorce in particular, i.e. one is allowed to use gestures instead of words in divorce cases.

13. A variant of the preceding ḥadīth.

14. i.e. "Does this divorce count as one of the three steps of Islamic divorce?"

15. On the other hand, this may also be interpreted as: "What else would you think—even if the husband is incompetent or acts like a fool?" Another Islamic interpretation is: "What else would you expect in someone who has been driven to his dotage to do it?"

16. 'Never'?

17. 29 days.

18. This was, and is, a serious step to take—particularly if a man did this to all of his wives at one and the same time.

19. The two verses that follow are: **But if they are then firmly resolved on divorce, God knows and hears all things.**

Divorced women shall have a waiting period of three months periods, and they may not marry again during this time; and it is not lawful for them to hide what God might have created in their wombs if they believe in God and the Day of Judgement. And their husbands have the most right to take them back during that period if they wish reconciliation. And the wives shall have rights to protect them equal to the rights their husbands have over them in accordance with just fairness. And God is Almighty and Wise. (Q2:227-8)

20. Four months.

21. The probable meaning here is that he must make a definite decision whether he is to divorce or not, and to inform his wife/wives accordingly (multiple divorces are permissible).

22. i.e. any woman already married to a prospective husband the first woman desires.

23. This refers to *khulʿa* (خلعة, also *khulʿ* خلع)—'divorce at the instance of the wife, who must pay a compensation' (Wehr).

24. The second Caliph.

25. The third Caliph.

26. Also 'women and children'.

27. *Janāba* (جنابة) is major ritual impurity of the body resulting from (particularly) sexual intercourse, requiring a full body wash for ritual cleansing before one can come into contact with other human beings or pray, and so on.

28. i.e. "I refuse to have sex with you again!"

29. Her name was probably Jamīla (7/151).

30. This is her indirect way of saying: "I am going to carry out some very un-Islamic deeds if I remain married to my present husband for one day more!"

31. In all the versions of this incident, she is described as graphically holding up the drooping, gathered-together corner of her shawl for all to see as she said this.

3. Widowhood & Death

1. Kohl (كحل) or antimony was, and is, used not only as a cosmetic (eyeliner) but also for its therapeutic and healing effects. A widow is not permitted to use kohl during mourning—since it doubles as make-up.

2. Note that the Prophet is not mentioned here (he had already died).

3. Always an odd number of times.

4. 2/197 adds: "*Umm ʿAṭiyya said:* The women undid the hair of the Prophet's daughter, and they washed it and then entwined her in three braids." 2/195 adds that the Prophet ordered: "Begin washing the right-hand side of her as well as the parts of her that are washed when one does the Islamic ritual ablutions."

5. Muḥammad had daughters but no sons that survived him—see pp. 10 & 175.

6. Or: "Ibnat Abū Ṣabra, the wife of Mu^cādh and another woman."

7. The case title of this ḥadīth is: 'Chapter of whoever (may) enter the grave of a female.'

8. Note that Islam does not prohibit the keeping of slaves, but makes provision for their care.

9. Presumably after having given birth.

10. Red or black stripes—a special Yemeni type of the period. It is difficult to hypothesize a modern equivalent for this stipulation.

11. Ambiguous, as the Arabic *armala* (أرملة) is also a collective noun meaning 'weak and destitute people' (by analogy).

4. The Day of Judgement

1. Of religion.

2. Or 'husband'.

3. See the entry 'Azd' in the *Encyclopaedia of Islam* (new edition).

4. Or 'idol'.

5. Heaven & Hell

1. 4/342 adds: ". . . and they shall be like their ancestor Adam—60 cubits high."

2. 4/310 says that they shall specifically be houris (plural: *ḥūr* حور)—the Nymphs or Maidens of Paradise. Although it has taken on a separate, derogatory meaning, the English 'whore' shares the same etymology.

3. 4/310 adds: ". . . and their bones."

4. This includes the irises of the eye, as most people of the region tend to have eyes of dark colouring—the darker they are, the more beautiful they are considered. In many parts of the Middle East, blue eyes are traditionally considered to be a mark of suspicion and deviousness.

5. Also implied here, according to most commentators, is an extremely fair complexion—i.e. a complexion that is neither weather-beaten nor sunburnt.

6. i.e. holy war (*jihād* جهاد) and martyrdom.

7. The verb here (*kafara* كفر) can also mean 'to disbelieve'.

8. This includes birds.

NOTES

6. Justice & the Law

1. The *hijra* (هجرة)was Muḥammad's flight from Mecca to Medina in 622 AD. It is therefore used also to denote any flight, exodus or journey of immense significance and consequence. The terms 'migration' and 'migrate' are also used in Islamic literature written in English.

2. i.e. one of the two women. The official view is that women are less experienced in business and legal affairs.

3. A group of men here, in all probability.

4. An obvious euphemism for rape.

5. i.e. 'raped'.

6. Presumably whipping.

7. *Thayyib* (see note 8, p. 183) can also be taken to mean a 'previously married man'—or both—while it can also imply a '(still) married person'. The Arabic text provides no further clarification. If *thayyib* refers to either sex here, then this is at variance with its use elsewhere in the ḥadīth texts included in this collection.

8. i.e. that her own tooth should be broken, or else a compensatory fine equivalent to this be paid—at the discretion of the injured party or her family.

9. Compensation or indemnity for bodily injury.

10. Another version (9/35) has the attacked woman die as well as miscarry—but the blood-wit is quoted as being the same.

11. Male witnesses (cf. Q2:282, p. 38).

12. The verb *jalada* (جلد) has a broad spread of meaning, e.g. 'scourge, lash, whip, beat, flog'.

13. This, and all other similar references in this ḥadīth, refer to a person whipped for making false accusations of unlawful sexual intercourse.

14. Or 'veiled'.

15. Or 'recognize'?

16. Stoning to death in the case of adultery.

17. For a first offence, technically, *according to custom*, it is the right hand which has to be chopped off.

18. i.e. the mistake of chopping off the wrong hand for her first offence should be left as it is, and is not to be rectified by then cutting off the right one.

19. Or 'to wink at'.

Women in Islam

7. Modesty & Clothing

1. *Lithām* (لثام)—a veil that covers the lower part of the face to the eyes

2. *Burqu*^{c} (برقع)—chadour, a long garment that covers the whole body leaving only the eyes uncovered.

3. Such a pilgrim usually has to wear two seamless woollen or linen sheets (waist and shoulder wrapping-cloths), usually white.

4. Born of another wife.

5. 'Slaves'.

6. This verse ends: **And, O believers, always repent and turn to God for mercy, and thus you shall all achieve happiness!**

7. Note that here 'to flee' may be read for 'to emigrate', and 'refugee' for 'emigrant'; cf. note 1, p. 181.

8. 'May God curse . . . !'

9. cf. 7/515, p. 126.

10. Note that Umm Ya^{c}qūb is a literate woman.

11. The Prophet Muḥammad.

12. Q59:7.

13. This could perhaps also be taken as: "I would divorce her!"

14. Umm Zufar?

15. i.e. her clothes slip away from her body on account of the violence of her fits.

16. 'Persians' or 'all non-Arabs'.

17. Or 'chests'.

18. See pp. 46-7.

19. Or 'scarlet fever', or 'smallpox'?

20. Or 'May God curse . . .'

21. The legal interpretation of this is: "A wife is not to obey her husband if he wants her to do something contrary to God's laws."

22. The case title of this ḥadīth is: "The clothing of women with customary kindness."

23. In connection with this, Abū Dāwūd is quoted as saying: "It is agreed by the majority of the Religious Scholars that a woman while praying should cover herself completely except her face, and it is better that she should cover her hands with gloves or cloth etc. but her feet must be covered either with a long dress or she must wear socks to cover her feet. This verdict is based on the Prophet's Statement."

8. Marriage

1. *Dhimmī* (ذمي)—'a free non-Muslim subject living in a Muslim country who, in return for paying capital tax, enjoys protection and safety' (Wehr).

2. 'Ritually forbidden'.

3. For her to complete one menstrual cycle.

4. This can also be interpreted as 'he *can* marry her' or 'he *should* marry her'.

5. Magian: an adherent of Mazdaism, i.e. a Zoroastrian.

6. Q60:10

7. The Quraish were the tribe who governed Mecca and vehemently opposed Muḥammad and his followers, even though he and many prominent Muslims were also Quraish.

8. 'A woman who has already been married' (*thayyib* ثيب—'a dowered and deflowered woman', cf. note 7, p. 181) is defined in Lane as: "A woman who has become separated from her husband in any manner; or a woman whose husband has died, or who has been divorced, and has then returned to the marriage-state; or one that is not a virgin; or a woman to whom a man has gone in; or a person who has married—applied to a man and to a woman." Having been married gives a woman respectability (so much so that a married girl of twelve, for example, may be held to have higher status than an unmarried virgin of fifty)—furthermore, divorce is considered an almost integral part of the marriage process, hence little stigma is attached to this.

9. The case title of this ḥadīth is: 'A woman's helping her husband with his children.'

10. 'Brother' and 'sister' are used here in a general sense, and applies to other Muslims.

11. i.e. to allow the former to marry the latter's husband.

12. i.e. 'on behalf of'.

13. i.e. only a formal wedding ceremony had occurred.

14. Presumably for marriage, since this would have been regarded as the highest honour—or an escape from dire circumstances.

15. *Shigār* (شغار) is where a man gives his daughter away in marriage to another man who gives his own daughter back in marriage in turn—and neither party pays any form of dowry.

16. *Mutʿa* (متعة): "muta, temporary marriage, usufruct marriage contracted for a specified time and exclusively for the purposes of

sexual pleasure" (Wehr). Although frowned upon by their peers, some Shi^c^i Muslims are said to still permit temporary marriage under certain circumstances.

17. An oasis 95 miles from Medina and the site of a battle where the Muslims defeated the Jewish tribes in 628.

18. As opposed to wild asses or onagers.

19. ^c^Ā'isha provides a further explanation: "This verse is about the female orphan who is in the ward of a man, and she may even perhaps be a partner in his estate. This man would have the most right to marry her—however, he is unwilling to marry her, and he prevents her from marrying anyone else and rigidly controls her estate, unwilling to have to share her wealth with any other man." (7/46)

20. Also 7/15: "The Prophet freed Ṣafiyya and he made manumitting her as her dowry."—This highlights the difference between marriage of a free woman and marriage of a slave girl. The former requires a formal dowry, the latter does not.

21. i.e. their honeymoon.

22. i.e. a woman/girl who has never been married before.

23. This ḥadīth is best taken without the first and third bracketed phrases.

24. The word used here (*ḍarra* ضرة—'wife other than the first of a plural marriage') shares the same root in Arabic as 'damage, harm, loss' etc.

25. Citing here Muḥammad's example.

26. As elsewhere, no comparable directives exist that are addressed specifically to women.

27. 7/24 quotes this verse as a prohibition against marriage between foster-children (i.e. those who have been suckled by the same woman although there is no blood relationship between them) thus placing them on the same level as blood relatives. This, however, holds force only if one has been suckled under the age of two years old (7/26ff; & cf. Q2:233, p. 17). The editors of *The Translation of the Meaning of Sahih Bukhari* add an intriguing footnote (7/25): "It is rather sad that now, all over the European and American countries there are Human Milk Banks and all the newly born babies are fed with this human milk from the Milk Bank which makes them as brothers and sisters. This means, a foster brother may marry his foster sister without being aware of the existence of such relationship, and such marriage is unlawful in Islam and even in other religions."

28. This could have the implication that a man is permitted to treat a slave ('one possessed by the right hand') as his wife in everything but name despite her being married to another man.

29. Either slaves or war-captives.

30. i.e. by being tempted to unlawful sex.

31. The verb used *(nazaʿa* نزع*)* suggests that the divorce of the slave couple or their permission is not required.

32. 7/23 has the case title of: 'Chapter of not marrying more than four wives, according to the words of God'—[and then two extracts from the Qur'ān are quoted]: ". . . **(one) two, three, or four (wives)** . . . (Q4:3)" and ". . . **the angels . . . endowed with wings, two, three, or four** (Q35:1)."

33. i.e. seven types related by blood and seven related by marriage.

34. They were not blood relations (i.e. not natural mother and daughter).

35. *Mutʿa*—see note 16 of this section

36. A touch of irony since ᶜAlī is the most important figure for Shiᶜi Muslims after the Prophet Muḥammad, yet they are the only Muslims alleged to still tolerate the practice.

37. This and the following item are now taken as the minimum requirements for a dowry (for a free woman), i.e. either a ring of iron or a verse of the Qur'ān.

38. Obscurely, this ḥadīth is used, in an abbreviated form (3/288), under the case title of: 'A woman can depute the ruler in the matter of marriage.'

Based on this ḥadīth is 7/53, 55 (Q4:3, p. 66 is quoted with it): "A man says to a guardian 'Give me So-and-So [a female] to me in marriage', and the guardian is then silent or else he asks 'What do you have to offer as a dowry?'—and the first man answers 'I have such-and-such to offer as a dowry', or else they both bide their time [and are silent?] and eventually the guardian says 'I have given her to you in marriage'. If the above occurs, it is considered a lawful marriage, even if the suitor has not stated whether he agrees to any dowry terms laid down by the guardian."

39. Lineage was, and still is, of great importance to the Arabs. Here, this could also mean 'personal eminence'.

40. The following verse is: **Therefore take from the good things which God grants you as lawful sustenance, and be aware of the God in whom you believe.** (Q5:88)

41. i.e. 'means for a dowry'.

42. Often wrongly translated as: "But you're as old as I!"—If there is some semblance of wealth, age is never questioned.

43. i.e. "religiously permitted and lawful—therefore there can be no objection to me marrying her." The case title of this ḥadīth is: "Chapter of the marrying of minors/young girls by seniors/old men."

44. Presumably this means concurrently only, so a man may marry one of them provided that he has divorced the other. This prohibition applies also to a wife, her father's paternal aunt and so on.

45. The official interpretation of this is: 'The marriage of young girls to men is permitted.'

46. = ᶜAbdullāh.

47. And "'not to gaze or behave lustfully in any way'.

48. This can also be taken as 'his wife's chastity'.

49. *Wijā'* (وجاء) is technically 'crushing testicles, especially of goats, so they cease to function'.

50. A case title for this is: 'Should a man get married if he has no aspiration for wedlock?'

51. This can also mean: ". . . And I bedded you with her and gave you the bounty of her . . . !"

52. This is considered to refer specifically to the Prophet expressing his love for all the Anṣārī people. The interpretation of this ḥadīth is, however, that "women and children may go to wedding parties."

53. This includes step-daughters and so on.

54. The distinction, here and elsewhere in the text, is often extremely unclear between a free wife, a concubine and a slave girl. 'Wife' is used unless the Arabic specifies otherwise.

55. The technical term is *istibḍāᶜ* (استبضاع).

56. This is also a euphemism for 'to have sexual intercourse with them'.

57. A physiognomist *(qā'if* قائف*)* uses facial and other physical features to divine another's character and/or origin.

58. Or 'disobeys'.

59. Interpreted as also pertaining to the divorced woman.

60. "*Some have said:* If a virgin's consent is not sought and she is not yet married, and a man deceitfully presents two witnesses who falsely claim that he has married her by her consent, and the judge then confirms the marriage while the husband knows that the evidence was worthless, then there is no legal objection to him having sexual

intercourse with her, and the marriage is considered to be valid." (9/80)

9/81 says: "If an individual deceitfully uses two witnesses to falsely claim that he has married a woman who has already been married with her full consent, and the judge then confirms the marriage, which the husband knows full well that he had never married her, then this marriage is lawful, and there is no legal objection to his living with her as man and wife."

9/82 adds: "If a man falls for an orphan slave girl or a virgin and she refuses his attentions, and he then deceitfully brings two witnesses to falsely testify that he has married the girl, and then she attains puberty and is willing [or: and *they claim* that she is willing (?)], and the judge accepts this false evidence, while the husband knows full well the worthlessness of this evidence, he is then permitted to have sexual intercourse with her."

61. Customs vary from country to country as to the actual Islamic marriage procedure, and there are no clear guidelines, least of all in the Qur'ān. Jurists and theologians are not even agreed as to whether witnesses are required—or, indeed, any form of presiding figure.

9. Prayer

1. Because the bloodflow of her period puts her into a state of major ritual impurity—this makes her unclean and thus in no condition to pray.
2. Or ". . . we never used to do that!"
3. i.e. the men
4. Of the waist-wrappers.
5. As they prayed *behind* all the men.
6. i.e. to make themselves clean and ritually pure for this most important prayer of the week.
7. The point ᶜĀ'isha is making here is that she (as a woman) never put herself in the Prophet's way when he prayed because she wanted to show him consideration, and *not* because he had decreed so.
8. In 1/294 she says: "The Prophet used to pray with me still asleep in bed, and his clothes would touch me, even when I had my period."
9. One of the points made here is that a menstruating woman may go into a spiritual retreat for prayer (and may do this with her husband).

10. Or 'the legs and labia majora of her vulva'.

11. Although it is not specified here, washing for both partners is obligatory.

10. Religion

1. Or 'the law'.

2. The word used, *hā'id* (هائد) is masculine in form (instead of the expected feminine *hā'ida* هائدة). The simpler masculine, closer to the *grammar* of deriving words in Arabic from a basic root meaning, is all that is required here, since there is no gender contrast amongst those who menstruate (i.e. men and women can steal, but only women can menstruate). This is a good example of how little apparent grammatical gender has to do with actual gender in Arabic.

3. i.e. the month of Dhū 'l-Ḥijja. The plural 'months' refers either to its annual recurrence or the final three months of the Islamic year (including Dhū 'l-Ḥijja).

4. This ḥadīth is titled: 'Chapter of performing the *ḥājj* on behalf of a dead person and fulfilling his vows. A man can perform the *ḥājj* on behalf of a woman.'

5. A personal description of attraction between the sexes rarely found in such literature.

6. 3/47 has the case title of: 'The *ḥājj* of one who cannot sit properly on one's mount.' 3/48 has: 'The *ḥājj* of a woman on behalf of a man.'

11. Sex, Unlawful Sex & Chastity

1. Stoning to death for unlawful sexual intercourse is a contentious issue. The so-called 'Verse of Stoning' is not included in the Qur'ān, so any judgement is based on ḥadīths alone, many of which show the influence of the Caliph ᶜUmar, who favoured this form of punishment. Moreover, one is able, with very little difficulty, to justify such a penalty under these conditions for those who have committed any form of unlawful sexual intercourse and not merely those who have committed adultery in its technical sense. (Conceivably 8/534, p. 44, could be a suggestion that sexual penetration is the benchmark for what constitutes unlawful sexual intercourse; however, aside from this,

no other reference is made as to what precisely defines unlawful sexual 'intercourse', although some have defined 'sexual penetration' as 'any further than the circumcision ring'.) The Qur'ān says: **As regards the adulterer and the adulteress, give each one of the a hundred lashes, and if you truly believe in God and the Day of Judgement you shall not allow pity for them prevent you from executing this commandment from God. Let a group of true believers witness their punishment. Know that they are as guilty as each other, for the adulterer couples with no one but the adultress—that is, a woman who places her lust on the same level as God; and with the adultress couples no one but the adulterer—that is, a man who places his lust on the same level as God. This is forbidden to the believers!** (Q24:2-3)

8/543 uses these two verses for the legal interpretation: "The unmarried couple [i.e. who are virgins and unmarried] who have committed unlawful sexual intercourse should be whipped and banished." In passing, it should be noted that few traditional cultures, if any, possessed a clear defined term for unlawful sex between unmarried people.

2. 8/527 & 535 add the following: ". . . And the Prophet ordered him to be stoned, and so he was—for he was married." And Jābir has added: "And I was amongst those who stoned him to death, and we stoned him at the mosque, and when the stones began to inflict actual harm on him, he ran and ran until we caught up with him at al-Ḥarra and there and then we stoned him to death." And ᶜAlī said to ᶜUmar: "Do you not know that as for the madman, the pen is not raised from him [i.e. he can neither sin nor do good deeds in terms of the Final Reckoning and no account will be made of them] until he recovers his sanity? And this is true also of the child, until he achieves the age of reason [or 'to attain puberty'], and of the sleeper, until he awakens."

The legal interpretation of this is: "The madman or the madwoman should not be stoned to death."

3. *Ghaira* (غيرة) is 'jealous pride and possessiveness'—the sense of honour or machismo that is required in being such a husband and a man.

4. The specific connotations of the word used here (*fawāhish* فواحش) are 'adultery, fornication, whoredom'.

5. ᶜUmar was the second Caliph after the Prophet's death.

6. Or 'not in his dialect', or 'unintelligibly'.

7. Or 'male companion', or 'lord', or 'owner'.

8. 'Raped'?

9. The case title of this ḥadīth is: 'The chapter of interpreting/translation for rulers, and whether it is permitted to have an interpreter/translator.'

10. Or 'child', or 'children'.

11. i.e. that you would have abstained from sex, not being aware that just as eating and drinking are permitted at night-time (between dusk and dawn) during the fast of Ramaḍān, so too is sex.

12. 3/135 adds, in connection with this verse: "*ʿĀ'isha said:* 'The Prophet used to go into spiritual retreat for prayer for the last ten days of every Ramaḍān until he died, and then his wives would go into spiritual retreat after he had passed away.'" These retreats are similar to those practised by Christians during the Lent fast in the lead-up to Easter.

13. Khan (3/518) expands on the term as follows: "Literally *liʿān* meaning cursing, legally it means an oath by which a husband claims that his wife has committed illegal sexual intercourse. The wife in her turn denies the accusation and takes a similar oath. In both oaths God is invoked to curse the liar. The case ends with divorce but no punishment is imposed on any of the two because there are no witnesses to confirm the accusation."

14. 3/292 has the version: "The Prophet said: 'O Unais—go to the wife of this man, and if she confesses (to adultery) then stone her to death.'" The legal interpretation of this version is: 'The deputizing of someone to enforce the penalties of God.' 9/273 has: "'Go to this woman tomorrow morning, and if she confesses then stone her to death.' So Unais went to her on the morrow and she confessed, so he stoned her to death."

15. 8/551 gives a version of the same ḥadīth with the case title of: "Chapter of when one accuses one's wife of unlawful sexual intercourse or the wife of another in the presence of the ruler and the people, is it then incumbent upon the ruler to send for the woman and to question her about what she has been accused of?" Note the very clear legal implication of this ḥadīth—the married culprit is judged differently to the unmarried one (cf. note 1, p. 188; & note 2, p. 189).

16. i.e. sexual.

17. This could be a garment or a simple sanitary towel. Tampons, in passing, are not un-Islamic, since there is no mention in the Qur'ān or the ḥadīths upon which to base a prohibition of them.

18. 8/548 gives a version of this ḥadīth with the legal interpretation of: "One should not upbraid a slave girl if she commits unlawful sexual intercourse, nor should she be banished."

19. The penalty for a slave who commits unlawful sexual intercourse is fifty lashes (half that given to a free unmarried person). Stoning is not required in the cases of actual adulterous slaves. Conceivably, rape, if ever proved, must be included under all these headings (but see 9/66, p. 39)—i.e. adultery of free person, adultery of slave, adultery of unmarried person, etc—thereby in itself holding little significance.

20. i.e. from this particular coupling.

21. This is interpreted as a command.

22. Note that there is no specific prohibition—an open-ended ḥadīth. In fact, contraception in any form for women (men tend not to view condoms or vasectomies favourably) is tolerated in most forms of Islam—for married women only (logically), and this is only provided that a reasonable number of children are produced (the ideal minimum varies). The main objection to birth-control pills is whether they change God's creation or not (e.g. changing a woman's body [cf. 3/379, p. 47 and so on] in which case most forms of modern medicine would have to be viewed in the same light)—or whether they are *ḥalāl* for consumption (cf. the charts produced by Islamic organizations indicating which food additives and preservatives are religiously permissable for consumption).

23. Or 'recited'?

24. 8/549 gives a similar version, with the case title of: 'Chapter of Islamic provisions concerning the *dhimmīs* (see note 1, p. 183) and their being married when they commit unlawful sexual intercourse and are taken before the Muslim leader.'

25. 7/93 has the variant: ". . . And the angels shall curse her until she goes back [to her husband]." Here 'goes back' also has the sense of 'retracts one's word' and 'relents'.

26. i.e. just after one has acquired her.

27. Chastity does not mean celibacy.

28. Despite being used in this ḥadīth to justify the harmlessness of such a sexual position, no commentator has satisfactorily explained the Qur'ān's words "**as you desire.**" This can be interpreted as an order to have sex whenever desired with one's wife, an order to use any sexual position desired, or to use any orifice desired (or even all of these combined)—subject of course to the accepted restrictions. As a general

note, there are no specific prohibitions of such issues as female circumcision.

29. The preceding verse is: **And the people will ask you concerning women's monthly periods—so say: "It is an affliction. So keep away from women when they are having their monthly periods, and do not approach them until they have become clean again. And when they have cleansed themselves, go unto them where God has ordered you to." Truly God loves those who have recourse to Him, and He loves those who make themselves pure.** (Q2:222)—The word 'affliction' is variously translated elsewhere as 'a filthy thing, a hurt and a pollution, a vulnerable condition'.

12. Status & Rights

1. i.e. of unlawful sexual intercourse.

2. 'Unmindful' (*ghāfilāt* غافلات)—this can mean women who have, through no fault of their own, made a slip or mistake, or women who are too chaste to be tempted to err.

3. A palm grove in Medina.

4. The case title for this is: 'The chapter of men greeting women and women greeting men.'

5. Ḥudaibiya was the place where the Prophet established a formal truce with the hostile Meccans in 628, thus guaranteeing the Muslims a secure period during which they were able to quietly consolidate their power, subsequently allowing them to conquer Mecca and the Meccans. Suhail ibn [c]Amr was the envoy of the Meccan rulers.

6. Abū Jandal was a son of Suhail ibn [c]Amr who had gone over to the Muslims.

7. His wives.

8. By this he means that he wishes that the Prophet would veil his wives so that impious or evil people coming to have an audience with the Prophet would not be able to look at those of his wives present with him.

9. See Q33:53, p. 135; cf. Q33:32, p. 153. These references, supposedly a result of [c]Umar's suggestion, are clearly directed at the wives of the Prophet only, but this soon became extended to all free Muslim women: "The wearing of the veil marks the transition from childhood to puberty, and from sisterhood to marriage" (*Encyclopaedia of Islam,* 2nd edition). 1/107, in connection with the Verses of the Veil, has the legal

interpretation of: "You (women) are allowed to go out to answer the calls of nature."

10. *Ruqya* (رقية) is the use of magic incantations—particularly through the recitation of particular sections of the Qur'ān to ward off illness and ill luck.

11. Both of which begin: "I seek refuge with the Lord . . ."

12. Abū Bakr—who was to become the first Caliph after the Prophet's death.

13. He was to become the second Caliph.

14. All of whom he nonetheless refused respectfully.

15. i.e. a full, legal wife.

16. He drew the veil over her.

17. Presumably without full sexual connection.

18. Or 'sexual member/organs' (male or female). The distinction between *irb* (إرب) and *arb* (ارب) is obscure.

19. The Persian emperor Chosroes.

20. The narrator relates this in connection with the choice he had to make of joining ᶜĀ'isha and her army or not. This was against ᶜAlī just before the Battle of the Camel (656), part of the lengthy struggle for power that followed the Prophet's death. ᶜĀ'isha lost.

21. i.e. these were the only people with the Prophet at the very beginning of Islam and his Flight.

22. This is interpreted as the 'offering of shelter and peace to someone by women'.

23. But 4/85 states: "The Prophet would get his wives to draw lots as to which of them would accompany him on his sorties [technically *jihād*]."—This includes *after* they had to wear the veil.

4/86 has: "Before the Veiling, the Muslim women carried the waterskins for the Muslim warriors and watered them in battle." The same ḥadīth adds: "The Muslim women watered the wounded, treated them and returned the slain to Medina during battle." It is uncertain if this was before or after the Veiling (or both). This ḥadīth is used also to justify the case title of: 'Can a man treat/nurse a sick woman and can a woman treat/nurse a sick man?'

24. See note 17, p. 190.

25. i.e. Jews, Muslims, Sabaeans and Christians.

26. This includes after having had sex.

27. *Ḥarām* (حرام)—'forbidden', 'unlawful', 'something forbidden or unlawful'.

28. *Ḥalāl* (حلال)—'permitted, 'lawful', 'something permitted or lawful', the opposite of *ḥarām* (see preceding note). The same root is found in *ḥalīl* (حليل)'husband' and the corresponding *ḥalīla* (حليلة)'wife'

29. In other words: *ḥarām* food is *ḥarām*, and will always be so, *ḥalāl* food is *ḥalāl* and will always be so; a woman, on the other hand, can be either, as circumstances dictate.

30. It is possible this is based on the fact that at that time each wife had her own dwelling, and the husband would move from dwelling to dwelling in turn.

31. The general interpretation (cf. elsewhere in this volume) is that this is spending for alms and other such charitable purposes.

32. Or specifically 'wives'.

33. i.e. 'we cannot trust our women with you'.

34. lit: 'speared in the anus'.

35. i.e. to lull Kaᶜb and his men into a false sense of security.

36. i.e. your body needs food.

37. i.e. the eye needs sleep.

38. This would appear to counter any self-imposed celibacy (i.e. the body needs sex). A longer version is found in 3/110.

39. The month of Shawwāl.

40. *Ghishā'* (غشاء)—perhaps a light veil that covered her completely, or merely a cloak or overdress.

41. i.e. that they would maintain ties of protection over her when she was freed—and thus maintain such ties as trade and service. This was a very important form of relationship at the time, and it was by no means restricted to freed slaves—anyone of lowly status (through lack of wealth or lineage, etc.) or those in real need of physical protection entered such patronage relationships with powerful individuals or clans (particularly important since the Arab society of the time was said to be vendetta-ridden).

42. The case title of this ḥadīth is: 'May the freed slave girls of the wives of the Prophet accept things given in charity?'

43. *Zakāt al-fiṭr* (زكاة الفطر, lit: 'alms-giving of breaking the fast')—'An obligatory donation of foodstuffs required at the end of Ramaḍān, the month of fasting' (Wehr).

44. This ḥadīth (and 3/514) later provides a tentative age of 15 for boys' coming of age (i.e. the age for entering the army).

45. The next verse (Q3:15) continues: **Say: "Shall I tell you of things better than these? For those who are righteous there are gardens**

under which rivers flow, near the presence of their Lord, and there shall they abide eternally with wives who are pure, and with God's favour . . ." [Note that these wives are not necessarily their earthly ones.]

46. Generally taken as 'for marriage'.

47. Needless to say, he turned down the woman's offer.

48. Q4:34, pp. 158-9 is quoted along with this ḥadīth. 6/439 says the same, but adds at the end: "And he exhorted them against their laughing at farts, saying: 'Why does any one of you laugh at what he himself does?' "

13. Travel

1. Or more.

2. *Maḥram* محرم—blood or foster relation who is male and thus unlawful for her to marry—or her husband. Note that 2/160 gives: The Prophet said: "A woman should not travel for a *two*-day journey unless in the presence of a *maḥram* or her husband."

3. i.e. he should send warning of his arrival and then come home properly the next morning.

4. Or 'do not enter at night' (7/124).

5. 7/123, 125-6 add: "And then the Prophet exclaimed: 'Finesse! Finesse!'—This is also interpreted as: 'Seek to have offspring! Seek to have offspring!' "

6. The legal interpretation of this is: 'One should not come by night to one's family if one has been absent for a long period of time, for fear that he should discover any betrayal in them or seek faults in them.'

15. Family & Care

1. ʿAlī was married to the Prophet's favourite daughter, Fāṭima.

2. The legal interpretation of this is: 'Freed female slaves or any other women can be wet-nurses.'

3. A wife of the Prophet. Legally, the child was her half-brother, but because the Prophet considered the real father to be ʿUtba, in practical terms the child was not a male blood-relative (*maḥram*—see note 2, previous section) of hers, and therefore she would have to observe all

the rules of behaviour required of a woman when in the presence of such a male.

4. The legal interpretation is: 'A child belongs to the owner of the bed—no matter whether the mother is a slave or a free woman.'

5. The legal interpretation is: 'It is obligatory to spend on one's family.'

6. Particularly widows and their dependants.

7. i.e. besides those of his wives.

8. Or, more generally: 'his household duties' (مهنة أهله *mihnatu ahlihi*).

9. Or 'wife'.

10. Unfortunately, it is not specified who is liable for this compensation.

16. Property, Possessions & Wealth

1. Or 'household'.

2. Or 'slave girls'—Note that it is only the *fees* for such practices which are banned (interest-free loans, for example, are not unIslamic)

3. *Sufahā'* (سفهاء) commonly also means 'women' by analogy, or even 'women and young children'.

4. In heaven.

5. It was granted.

6. *'Ā'id* (عائد) can also mean 'one who visits the sick'.

7. The Prophet is saying that if they permit his request, then they are not to complain about it afterwards.

8. i.e. cheap and humble.

9. Weddings would have been a common reason.

17. Social Conduct

1. i.e. 'seclusion'.

2. But the three groups of women were allowed to participate together in all other aspects of such festivals.

3. The legal interpretation is: 'A man is not allowed to be alone with a woman unless that man be a *maḥram* [see note 2, p. 195], nor to enter the house of a woman whose husband is absent.'

4. Possibly the only reference to such women in the Qur'ān and ḥadīths.

5. One of the many indicators that in those days life was hard for

almost all—and this included the Prophet and his family. It should be noted, however, the tradition is that the Prophet imposed the standard of living of the most lowly of his subjects upon himself and his family out of humility.

18. Mothers & Children

1. Or 'daughters'.

2. 4/158, however, gives: "The Prophet was asked about his own people attacking the pagans at night and the pagans and their women and children getting hurt, and his reply was: 'They belong to them!' [Also quoted is: 'They are from their parents!']—And he was heard to say: 'There is no sanctuary except in God and His Apostle!'"

3. The case title of this ḥadīth is: 'A man's protecting his daughter from jealousy and his seeking justice for her.'

4. i.e. praying out aloud.

5. A John the Baptist-like figure who died shortly before the advent of Islam.

6. Nicholson, in *A Literary History of the Arabs*, pp. 90-1, says: "The custom which prevailed in the Jáhiliyya of burying female infants alive, revolting as it appears to us, was due partly to lack of rain, and partly due to a perverted sense of honour. Fathers feared lest they should have useless mouths to feed, or lest they should incur disgrace in consequence of their daughters being made prisoners of war. Hence the birth of a daughter was reckoned calamitous, as we read in the Qur'ān: **And they ascribe unto God daughters—far be it from Him!—yet they themselves desire only sons! When the news of the birth of a female child is brought to one of them, his face darkens with rage and he grieves within. In his shame he hides himself from his people because of the bad news he has received. Should he keep the child and suffer disgrace or should he bury it in the dust?** (Q16:57-9). It was said proverbially, 'The despatch of daughters is a kindness' and 'The burial of daughters is a noble deed'. Islam put an end to this barbarity, which is expressly forbidden by the Qur'ān: **Do not kill your children out of fear of poverty: We shall provide for them as well as for you—Truly the killing of them is a terrible sin.** (Q17:31; cf. 81:8-9 [a description of the Last Judgement]: **When the infant girl who was buried alive shall be asked for what crime was she killed.**)"

This feeling against the burying of baby girls was linked closely with the general movement against pre-Islamic customs instigated and rigidly enforced by the Prophet and his successors. See also the entries in Lane's *Lexicon* under the root *wa'ada* (وأد)—'to bury alive a daughter'.

The 'daughters' ascribed to God in (Q16:57-9) quoted above are mentioned because the pagan Arabs believed in pantheons of gods—the main one comprising Alāh with his three powerful daughters, Alāt, Al^{c}uzzā and Manāt [*allāh* technically means 'the god', *alāt* 'the goddess']. Moreover, the common belief was that the angels were all female as well. There are several damning references to these daughters in the Qur'ān, including: **Or has God only daughters and you have sons?** (Q52:39); and **And have you seen Allāt and Al^{c}uzzā and the third member of this trinity, Manāt? Is it true that for you are male offspring, yet for Him are female? That indeed would be a most unfair division!** (Q: 53:19-22). When Muḥammad broke the belief in these goddesses, he also broke the power of his principal opponents in Mecca, since it was they who adhered to this belief and used it politically, socially as well as commercially.

19. General

1. *Ruqya*—see note 10, p. 193.
2. The Arabic word used here, *saf‘a* (سفعة), has also connotations of evil caused by Satan or the Evil Eye.
3. This can also mean 'an evil look'.
4. *Fiṭra* (فطرة) can be the natural/innate disposition of all true Muslims; or the natural/innate disposition of all human-beings.
5. Two reasons for this are because it is considered to be more comfortable on hot, muggy weather, and because of the sweat (a ritually impure substance) that gathers in the areas where such hair is found.
6. As in the preceding note.
7. In all probability this means the clipping of the moustache away from the mouth so that food and drink will not get caught up in it—rather than shaving it off completely. In many parts of the Middle East, it is traditionally held that only Kurdish and Christian men wore bushy moustaches.

8. For obvious reasons, not all these rules apply to women.

9. This should be taken as any human being (i.e. 'slave of God').

10. 'Glory be to God!'

11. Another ḥadīth says: "The Prophet said: 'Men can say "Glory be to God!" as an exclamation of surprise in the congregation of prayer, but women should clap'." (2/165).

12. It is more likely that it is ^{c}Ā'isha who is speaking. Although it is impossible to confirm this, the direct speech is kept for its freshness and immediacy.

13. 'God is greatest!'

14. 'Praise be to God!'

15. See note 10, this section.

16. The interpretation of this ḥadīth is that the one-fifth of all war booty which automatically goes to the Prophet (or subsequent leader of the Muslims) is meant only for himself and the poor and needy.

17. See note 2, p. 195.

18. The case title of this ḥadīth is: 'If a man has been enlisted in the army and his wife goes off to do the *ḥājj*, or he has another excuse, can he be made exempt?'—The answer is clearly 'yes'.

19. i.e. 'all human beings'.

20. 4/426 adds: ". . . and upon the touch of Satan, the newborn child screams out loudly."

21. Or 'diaphragm' or 'placenta'. The folklore behind this particular ḥadīth is obscure.

22. 'Smiled'?

23. Also implied are 'discreet, reticent, accommodating'.

24. The Prophet had eleven wives (although not more than nine at one time) for two connected reasons: he was the most important man of his community, and he was thus the most responsible for the welfare of this community—so giving needy women the security of marriage was one such (voluntary) responsibility. Of his wives, ^{c}Ā'isha was a virgin (i.e. never married before), Zainab was a divorcee (see note 18, p. 203), all the others were widows. He did not divorce any of them. Khadīja (not a needy woman, in fact quite the opposite) was the first, Maimūna the last (see 'The Family of the Prophet', p. 10).

25. This ḥadīth, and all others similar to it, are quoted with the legal verdict of: 'Those (other) wives will have no right to claim back their lost turns (of having their husband stay with them).'

26. A much larger area than the present-day nation—the Levant.

27. *ʿAṣr* (عصر).

28. Commentators say that this is not a reference to ^{c}Ā'isha, but to the direction in which her house lay—east, commonly alluded to in ḥadīth literature as 'where the horn of Satan arises' (clearly there is a connection with the rising sun). Shi^{c}ī Muslims, however, would find great portend in this ḥadīth since they view ^{c}Ā'isha unfavourably, being as she was one of the principal opponents of ^{c}Alī in his struggles to succeed to the leadership of the Muslims after the Prophet's death.

29. 'People'?

30. This is referred to in other ḥadīths, leading to the assumption that this must have been a familiar situation for Muḥammad, either personally or as a regular feature of the culture of his day.

31. i.e. ". . . and I therefore (neither my wife nor I being black) have grave doubts concerning my having fathered this child."

32. A clear reference to the situation described in 7/443 where a spell was cast on the Prophet so that he kept thinking that he had slept with his wives, when in fact he had not.

33. See 3/461, p. 114.

34. The ḥadīth that follows in al-Bukhārī's collection says that the Prophet had nine wives and he used to visit them all (sexually) in one night.

35. The interpretation of this is: 'Effeminate men are forbidden to visit women.'

20. Islamic Women

1. Also called al-Juhfa, a place near Medina.

2. This, and ^{c}Alī's action related here, formed part of the power struggle between ^{c}Ā'isha's cause and that of ^{c}Alī in the period after the Prophet's death.

3. The Ka^{c}ba. In fact, the Prophet, Abū Bakr and others are buried in present-day Medina.

4. Including the Prophet and Abū Bakr.

5. The first ^{c}Umayyad Caliph and a renowned general.

6. The Prophet's first wife.

7. Note that the "old woman" referred to is the Prophet's wife Khadīja, variously said to have been five to fifteen years older than him and twice-married already. He subsequently married ^{c}Ā'isha—a child-

bride and a virgin. Both were the most influential women in his life, although his daughter Fāṭima perhaps should be included here too. See, however, note 1, p. 205 on the 'Four Perfect Women'.

8. The senior wife.

9. Divine revelations of the Qur'ān in particular.

10. This took place in the days when Muḥammad and his followers were persecuted.

11. i.e. all the worst parts of it—which are also the most ritually impure and contaminating parts (even before the coming of Islam).

12. The legal interpretation of this is: 'A woman may remove anything noxious from one who is praying.' The Battle of Badr was the first great battle for the Muslims in 625.

13. 4/448-9 say that she was an Israelite.

14. Are such 'sins' to be equated with adultery?

15. Or 'eaten *from*.'

16. i.e. before he was married to her, and perhaps even before he met her.

17. This section is used in 7/42 with the case title of: 'The permissibility of a man being able to look at women before getting married to them.'

18. i.e. the original inhabitants of Paradise.

19. i.e. to a girl.

20. Muslims believe in and accept Mary (Maryam) and Jesus (Yasū^{c})—indeed, Mary is the only woman, bar Potiphar's (^{c}Azīz) wife, with any tangible character or personality in the Qur'ān. What is not accepted, however, is the divinity of Jesus. He was the last but one prophet, heralding the Seal of the Prophets, Muḥammad. Mary, although not revered at the same level as in Christianity, also has a Virgin Birth in the Qur'ān, caused by God: **. . . Mary . . . who guarded her chastity—and We then breathed Our Spirit into her womb . . .** (Q66:12); and see the entry for Mary in Appendix 2.

21. Q3:33-44 is quoted with 4/427 on p. 138.

22. The Prophet Ibrāhim.

23. Ishmael's mother.

24. Otherwise the sheep would have died of its own accord and in the process become carrion, which ritually may not be eaten according to Islam.

25. This ḥadīth is interpreted as a recommendation for the best type of woman to marry.

26. Contrasted is the preceding verse: **And God has produced for the Unbelievers the parables of the wife of Noah and the wife of Lot. They were the wives of two of our righteous servants, and each proved false to her husband. And they availed naught from their husbands when they were told: "Enter the Fire alongside all the other sinners who enter it!"** (Q66:10)

27. Prophets and other such people are referred to here. There are no prophetesses in Islam.

28. And mother of Jesus.

29. *Tharīd* (ثريد)—a kind of broth made with bread and meat.

APPENDIX 1: Further selections from the Qur'ān

1. i.e. 'consummated your marriage with them'.

2. Lit: 'the gardens of Eden'.

3. These verses concern what God will say to all the people gathered before Him on the Last Day.

4. The common belief is that men shall in fact have unlimited numbers of houris as their companions—each one a virgin; women, on the other hand, will have a single *ghulām* (غلام 'strapping serving youth'), furthermore they will continuously and forever be remade virgins. The houris are mentioned in this respect in the Qur'ān, the youths are not (see p. 150, Q52:24; & p. 151, Q56:17).

5. The houris.

6. These youths shall serve both men and women.

7. See the preceding note.

8. Again: 'houris'.

9. A reference to virginity.

10. See note 4 of this section (omitting the 'continuously and forever').

11. Variously interpreted as 'until God helps them see the error of their ways' or more simply 'until God issues clearer instructions on how to deal with their case'.

12. i.e. homosexuals.

13. This must mean after punishment has been inflicted.

14. Christians, Jews and Sabeans.

15. Aside from pork, this was in keeping with contemporary customs of the Middle Eastern peoples—Judaism has even more rigorous food taboos in the same vein as Islam, while the New Testament, for

example, says: **For it seems good to the Holy Spirit, and on us, to lay upon you no greater burden than these necessary things: That ye abstain from meats offered to idols, and from blood and from things strangled, and from fornication: from which if ye keep yourselves, ye shall do well. Fare ye well.** (Acts, 15:28-9—echoed perfectly in Q5:3).

16. Asad's translation of the Qur'ān adds the note (p. 142), quoted here in full: "Whereas Muslim men are allowed to marry women from among the followers of another revealed religion [i.e. Peoples of the Book], Muslim women may not marry non-Muslims: the reason being that Islam enjoins reverence of *all* the Prophets, while the followers of other religions reject some of them—e.g. the Prophet Muḥammad or, as is the case with the Jews, both Muḥammad and Jesus. Thus, while a non-Muslim woman who marries a Muslim can be sure that—despite all doctrinal differences—the prophets of her faith will be mentioned with utmost respect in her Muslim environment, a Muslim woman who would marry a non-Muslim would always be exposed to an abuse of him whom she regards as God's Apostle."—The point made, however, of Islam enjoining reverence of all the prophets is perhaps something of a grey area.

17. The official reasoning behind the wives of the Prophet not being permitted to marry again after his death is that since they were given the title of 'Mothers of the Faithful', all Muslims aside from the Prophet technically became their 'children'.

18. This latter part is based on the fact that the Prophet had been given a captive slave boy called Zaid (ibn Ḥāritha) by his first wife, Khadīja. Muḥammad promptly freed the boy and adopted him. When Muḥammad became leader of the Muslims and had consolidated his power and authority, he married his cousin Zainab off to Zaid—supposedly to break down the ancient Arabian prejudice against a slave's or even a freed man's marrying a freeborn woman. Zainab had done this begrudgingly—nor was Zaid happy at this match, and eventually, after threatening to do so many times, he divorced her, in spite of the Prophet's attempts at reconciliation. The Prophet then felt obliged to marry Zainab himself, which he did.

19. It must be up to one's personal discretion to decide which of the following orders are applicable to men in general or to the Prophet only.

20. This could also imply offering oneself up without any demand for a dowry—something normally never done.

21. As slave girls, etc.

22. i.e. the state of total bodily uncleanliness resulting principally from sexual intercourse. *Ghusl* (غسل) is required in this case—the religious act of bathing the whole body—"the believer has to be careful that not only is every impurity removed from his body but also that the water moistens every part of his body and his hair" (*Shorter Encyclopaedia of Islam*—'Ghusl'). This is required after menstruation, puerperium, sexual intercourse and sexual emissions during sleep.

23. This is in place of the ablutions with water described in the next verse (Q5:6) which all Muslims must carry out in order to ritually cleanse themselves each time they pray.

24. See note 22 of this section.

25. This continues as in Q4:43 above.

26. Asad's translation of the Qur'ān adds the following note (p. 105): "In the event that a wife's immoral conduct has been proved by the direct evidence of four witnesses . . . the husband has the right, on divorcing her, to demand the return of the whole or of part of the dower which he gave her at the time when the marriage was contracted. If, as is permissible under Islamic Law—the dower has not been actually handed over to the bride at the time of marriage but has taken the form of a legal obligation in the part of the husband, he is absolved of this obligation in the case of proven immoral conduct on the part of the wife."

27. See the preceding note.

28. i.e. sexually.

29. Despite the existence of ḥadīths contrary to this, since there is no counter order provided in the Qur'ān, there is a strong argument that one is bound take the beating of one's wife under these conditions as law.

30. This concerns polygamous marriages, and is said to concern the inequality of personal feelings towards each of a man's wives as against the equality of treatment that is their right in every other respect.

31. An irrevocable form of divorce practised by the pre-Islamic Arabs, which was forbidden by Muḥammad in no uncertain terms. This procedure was particularly harsh as the woman would not be allowed to remarry and had to remain under her former husband's absolute control.

32. Note that fathers are not referred to in the way mothers are.

33. 'Those who cry unto God.'

34. i.e. 'camels, cows, goats, sheep'.

35. i.e. 'to eat'.

36. Q39:6 says: **And He created you from a single living being, and from it fashioned its mate—and He has granted you four types of cattle of either sex, and he creates you in your mothers' wombs in one stage after another, through three veils of darkness.**

37. i.e. 'daughters'.

38. This is a general term for livestock.

39. This often-seen exclamation of irony refers principally to the pre-Islamic Arabs's belief in a pantheon of Allāh and his daughters (see note 6, p. 197). A secondary, less important emphasis may be applied concerning the Christian belief of Jesus Christ as the son and equal of God.

40. Q37:149-51 gives us: **Now ask them for their opinion: Is it the case that your Lord has daughters while you yourselves have only sons? Or is it the case that We created all the angels female, and that they were witnesses to this fact? Truly, it is out of their lying that they say: "God has begotten offspring!" And truly they are liars also when they say: "He has chosen daughters for himself over sons!"**

41. See note 31 of this section.

APPENDIX 2: Women in the Qur'ān

1. The Four Perfect Women in Islam are Āsiya (Pharaoh's wife), Mary (the mother of Jesus), Khadīja (first wife of the Prophet, and Fāṭima (the Prophet's favourite daughter). Note that ᶜĀ'isha is not one of their number. Islamic thought has always had mixed reactions towards her—no doubt because she became politically active after the Prophet's death—many Shiᶜi Muslims, for example, traditionally consider her a 'red-haired hussy'. (Note that in the Qur'ān itself there are comparatively few women, named or unnamed, and that there are no prophetesses or great heroines.)

2. See note 26, p. 202.

3. Q11:78, incidently, relates the words of Lot (Lūṭ) to his people who were spurred on by desire at what they had seen in Sodom: **Lot said: "O my people! Here are my daughters—take them instead, for they are purer for you than men are . . . !"**

4. The nature of translations made in this volume, of course, cannot convey the great poetry of these extracts.

5. The actual word used here (*baghī* بغي) means 'prostitute'.

6. See note 5 of this section.

7. . . . **They said: "How can we talk to who is still a child in the cradle?" He said: "Indeed I am a servant of God, and He has given me Revelation and made me a prophet; and He has made me blessed wherever I may be; and He has enjoined upon me the performing of prayer and charity for as long as I live; and He has filled me with pious respect for my mother, and has not made me arrogant or base. Thus peace is upon me on the day that I was born, and on the day that I die and on the day when I shall again arise living!"** (Q19:29-33)—The words of the final verse are not interpreted as having great significance.

8. Noah's Ark appears in Q11:40: **And so on until there came Our judgement to pass and the earth gushed forth torrents across the earth! And We said to Noah: "Put aboard your Ark two of each kind of animal, a male and a female, as well as your family."**

9. According to popular tradition her name was Zulaikhā.

10. i.e. 'husband'.

11. According to popular tradition this was a child.

References

Asad, Muhammad (trans.), *The Message of the Qur'ān*, Gibraltar, 1980.

Bell, R., *A Commentary on the Qur'ān*, Manchester, 1991.

al-Bukhārī, *Al-Jāmi^{c} al-Ṣaḥīḥ* (various editions).

al-Bukhārī, *Sahih: Le recueil de Traditions Musulmanes*, ed. L. Krehl & F. W. Juynboll, Leiden, 1862-1908.

al-Bukhārī, *The Translation of the Meaning of Sahih Bukhari*, ed. Muhammad Muhsin Khan, 1973 (Arabic-English).

EI1 = *The Encyclopaedia of Islam* (1st edition), Leiden, 1913-36.

EI2 = *The Encyclopaedia of Islam* (2nd edition), Leiden, 1960/2002.

Fluegel, G., *Corani Textus Arabicus*, Leipzig, 1898.

Fraenkel, S., *De Vocabulis in Antiquis Arabum Carminibus et in Corano Peregrinis*, Leiden, 1880.

Guillaume, A., *The Life of Muhammad*, London, 1955.

Hava, J. G., *Arabic-English Dictionary*, Beirut, 1915 [1964].

Jeffery, A., *The Foreign Vocabulary of the Qur'ān*, Baroda, 1938.

Lane, E. W., *An Arabic-English Lexicon*, 8 vols, London, 1863-93.

Muhammad: Encyclopedia of Seerah (Sunnah, Da^{c}wah & Islam), London, 1987 —Vol. 5: *Role of Muslim Women in Society.*

Muslim, *Al-Jāmi^{c} al-Ṣaḥīḥ* (various editions).

Muslim, *Sahih Muslim*, ed. Abdul Hamid Siddiqi, 1972-75 (Arabic-English).

Nicholson, R. A., *A Literary History of the Arabs*, Cambridge, 1930.

Shorter Encyclopaedia of Islam, ed. H. A. R. Gibb & J. H. Kramers, Leiden, 1961.

Wehr, H., & Cowan, J. M., *A Dictionary of Modern Written Arabic*, Wiesbaden, 1979.

Wright, W., *A Grammar of the Arabic Language*, Cambridge, 1894-8.

Women in Islam: A Select Bibliography of Works

Abadan-Unat et al, *Women in Turkish society*, E. J. Brill, 1981.

Abbott, Nabia, *Aishah: the Beloved of Mohammed*, Al Saqi, 1985.

Abbott, Nabia, *Two queens of Baghdad*, Al Saqi, 1986.

Abdalati, Hammudah, *Islam in focus*, American Trust Publications, 1975.

Abdalati, Hammudah, *The family structure in Islam*, American Trust Publications, 1977.

Abd al-Rahman, A'isha, *The wives of the Prophet*, Lahore, 1971.

Abdella Doumato, Eleanor, *Getting God's ear: women, Islam, and healing in Saudi Arabia and the Gulf*, Columbia University Press, 2000.

Abdel-Wahab, Ahmad, *La situation de la femme dans le judasme, le christianisme et l'islam*, A.E.I.F., 1994.

Abdul-Rauf, M., *Marriage in Islam: a manual*, Exposition Press, 1972.

Abdul-Rauf, M., *History of the Islamic Center*, Islamic Center, Washington D.C., 1978.

Abdul-Rauf, M., *The Islamic view of women and the family*, Al-Saadawi, 1995.

Abdur Rahim, M. A., *The principles of Islamic jurisprudence according to the Hanafi, Maliki, Shafi'i and Hanbali schools*, Kitab Bhavan, 1994.

Abou El Fadl, Khaled, *Speaking in God's Name: Islamic law, authority and women*, Oneworld Press 2001.

Abou El Fadl, Khaled, *The place of tolerance in Islam*, Beacon Press, 2002.

Abouzeid, Leila, *Year of the elephant: a Moroccan woman's journey toward independence, and other stories*, University of Texas Press, 1989.

Abouzeid, Leila, *Return to childhood: the memoir of a modern Moroccan woman,* University of Texas Press, 1998.

Abraham, Sameer Y., & Nabeel Abraham (eds.), *The Arab World and Arab-Americans: understanding a neglected minority*, Wayne State University, Center for Urban Studies, 1981.

Abu Sulayman, AbdulHamid A., *Chastising wives: Quranic verse re-interpreted: women* [sic] *dignity reconsidered*, International Institute of Islamic Thought, 2002.

Abu Zahra, Muhammad, 'Family Law', in Majid Khadduri & Herbert J. Liebesney (eds.), *Law in the Middle East*, Middle East Institute, 1955.

Abu-Lughod, Lila, *Veiled sentiments: honor and poetry in a Bedouin society*, University of California Press, 1986.

Abu-Lughod, Lila, *Writing women's worlds: Bedouin stories*, University of California Press, 1992.

Abu-Lughod, Lila (ed.), *Remaking women: feminism and modernity in the Middle East*, Princeton University Press, 1998.

Abu-r-Rida', Muhammad, *Handbuch der muslimischen Frau,* Islamische Bibliothek, 1996.

Adamgy, M. Yiossuf M., *A mulher no islão: como a muhler era considerada nas civilizações antigas e de que forma o islão elevou a sua posição,* Al Furqán, 2000.

Adelabu, Habeeba Abdur-Razaq, *Islamic awareness in women*, Centre for Islamic Education and Propagation, 1995.

Adeney, Miriam, *Daughters of Islam: building bridges with Muslim women*, InterVarsity Press, 2002.

SELECT BIBLIOGRAPHY

Afary, Janet, 'Feminism and the challenge of Muslim fundamentalism', in T. Denean Sharpley-Whiting (ed.), *Spoils of war: women of color, cultures and revolutions*, Rowman & Littlefield, 1997.

Afkhami, Mahnaz (ed.), *Faith and freedom: women's human rights in the Muslim world*, Syracuse University Press, 1995.

Afkhami, Mahnaz & Erika Friedl (eds.), *Muslim women and the politics of participation: implementing the Beijing Platform*, Syracuse University Press, 1997.

Afsar, Bano (ed.), *Status of women in Islamic society*, Anmol, 2004.

Afsaruddin, Asma (ed.), *Hermeneutics and honor: negotiating female 'public' space in Islamic/ate societies*, Harvard University Press, 1999.

Afshar, Haleh, *Women and gender in Islam: historical roots of a modern debate*, University of York, Department of Politic, 1992.

Afshar, Haleh, *Why fundamentalism?: Iranian women and their support for Islam*, University of York, Department of Politics, 1994.

Afshar, Haleh, 'Islam and feminism: an analysis of political strategies', in M. Yamani (ed.), *Feminism and Islam*, Garnet, 1996.

Afshar, Haleh (ed.), *Women and politics in the Third World*, Routledge, 1996.

Afshar, Haleh, *Islam and feminisms: an Iranian case-study*, Macmillan, 1998.

Afza, Nashat, & K. Ahmed, *The position of women in Islam*, Islamic Book Publishers, Kuwait, 1982.

Agmon, Iris, 'Women, class and gender: Muslim Jaffa and Haifa at the turn of the 20th century', *International Journal of Middle East Studies*, 30, 4, pp 477-500.

Ahmad, Imtiaz (ed.), *Divorce and remarriage among Muslims in India*, Manohar, 2003.

Ahmad, Leila, *Women and gender in Islam*, Yale University Press, 1992.

Ahmad, Maulana, *Islam on marital rights*, London Mosque, 1976.

Ahmad, Naseem, *Liberation of Muslim women*, Kalpaz, 2001.

Ahmad, Naseem, *Women in Islam*, Anmol, 2003.

Ahmad, Naseem, *Islamic manners*, Anmol, 2003.

Ahmad, Shahnon, & Harry Aveling, *Islam, power, and gender*, Penerbit Universiti Kebangsaan Malaysia, 2000.

Ahmed, Akbar, *Postmodernism and Islam*, Taylor & Francis, 1992.

Ahmed, Akbar, *Living Islam*, Penguin, 1995.

Ahmed, Akbar, *Islam Today*, I. B. Tauris, 1999.

Ahmed, Akbar, *Islam under siege: living dangerously in a post-honor world*, Polity, 2003.

Ahmed, Akbar, & Donnan, Hastings, *Islam, globalization and postmodernity*, Routledge, 1994.

Ahmed, Anis, *Women and social justice: an Islamic paradigm*, Institute of Policy Studies/The Islamic Foundation, 1996.

Ahmed, Leila, *Women and gender in Islam: historical roots of a modern debate*, Yale University Press, 1993.

Ahmed, Leila, *A border passage: from Cairo to America: a woman's journey*, Penguin, 2000.

Ahmed, Rafiuddin, *Understanding the Bengal Muslims: interpretative essays*, Oxford University Press, 2001.

Akhenaton, Jamal G., 'Islam in the State of California', *Pluralism project research notes*, 1991.

Akhenaton, Jamal G., 'African American Islam in Houston', *Pluralism project research notes*, 1992.

Akhtar, Shabbir, *Be careful with Muhammad*, Bellew, 1989.
Akhtar, Shabbir, *A faith for all seasons*, Bellew, 1990.
El Alami, Dawoud, & Doreen Hinchcliffe, *Islamic marriage and divorce laws in the Middle East*, Kluwer, 1996.
Aldeeb Abu Sahlieh, Sami A., *Male and female circumcision among Jews, Christians and Muslims*, Shangri-La, 2001.
Ali, A. Yusuf, *The Holy Qur'an: translation and commentary*, Tahrike Tarsile Qur'an, 1987.
Ali, Ameer, *The legal position of women in Islam*, University of London Press, 1912.
Ali, Azra Asghar, *The emergence of feminism among Indian Muslim women, 1920-1947*, Oxford University Press, 2000.
Ali, Maulana Muhammad, *A manual of Hadith*, Ahmadiyya Anjuman Ishaat, 1977.
Ali, Maulana Muhammad, *The religion of Islam: a comprehensive discussion of the sources, principles and practices of Islam*, Ahmadiyya Anjuman Ishaat, 1983.
Ali, Nadje Sadig, *Secularism gender and the state in the Middle East: the Egyptian women's movement*, Cambridge University Press, 2000.
Ali, Syed Ameer, *The spirit of Islâm: or the life and teachings of Mohammed*, S. K. Lahiri, 1902.
Ali, Shaheen Sardar, *Gender and human rights in Islam and international law: equal before Allah, unequal before man?*, Kluwer Law International, 2000.
Ali, Syed Anwer, *Qur'an: the fundamental law of human life*, Kazi, 1982-1994.
Ali, Thanwi Asharaf (trans. Ansari Iqbal Husain), *Muslim way of life*, Right Way, 2001.
Ali, Zaheer, 'African American Islam in New York', *Pluralism project research notes*, 1993.
Ali, Zeenat Shaukat, *The empowerment of women in Islam: with special reference to marriage & divorce*, Gopi Books, 1997.
Alkan, Metin, et al., *Islam in een ontzuilde samenleving: discussies over vrouwenemancipatie, kunst en onderwijs*, Koninklijk Instituut voor de Tropen/Soeterijn, 1996.
Allami, Noria, *Voilées, dévoilees: être femme dans le monde arabe*, L'Harmattan, 1988.
Allana, Mariam, *Muslim women and Islamic tradition: studies in modernisation*, Kanishka, 2000.
Alliata, Victoria, *Harem: Die Freiheit hinter dem Schleier*, Rogner & Bernhard, 1981.
Altorki, Sorya, & Camillia Fawzi el-Solh, *Arab women in the field: studying your own society*, Syracuse University Press, 1983.
El-Amin, Mildred M., *Family roots: the Qur'anic view of family life*, International Ummah Foundation, 1991.
Amin, Qasim, *Die Befreiung der Frau*, Echter/Oros, 1992.
Amin, Qasim (trans. Samiha Sidhom Peterson), *'The liberation of women' and 'The new woman': two documents in the history of Egyptian feminism*, American University in Cairo Press, 2000.
Amin, S., *The world of Muslim women in colonial Bengal, 1876-1939*, E. J. Brill, 1996.
Amri, Nelly, & Laroussi Amri, *Les femmes soufies, ou la passion de Dieu*, Dangles, 1999.
Andall, Jacqueline, *Gender and ethnicity in contemporary Europe*, Berg, 2003.
Anderson, N., *Law Reform in the Muslim World*, Athlone Press, 1976.
Andrae, Tor, *Mohammed: the man and his faith*, Harper Torchbook, 1960.
Aniba, Mokhtar, *L'Islam et les droits de la femme*, Dar Najib lil-Tiba'ah wa-al-Nashr, 1991.
Anjum, Mohini, *Muslim women in India*, Sangam, 1992.
Ansari, Sarah, & Vanessa Martin (eds.), *Women, religion and culture in Iran*, Curzon, 2002.
Anway, Carol L., *Daughters of another path: experiences of American women choosing Islam*, Yawna, 1996.

SELECT BIBLIOGRAPHY

'Arab Draft Unified Code of Personal Status, 1986', in J. Nasir, *The Islamic law of personal status*, Graham & Trotman, 1990.

Arat, Yeşim, *Political Islam in Turkey and women's organizations*, Turkish Economic and Social Studies Foundation, 1999.

Arberry, A. (trans.), *The Koran interpreted: a translation*, George Allen Urwin,1980.

Arebi, Saddeka, *Women and words in Saudi Arabia: the politics of literary discourse*, Columbia University Press, 1994.

Ariff, Mohamed (ed.), *The Muslim private sector in Southeast Asia: Islam and the economic development of Southeast Asia,* Institute of Southeast Asian Studies, 1991.

Armstrong, Karen, *Islam: a short history*, Modern Library, 2002.

Asad, Muhammad, *The principles of state and government in Islam*, Dar al-Andalus, 1980.

Asad, Muhammad (trans.), *The Message of the Qur'an*, The Book Foundation, 2004.

Asayesh, Gelareh, 'Iran: the rules of courtship', *Toronto Star*, Feb. 4, 1991.

Asayesh, Gelareh, *Saffron sky: a life between Iran and America*, Beacon Press 1999.

Ascha, Ghassan, *Du statut inférieur de la femme en Islam*, L'Harmattan, 1987.

Ask, Karin, & Marit Tjomsland (eds.), *Women and Islamization: contemporary dimensions of discourse on gender relations*, Berg, 1998.

Assouline, Florence, *Musulmanes: une chance pour l'Islam,* Flammarion, 1992.

Aswad, Barbara, & Barbara Bilge (eds.), *Family and gender among American Muslims: issues facing Middle Eastern immigrants and their descendants*, Temple University, 1996.

Atiya, Nayra, *Khul-Khaal: five Egyptian women tell their stories*, Syracuse University Press, 1982.

Augustin, Ebba (ed.), *Palestinian women: identity and experience*, Zed Books, 1993.

Austin, A. D., *African Muslims in antebellum America: a sourcebook*, Garland, 1984.

Aveling, Harry, *Shahnon Ahmad: Islam, power, and gender*, UKM Press, 2000.

El-Awa, M., *Punishment in Islamic law*, American Trust Publications, 1982.

Azami, M. M., *Studies in early Hadith literature*, American Trust Publications, 1992.

Azami, M. M., *On Schacht's Origins of Muhammadan Jurisprudence*, Islamic Texts Society, 1996.

Azari, Farah, *Women of Iran: the conflict with fundamentalist Islam*, Ithaca Press, 1983.

Azim, Saukath, *Muslim women: emerging identity*, Woodrow Wilson Center Press, 1997.

al-Azmeh, Aziz, *Islams and modernities*, Verso, 1996.

Badamasiuy, Juwayriya Bint, *Status and role of women under the Shari'ah*, Zakara, 1998.

Badawi, Jamal, *Status of women in Islam*, American Trust Publications, 1971.

Badawi, Jamal, *Gender equity in Islam: Basic Principles*, American Trust Publications, 1995.

Badran, Margot, *Harem years: the memoirs of an Egyptian feminist (1879-1924)*, Feminist Press at the City University of New York, 1987.

Badran, Margot, *Feminists, Islam, and nation: gender and the making of modern Egypt*, Princeton, Princeton University Press, 1995.

Badran, Margot, & Miriam Cooke (eds.), *Opening the gates: a century of Arab feminist writing*, Indiana University Press, 1990.

el Bahnassawi, Salem (trans. Abdul Fattah el-Shaer), *Woman between Islam and world legislations: a comparative study*, Dar al-Qalam, 1985.

Baker, A., *Voices of resistance: oral histories of Moroccan women*, State University of New York Press, 1998.

Bakhtiar, Laleh, *Encyclopedia of Islamic law: a compendium of the major schools (Hanafi, Hanbali, Shafii, Maliki and Jafari)*, Kazi, 1996.
Bakhtiar, Laleh, *Sufi women of America, angels in the making*, Institute of Traditional Psychoethics and Guidance, 1996.
Barazangi, Nimat, 'Parents and youth: perceiving and practicing Islam in North America', in Barbara Aswad & Barbara Bilge (eds.), *Family and Gender among American Muslims: issues facing Middle Eastern immigrants and their descendants*, Temple University, 1996.
Barboza, Steven, *American Jihad: Islam after Malcolm X*, Doubleday, 1994.
Barlas, Asma, *'Believing women' in Islam: unreading patriarchal interpretations of the Quran*, University of Texas Press, 2002.
Baron, Beth, *The Women's Awakening in Egypt: Culture, Society and the Press*, Yale University Press, 1994.
Bashier, Zakaria, *Muslim women in the midst of change*, Islamic Foundation, 1980.
Bauer, Kirsten, *Frauen im Islam*, Wilhelm Heyne, 1994.
Baveja, Malik Ram (ed. M. A. Ali), *Women in Islam*, Advent Books, 1988.
Bayes, Jane H., & Nayereh Tohidi (eds.), *Globalization, gender and religion: the politics of women's rights in Catholic and Muslim contexts*, Palgrave, 2001.
Beck, Lois, & Nikki Keddie (eds.), *Women in the Muslim world*, Harvard University Press, 1978.
Beinin, Joel, & Joe Stork, *Political Islam*, I. B. Tauris, 1996.
Bell, R., *Introduction to the Qur'an*, (revised by W. M. Watt), Islamic Surveys, Edinburgh University Press, 1997.
Belt, Don, *The world of Islam*, National Geographic Books, 2001.
Bendt, Ingala, & James Downing, *We shall return: women of Palestine*, Zed Books/Lawrence Hill, 1980.
Benedek, Wolfgang, Esther M. Kisaakye & Gerd Oberleitner (eds.), *The Human rights of women: international instruments and African experiences*, Zed Books, 2002.
Benguigui, Yamina, *Femmes d'Islam*, A. Michel, 1996.
Benkheira, Mohammed H., *L'amour de la loi: essai sur la normativité en Islam*, PUF, 1997.
Bennett, Sophie, *Gender and identity in the modern Egyptian short story (1954-1992)*, thesis, SOAS, 1993.
Bennoune, Karima, 'S.O.S. Algeria: Women's Human Rights under Siege', in *Faith and freedom: women's human rights in the Muslim world*, ed. Mehnaz Afkhami, Syracuse University Press, 1995.
Berg, Herbert, *The Development of exegesis in early Islam: the authenticity of Muslim literature from the formative period*, Curzon, 2000.
Bergstrasser, G. (ed. Joseph Schacht), *Grundzüge des islamischen Rechtes*, Berlin, 1935.
Berkey, Jonathan, 'Women and Islamic education in the Mamluk period', in Nikki Keddie & Beth Baron (eds.), *Women in Middle Eastern history: shifting boundaries in sex and gender*, Yale University Press 1991, pp 143-157.
Berkey, Jonathan, 'Circumcision circumscribed: female excision and cultural accommodation in the Medieval Near East', *International Journal of Middle East Studies*, 28, 1996, pp 19-38.
Berkey, Jonathan. 'Women in medieval Islamic society', in Linda E. Mitchell (ed.), *Women in medieval Western European culture*, Garland Publishing, 1999, pp 95-116.
Berry, Abdullatif, *Temporary marriage in Islam*, Az-Zahara International, 1989.

SELECT BIBLIOGRAPHY

Beshir, Ekram & Mohamed R., *Blissful marriage: a practical Islamic guide*, Amana, 2003.

Bevan Jones, V. R. & L., *Woman in Islam: a manual with special reference to conditions in India*, Hyperion Press, 1981.

Bewley, Abdal-Haqq, Aisha Bewley & Ahmad Thompson, *The Islamic will: a practical guide to being prepared for death*, Dar al-Taqwa, 1995.

Bewley, Aisha, *Islam: the empowering of women*, Ta-Ha, 1999.

Bhutto, Benazir, 'The Prophet preached equal rights; now the task is to restore them', *Asiaweek*, August 25, 1995.

Bibars, Iman, *Victims and heroines: women, welfare and the Egyptian state*, Zed Books, 2001.

Bingham, Marjorie Wall, & Susan Hill Gross, *Women in Islam: the Ancient Middle East to modern times*, Glenhurst Publications, 1980.

el-Bizri, Dalal, *L'ombre et son double: femmes islamistes, libanaises et modernes*, Cermoc, 1995.

Bin Ladin, Carmen, *Inside the kingdom; my life in Saudi Arabia*, Warner, 2004.

Blackwell, C., *Tradition and society in Turkmenistan: gender, oral culture and song*, Curzon, 2000.

Blakely, Thomas D., et al. (eds.), *Religion in Africa: experience & expression*, Heinemann, 1994.

Boddy, Janice Patricia, *Wombs and alien spirits: women, men, and the Zar cult in northern Sudan*, University of Wisconsin Press, 1989.

Bodman, Herbert L., & Nayereh Tohidi (eds.), *Women in Muslim societies: diversity within unity*, Lynne Reinner, 1998.

Borresen, Kari Elisabeth, & Kari Vogt, *Women's studies of the Christian and Islamic traditions: ancient, medieval, and Renaissance foremothers*, Kluwer Academic, 1993.

Boullata, I. J., *Literary structures of religious meaning in the Qur'an*, Curzon, 2000.

Bowen, Donna Lee, 'Abortion, Islam and the 1994 Cairo Population Conference', *International Journal of Middle East Studies*, vol. 29, no. 2, pp 161-184.

Boyd, J., *The Caliph's sister: Nana Asma'u, 1793-1865, teacher, poet and Islamic leader*, W estview, 1995.

Brand, L., *Women, the state, and political liberalization: Middle Eastern and North African experiences*, Columbia University Press, 1998.

Breitman, George (ed.), *Malcolm X speaks: selected speeches and statements*, Pathfinder, 1989.

Brooks, Geraldine, *Nine parts of desire: the hidden world of Islamic women*, Anchor, 1995.

Brown, Daniel, *Rethinking tradition in modern Islamic thought*, Cambridge University Press, 1996.

Brown, Nathan, *The rule of law in the Arab World: courts in Egypt and the Gulf*, Cambridge University Press, 1997.

Buckley, Silma, *Islamic parenting: the natural alternative*, Muslim Converts Association, 1991.

Buitelaar, Marjo, *Fasting and feasting in Morocco: women's participation in Ramadan*, Berg, 1993.

Buonaventura, W., *The Book of Oriental Body Care*, Al Saqi, 1998.

Bürgel, Johann Christoph, *Allmacht und mächtigkeit; Religion und Welt im Islam*, C. H. Beck, 1991.

Burton, Antoinette, *Burdens of history: british feminists, Indian women and imperial culture (1865-1915)*, University of North Carolina Press, 1994.

Burton, J., *The collection of the Qur'an*, Cambridge University Press, 1977.

Burton, J., *An introduction to the Hadith*, Edinburgh University Press, 1994.

Burton, J., *Introduction to the tradition*, Edinburgh University Press, 2000.

Burton, J., *The sources of Islamic law: Islamic theories of abrogation*, Edinburgh University Press, 1990.
Cadavid, Leslie, *Two twentieth-century muslim saints: Sayyida Fatima al-Yashrutiyya and Shaikh Ahmed al-Alawi*, Fons Vitae, 2004.
Caesar, Judith, *Crossing borders: an American woman in the Middle East*, Syracuse University Press, 1999.
Calder, Norman, *Studies in early Muslim jurisprudence*, Oxford University Press, 1993.
Calder, Norman, 'shari'a', in *Encyclopedia of Islam*, 2nd edition.
Calder, Norman, Farhat J. Ziadeh, Abdulaziz Sachedina & Ann Elizabeth Mayer, 'Law', in *Oxford encyclopedia of the modern Islamic world*, Oxford University Press, 1995.
Callaway, Barbara, & Lucy Creevey, *The heritage of Islam: women, religion, and politics in West Africa*, Lynne Rienner, 1994.
Canadian Journal of African studies/Revue Canadienne des Études Africaines, 34-3 (special issue on slavery and Islam in African history: a tribute to Martin Klein), 2000.
Carré, Olivier (trans. Carol Artigues; ed. W. Shepard), *Mysticism and politics: a critical reading of 'Fi Zilal al-Qur'an' by Sayyid Qutb (1906-1966)*, E. J. Brill, 2003.
Caspi, Mishael Maswari, & Julia Ann Blessing, *Weavers of the songs: the oral poetry of Arab women in Israel and the West Bank*, Three Continents Press, 1991.
Chafiq, Chahla, *La femme et le retour de l'Islam: l'expérience iranienne,* Le Félin, 1991.
Chafiq, Chahla, & Farhad Khosrokhavar, *Femmes sous le voile face la loi islamique*, Editions du Flin, 1995.
Chatty, Dawn, 'Women working in Oman: individual choice and cultural constraints', in *International Journal of Middle East Studies*, May 2000, vol. 32, no. 2, pp 241-254.
Chatty, Dawn, & Annika Rabo (eds.), *Organizing women: formal and informal women's groups in the Middle East*, Berg, 1997.
Chaturvedi, Archna (ed.), *Muslim women and development*, Commonwealth, 2004.
Chaturvedi, Archna (ed.), *Muslim women and law*, Commonwealth, 2004.
Chaturvedi, Archna (ed.), *Muslim women in global perspectives*, Commonwealth, 2004.
Chaturvedi, Archna (ed.), *Muslim women: from tradition to modernity*, Commonwealth, 2004.
Chaudhry, Muhammad Sharif, *The woman in a Muslim society*, al-Matbaat-ul-Arabia, 1995.
Chaudhry, Muhammad Sharif, *Women's rights in Islam*, Commonwealth, 2003.
Chavis, Melody Ermachild, *Meena, heroine of Afghanistan: the martyr who founded RAWA, the Revolutionary Association of the Women of Afghanistan*, St Martin's Press, 2003.
Chebel, Malek, *La féminisation du monde: essai sur les 'Mille et une nuits'*, Payot, 1996.
Cherif Bassiouni, M., *The Islamic criminal justice system*, Oceana, 1982.
Chishti, Hakim G. M., *The traditional healer's handbook; a classic guide to the medicine of Avicenna*, Healing Arts Press, 1988.
Choudhury, M., *Studies in Islamic political science*, Macmillan, 1998.
Cilardo, Agostino, 'Historical development of the legal doctrine relative to the position of the hermaphrodite in the Islamic law', in *The Search: Journal for Arab and Islamic Studies*, winter 1986, pp 128-170.
Clarke, John H., *Malcolm X: the man and his times,* Macmillan, 1969.
Clarke, Peter G. (ed.), *New trends and developments in the world of Islam*, Luzac Oriental, 1998.
Cohn-Sherbok, Dan, *Islam in a world of diverse faiths*, Palgrave Macmillan, 1997.

SELECT BIBLIOGRAPHY

Cook, Miriam, *Commanding right and forbidding wrong in Islamic thought*, Cambridge University Press, 2000.

Cooke, Miriam, *Women claim Islam: creating Islamic feminism through literature*, Routledge, 2001.

Coomaraswamy, Radhika, *The impact of tradition, culture and religion on women in South Asia*, International Centre for Ethnic Studies, 1988.

Cooper B., *Marriage in Maradi: gender and culture in a Hausa society in Niger 1900-89*, Heinemann, 1997.

Cornell, Rkia, *Early Sufi women*, Fons Vitae, 1999.

Cotran, Eugene, & Adel Omar Sherif (eds.), *Democracy, the rule of law and Islam*, Kluwer Law International, 1999.

Cotran, Eugene, & Mai Yamani (eds.), *The rule of law in the Middle East and the Islamic world: human rights and the judicial process*, I. B. Tauris, 2000.

Coulon, Christian, & Odile Reveyrand, *L'Islam au féminin: Sokhna Magat Diop, cheikh de la confrérie mouride*, Centre d'Etude d'Afrique Noire, 1990.

Coulson, Noel, 'The state and the individual in Islamic law', *International and Comparative Law Quarterly*, 6, 1957.

Coulson, Noel, *Succession in the Muslim family*, Cambridge University Press, 1971.

Coulson, Noel, *A history of Islamic law*, Edinburgh University Press, 1995.

Crone, Patricia, *Roman, provincial and Islamic Law: The origins of the Islamic patronate*, Cambridge University Press, 1987.

Crone, Patricia, & Michael Crone, *Hagarism: the making of the Islamic polity*, Cambridge University Press, 1977.

Da Costa, Yusuf, *The honor of women in Islam*, Islamic Supreme Council of America, 2002.

Dagher, Hamdun, *The position of women in Islam*, Light of Life, 1995.

Dahl, Tove Stang, *The Muslim family: a study of women's rights in Islam*, Scandinavian University Press, 1997.

Dalacoura, Katerina, *Islam, liberalism and human rights*, I. B. Tauris, 1998.

Damodaran, Vinita, & Maya Unnithan-Kumar, *Postcolonial India: history, politics, and culture*, Manohar, 2000.

Das, Man Singh, *Roles of women in Muslim countries*, MD Publications, 1991.

Dauda, Aliyu, *Women's education: its problems and prospects*, Manifold, 1999.

Daure-Serfaty, Christine (trans. Paul Raymond Côté & Constantina Mitchell), *Letter from Morocco*, Michigan University Press, 2003.

Deen, Hanifa, *Broken bangles*, Penguin, 1999.

Degand, Angela, *Geschlechterrollen und familiale Strukturen im Islam*, Frankfurt, 1988.

Delaney, Carol Lowery, *The seed and the soil: gender and cosmology in Turkish village society*, University of California Press, 1991.

Delcroix, C., *Espoirs et réalités de la femme arabe*, L'Harmattan, 1986.

DeLong-Bas, Natana J., *Wahhabi Islam: from revival and reform to global Jihad*, Oxford University Press, 2004.

Dhina, Amar, *Femmes illustres en Islam*, Entreprise nationale du livre, 1991.

Diallo, Yacine Marius, & Idrissa Alichina Kourguni (eds.), *Report of the regional conference on women, Islam, and family planning: Niamey, Niger, October 23 to 25, 1995*, International Planned Parenthood Federation, 1996.

Dialmy, Abdessamad, *Féminisme soufi: conte Fassi et initiation sexuelle*, Afrique Orient, 1991.

Dialmy, Abdessamad, *Féminisme, islamisme, soufisme,* Publisud, 1997.
Djebar, Assia (trans. Jean MacGibbon), *Women of Islam*, André Deutsch, 1961.
Djebar, Assia (trans. Dorothy S. Blair), *A sister to Scheherazade*, Heinemann, 1987.
Djebar, Assia (trans. Dorothy S. Blair), *Fantasia: an Algerian cavalcade*, Heinemann, 1993.
Doi, A. R. I., *Women in Shari'ah*, Ta-Ha, 1989.
Donnan, Hastings, *Interpreting Islam*, Sage, 2001.
Dore-Audibert, Andrée, & Souad Khodja, *Etre femme au Maghreb et en Méditerranée: du mythe à la réalité,* Karthala, 1998.
Dori, Muhammed, *Women, feminism, and Islam*, Muhmmad Mustapha Ladan, 1998.
Dorsky, Susan, *Women of Amran: a Middle Eastern ethnographic study*, University of Utah Press, 1986.
Dossier d'information sur la situation en Algérie: résistance des femmes et solidarité internationale (Compilation of information on the situation in Algeria: women's resistance and solidarity around the world), Women Living Under Muslim Laws, 1995.
Doumato, Eleanor Abdella, *Getting God's ear: women, Islam and healing in Saudi Arabia and the Gulf*, Columbia University Press, 2000.
Draft Charter on Human and People's Rights in the Arab World, Arab League, 1987.
Draz, M., *Introduction the Qur'an*, I. B. Tauris, 2000.
Draz, M., *The moral world of the Qur'an*, I. B. Tauris, 2004.
Dunne, B., 'Power and Sexuality in the Middle East', *The Middle East Report,* Spring 1998.
Dwyer, Daisy Hilse, *Images and self-images: male and female in Morocco*, Columbia University Press, 1978.
Dwyer, Daisy Hilse, *Law and Islam in the Middle East*, Bergin & Garvey, 1990.
Dwyer, K., *The human rights debate in the Middle East*, London, 1991.

Early, Evelyn A., *Baladi women of Cairo: playing with an egg and a stone*, Lynne Rienner, 1993.
Easterman, Daniel, *New Jerusalems*, HarperCollins, 1993.
Ebrahim, A., *Abortion, birth control and surrogate parenting: an Islamic perspective*, American Trust Publications, 1989.
Edith Laudowicz, Edith, Rukhsana Ahmad et al. (eds.), *Fatimas Töchter: Frauen im Islam*, PapyRossa, 1992.
Egyptian Women in social development: a resource guide, The American University Press: Cairo, 1998.
Eissa, Dahlia, *Constructing the notion of male superiority over women in Islam: the influence of sex and gender stereotyping in the interpretation of the Qur'an and the implications for a modernist exegesis of rights*, Women Living Under Muslim Laws, 1999.
Elias, Jamal J., *Islam,* Taylor & Francis, 1999.
Ellis, Deborah, *Women of the Afghan War*, Praeger, 2000.
Emadi, Hafizullah, *Repression, resistance, and women in Afghanistan*, Praeger, 2002.
Emmett, Ayala H., *Our sisters' promised land: women, politics, and Israeli-Palestinian coexistence*, University of Michigan Press, 1996.
Engineer, Asghar Ali, *Status of women in Islam*, Ajanta, 1987.
Engineer, Asghar Ali, *Justice, women, and communal harmony in Islam*, Indian Council of Social Science Research, 1989.
Engineer, Asghar, Ali, *The rights of women in Islam,* Hurst, 1992.
Engineer, Asghar Ali, *Problems of Muslim women in India*, Orient Longman, 1998.

Engineer, Asghar Ali, *The Qur'an, women, and modern society*, Sterling, 1999.
Engineer, Asghar Ali, *Islam, women and gender justice*, Gyan, 2002.
Esack, Farid, *Quran, liberation and pluralism: an Islamic perspective of interreligious solidarity against oppression*, Oneworld, 1997.
Esfandiari, Haleh, *Reconstructed lives: women and Iran's Islamic revolution*, John Hopkins University Press, 1997.
Esposito, John, *Women in Muslim family law*, Syracuse University Press, 1982.
Esposito, John (ed.), *Voices of resurgent Islam*, Oxford University Press, 1983.
Esposito, John, *Islam: the Straight Path*, Oxford University Press, 1998.
Esposito, John (ed.), *Oxford history of Islam*, Oxford University Press, 2000.
Esposito, John, & John Voll, *Makers of contemporary Islam*, Oxford University Press, 2001.

Fadel, Mohammad, 'Two women, one man: knowledge, power and gender in medieval Sunni legal thought', *International Journal of Middle East Studies*, 29-2, pp 185-204.
El Fadl, Khaled Abou, *Speaking in God's Name: Islamic law, authority and women*, Oneworld, 2001.
Fahmy, Mansour, *La condition de la femme dans l'Islam*, Allia, 2002.
Fakhro, M., *Women at work in the Gulf*, Kegan Paul International, 1990.
Faqir, Fadia, *Nisanit*, Penguin, 1987.
Faqir, Fadia, *In the house of silence: autobiographical essays by Arab women writers*, Garnet, 1998.
Farid, Arifa, *Muslim woman in world religions' perspective*, Bureau of Composition, Compilation & Translation, University of Karachi, 1994.
al Faruqi, Lamya, *Women, Muslim society and Islam*, American Trust Publications, 1988.
Faris, Mohamed A., & Mahmood Hasan Khan, *Egyptian women in agricultural development: an annotated bibliography*, Lynne Rienner, 1994.
Farmaian, Sattareh Farman, with Dona Munker, *Daughter of Persia: a woman's journey from her father's harem through the Islamic revolution*, Crown, 1992.
Faruqi, Lois Lamya, *Women, Muslim society and Islam*, American Trust Publications, 1988.
Fathi, A., *Women and the family in Iran*, E. J. Brill, 1985.
Fayyad, Muna, *The road to feminism: Arab women writers*, Michigan State University, 1987.
Ferdows, Adele K., & H. Amir, 'Women in Shi'i fiqh: images through the Hadith', in *Women and revolution in Iran*, ed. Guity Nashat, Westview Press, 1983.
Fernea, Elizabeth, *Middle Eastern Muslim women speak*, University of Texas Press, 1977.
Fernea, Elizabeth, *A street in Marrakech*, Anchor Press, 1980.
Fernea, Elizabeth (ed.), *Women and the family in the Middle East: new voices of change*, University of Texas, 1985.
Fernea, Elizabeth, *In search of Islamic feminism: one woman's global journey*, Doubleday, 1998.
Fernea, Elizabeth, & Basima Bezirgan, 'The Koran on the subject of women', in Elizabeth Fernea & Basima Bezirgan (eds.), *Middle Eastern Muslim women speak*, University of Texas, 1977, pp 7-26.
Fernea, Elizabeth, & Basima Bezirgan (eds.), *Middle Eastern Muslim women speak*, University of Texas, 1977.
Fleischmann, Ellen L., *The nation and its 'new' women: the Palestinian women's movement, 1920-48*, University of California Press, 2003.
For ourselves: women reading the Quran, Women Living Under Muslim Laws, 1997.
Forte, David F., 'Islamic law in American courts', *Suffolk Transnational Law Journal*, 7, 1983, pp 1–33.

Forte, David F., 'The comparative lawyer and the Middle East', *American Journal of Comparative Law*, 26, 1978, pp 305–307.
Franks, Myfanwy, *Women and revivalism in the West*, Palgrave Macmillan, 2001.
Friedl, Erika, *Women of Deh Koh: lives in an Iranian village*, Penguin, 1991.
Frith, Tabitha, *Constructing Malay Muslim womanhood in Malaysia*, Centre of Southeast Asian Studies, Monash Asia Institute, Monash University, 2002.
Fyzee, A. (ed.), *Outlines of Muhammadan law*, Oxford University Press, 1974/1999.

Gani, H. A., *Reform of Muslim personal law: the Shah Bano controversy and the Muslim Women (Protection of Rights on Divorce) Act, 1986*, Deep & Deep, 1988.
Gaudio, Attilio, *La révolution des femmes en Islam*, R. Julliard, 1957.
Geadah, Yolande, *Femmes voilées, intégrismes démasqués*, VLB, 1996.
Genia, *Single in Saudi*, Authorhouse, 2002.
Gerami, Shahin, *Women and fundamentalism: Islam and Christianity*, Garland, 1996.
Gerber, H., *Islamic law and culture, 1600-1840*, E. J. Brill, 1999.
Ghanem, I., *Outlines of Islamic jurisprudence (Islamic law in a nutshell)*, Express Printing Services, 1983.
al-Ghazali (trans. T. J. Winter), *Muhammad: disciplining the soul*, Islamic Texts Society, 1995.
al-Ghazali (trans. M. Holland), *The proper conduct of marriage in Islam (adab an-nikah)*, Al-Baz, 1998.
Ghazi, Abidullah, 'Problems of religious instruction and textbooks in North America', *Journal of the Institute of Muslim Minorities Affairs*, 5, 1983-84, pp 67-70.
Ghodsi, Tamilla F., 'Tying a slipknot: temporary marriages in Iran', *Michigan Journal of International Law*, 645, 1994.
Ghouri, Umer Hayat Khan (trans. Maqbool Ahmed Siraj), *Dowry and Islamic social system*, Markazi Maktaba Islami, 1992.
Glander, Annelies, *Inheritance in Islam: women's inheritance in Sana'a (Republic of Yemen): law, religion, and reality*, Peter Lang, 1998.
Gleave, R., & E. Kermeli (eds.), *Islamic law: theory and practice*, I. B. Tauris, 1997.
Gluck, Sherna Berger, *An American feminist in Palestine: the Intifada years*, Temple University Press, 1994.
Goitein, S. D., 'The birth-hour of Muslim Law', *The Muslim World*, 1960, pp.23-29.
Goldziher, Ignaz, *Introduction to theology and law*, Princeton University Press, 1981.
Göle, Nilüfer, *The forbidden modern: civilization and veiling*, University of Michigan Press, 1996.
Goodwin, Jan, *Price of honor: Muslim women lift the veil of silence on the Islamic world*, Little, Brown, 1994.
Gorkin, Michael, & Rafiqa Othman, *Three mothers, three daughters: Palestinian women's stories*, University of California Press, 1996.
Grima, Benedicte, *The performance of emotion among Paxtun women: 'the misfortunes which have befallen me'*, University of Texas Press, 1992.
Grob, Leonard, Riffat Hassan, & Haim Gordon (eds.), *Women's and men's liberation: testimonies of spirit, Vol. 45*, Greenwood Press, 1991.
Guillaume, A., *The traditions of Islam*, Khayyat, 1961.
El Guindi, Fadwa, *Veil: modesty, privacy and resistance*, Berg, 1999.
Gusau, Sule Ahmed (ed.), *Perspectives on purdah, working women and family planning in Islam*, Department of Economics, Usmanu Danfodiyo University, 1995.

Guthrie, Shirley, *Arab women in the Middle Ages: private lives and public roles*, Al Saqi, 2000.

Haddad, Yvonne Yazbeck, 'Muslims in America: a select bibliography', *Muslim World*, 76, 1986, pp 93-122.

Haddad, Yvonne Yazbeck, *The Muslims of America*, Oxford University Press, 1991.

Haddad, Yvonne Yazbeck, & John Esposito (eds.), *Daughters of Abraham: feminist thought in Judaism, Christianity, and Islam*, University Press of Florida, 2001.

Haddad, Yvonne Yazbeck, & John Esposito, *Islam, gender and social change*, Oxford University Press, 1997.

Haddad, Yvonne Yazbeck, & A. T. Lummis, *Islamic values in the United States: a comparative study*, Oxford University Press, 1987.

Haddad, Yvonne Yazbeck, & Jane I. Smith, *Mission to America: five Islamic sectarian communities in North America*, University Press of Florida, 1993.

Haddad, Yvonne Yazbeck, & Jane I. Smith (eds.), *Muslim minorities in the West*, AltaMira, 2001.

Haeri, S., *Law of desire*, I. B. Tauris, 1989.

Hafez, Kai (ed.), *Islam and the West in the mass media*, Hampton Press, 1999.

Hafez, Sherine, *The terms of empowerment: Islamic women activists in Egypt*, Eurospan, 2003.

Hale, Sondra, *Gender politics in Sudan: Islamism, socialism, and the state*, Westview Press, 1996.

Haleem, M. A., *Understanding the Qur'an: themes and style*, I. B. Tauris, 1999.

Hallaq, Wael, 'Was al-Shafi'i the master architect of Islamic jurisprudence', *International Journal of Middle East Studies*, 25, 1993, pp 587-605.

Hallaq, Wael, *A history of Islamic legal theories: an introduction to Sunni 'usul al-fiqh'*, 1997.

Hambly, Gavin (ed.), *Women in the Medieval Islamic world*, St Martin's Press 1998.

Haneef, Sayed, *Islamic law of evidence*, Pelanduk, 1997.

Haneef, Suzanne, *What everyone should know about Islam and Muslims*, Library of Islam, 1993.

Hanifi, Manzoor Ahmad, *A survey of Muslim institutions and culture*, Kitab Bhavan, 1992.

Haque, Mozammel, *Islam, socialism, and women*, Society for Pakistan Studies, 1970.

Hargraves, Orin, *Culture shock! Morocco*, Graphic Arts Center, 2001.

Harris, Lillian Craig, *Am I my sister's keeper?: building bridges between Muslim and Christian women*, Centre for the Study of Islam and Christian-Muslim Relations, 1996.

Harrow, Kenneth W. (ed.), *Faces of Islam in African literature*, Heinemann, 1991.

Hasan, Zoya, & Ritu Menon, *Unequal citizens: a study of Muslim women in India*, Oxford University Press, 2004.

Hashmi, Taj I., *Women and Islam in Bangladesh: beyond subjection and tyranny*, St Martin's Press, 2000.

Hassan, Sharifah, & Sven Cederroth (eds.), *Managing marital disputes in Malaysia: Islamic mediators and conflict resolution in courts*, Curzon, 1997.

Hassan, Riaz, *Faithlines*, Oxford University Press, 2002.

Hassan, Riffat, 'Equal before Allah?: woman-man equality in the Islamic tradition', *Harvard Divinity Bulletin*, Jan-May, 1987, pp 1-4.

Hassan, Riffat, 'Women and sexuality: normative Islam versus Muslim practice', paper presented at 2nd International Muslim Leaders Consultation on HIV and Aids, 2003.

Hatem, Mervat, 'Modernization, the state, and the family in Middle East women's

studies', in Margaret Meriwether & Judith Tucker (eds.), *Social history of women and gender in the modern Middle East*, Westview Press, 1999.
Hathout, Hassan, *Reading the Muslim mind*, Minaret, 1995.
Hathout, Hassan, Fathi Osman, & Maher Hathout, *In fraternity: a message to Muslims in America*, Minaret, 1989.
al-Hatimy, Said Abudullah Seif, *Woman in Islam: a comparative study*, Islamic Publications, 1979.
Hawfy, A. M., *Why the Prophet Muhammad married more than one*, Cairo, 1976.
Hawley, John Stratton, *Fundamentalism and gender*, Oxford University Press, 1994.
Hawting, G., & A. Sharif (eds.), *Approaches to the Qur'an*, Routledge, 1993.
Heath, Jennifer, *The scimitar and the veil: extraordinary women of Islam*, Hidden Spring Books, 2004.
Heine, I., *Oh Ihr Musliminnen!: Frauen in islamischen Gesellschaften*, Freiburg, 1993.
Hekmat, Anwar, *Women and the Koran: the status of women in Islam*, Prometheus Books, 1997.
Hélie-Lucas, M. A., *L'internationalisme dans le mouvement de femmes: les réseaux internationaux de femmes*, Women Living Under Muslim Laws, 1994.
Hermansen, M. K., 'Some Observations on the Situation of Muslim Women in North America', *Muslim Education Quarterly*, 5ii, 1988, pp 81-88.
Hessini, Leila, *Living on a fault line: political violence against women in Algeria*, Population Council: UNIFEM/AFWIC, 1996.
Hessini, Leila, *From uncivil war to civil peace: Algerian women's voices*, Population Council: UNIFEM/AFWIC, 1998.
al-Hibri, Azizah (ed.), *Women and Islam*, Pergamon Press, 1982.
al-Hibri, Azizah, 'Islam, law and custom: redefining Muslim women's rights', *American University Journal of International Law and Policy*, 306, 1997.
al-Hibri, Azizah, 'An introduction to Muslim women's rights', in Gisela Web (ed.), *Windows of faith*, Syracuse University Press, 2000.
Hijab, Nadia, *Womanpower: the Arab debate on women at work*, Cambridge University Press, 1988.
Hijab, Nadia, 'Women and work in the Arab world', in Suha Sabbagh (ed.), *Arab women: between defiance and restraint*, Olive Branch Press, 1997.
Hikmat, Anwar, *Women and the Koran: the status of women in Islam*, Prometheus Books, 1997.
Hill, Fred James, & Nicholas Awde, *A history of the Islamic world*, Hippocrene Books, 2004.
Hillmann, Michael C., *A lonely woman: Forugh Farrokhzad and her poetry*, Three Continents Press & Mage Publishers, 1987.
Hiltermann, Joost, *Behind the Intifada: labor and women's movement in the Occupied Territories*, Princeton University Press, 1991.
Hodgson, Marshall G. S., *The venture of Islam: conscience and history in a world civilization*, University of Chicago Press, 1977.
Hoffman-Ladd, Valerie, 'Polemics on the modesty and segregation of women in contemporary Egypt', *International Journal of Middle East Studies*, 19- 1, pp 23-50.
Holf, Maria, *Half the people: women, history and the Palestinian Intifada*, Passia, 1990.
Höll, R., *Die Stellung der Frau im zeitgenössischen Islam, dargestellt am Beispiel Marokkos*, Bern, 1979.

Holmes-Eber, Paula, *Daughters of Tunis: women, family, and networks in a Muslim city*, Westview Press, 2002.
Holton, Patricia, *Mother without a mask: a Westerner's story of her Arab family*, Cathie Kyle, 2001.
Hoodfar, H., *Between marriage and the market: intimate politics and survival in Cairo*, University of California Press, 1996.
Hooglundm Eric (ed.), *Twenty years of Islamic revolution: political and social transition in Iran since 1979*, Syracuse University Press, 2002.
Hopkins, Nicholas S., & Saad Eddin Ibrahim (eds.), *Arab society: class, gender, power, and development*, American University in Cairo Press, 1997.
Hourani, Albert, *A history of the Arab peoples*, Faber & Faber, 1991.
Hourani, Albert, *Islam in European thought*, Cambridge University Press, 1991.
Hoyland, Robert G., *Arabia and the Arabs: from the Bronze Age to the coming of Islam*, Routledge, 2001.
Hübsch, Hadayatullah, *Frauen im Islam: 55 Fragen und Antworten*, Betzelverlag, 1997.
Humphreys, R. S., *Islamic history: a framework for inquiry*, I. B. Tauris, 1995.
Hurley, Jennifer A. (ed.), *Islam: opposing viewpoints*, Greenhaven Press, 2000.
Husain, Murteza, *Le statut de la femme marice en droit shyite*, Domat-Montchrestien, 1935.
Hussain, Aftab, *Status of women in Islam*, Law Pub. Co., 1987.
Hussain, Freda (ed.), *Muslim women*, St Martin's Press, 1984.
Hussain, S., *Islam: women modernization in India*, Delhi, 1998.
Hussain, Sabiha, *The changing half: a study of Indian Muslim woman*, Classical Publishing Company, 1998.
Hussein, Aamer (ed.), *Hoops of fire: fifty years of fiction by Pakistani women*, Al Saqi, 1999.

Ide, Arthur Frederick, *Islam and woman*, Monument Press, 1985.
Ilkkaracan, Pinar (ed.), *Women and sexuality in Muslim societies*, Women for Women's Human Rights (WWHR)/Kadının Insan Hakları Projesi (KIHP), 2000.
Ilkkaracan, Pinar, *A brief overview of women's movement(s) in Turkey (and the influence of political discourses)*, Women for Women's Human Rights, 1997.
Imache, Djedjiga, & Inès Nour, *Algériennes entre Islam et islamisme*, Edisud, 1994.
Imam, A. A., *The variant readings of the Quran*, International Institute of Islamic Thought, 1998.
Imran, Muhammad, *Ideal woman in Islam*, Islamic Publications, 1979.
Iqbal, M., *The rights of Women*, Montreal, 1988.
Iqbal, Safia, *Woman and Islamic law*, Al-Asr Publications, 1988.
Islam, Mahmuda, et al., *Training course on research methodology and women's issues, coordinators*, Women for Women, 1985.
Islam, Mahmuda, *Women, health, and culture: a study of beliefs and practices connected with female diseases in a Bangladesh village*, Women for Women, 1985.
Islam, Mominul, & Sameena Bary Alam (eds.), *Movement against flesh trade*, Bangladesh National Women Lawyers Association, 1996.
Islam, Mominul, Sudhangshu Sekhar Roy & Muhammed Shahriar Haque (eds.), *Prostitution: women, society, state, and law*, Bangladesh National Women Lawyers Association, 1997.
Islam, Shamina, *Indigenous abortion practitioners in rural Bangladesh: women abortionists, their perceptions and practices*, Women for Women, 1981.

Islam, Shamima, & Jowshan A. Rahman (eds.), *Mid-decade world conference on women: Bangladesh perspective, 1980*, Women's Development Unit, UNICEF, 1981.
Islam and equality: debating the future of women's and minority rights in the Middle East and North Africa, Lawyers Committee for Human Rights, 1999.
Islam and the advancement of women: a compilation of papers presented at the Workshop on Islam and the Advancement of Women, Jakarta, 21-24 April 1994, Forum for Islam and the Advancement of Women, 1994.
Islam, Islamisation and women in Africa, WLUML Research, Information & Documentation Unit, Women Living Under Muslim Laws, 1994.
Islam, reproductive health, and women's rights: report of proceedings on the regional workshop organised by SIS Forum (Malaysia) Berhad (Sisters in Islam), SIS Forum (Malaysia), 1998.
Islamic Council of Europe, *Universal Islamic Declaration of Human Rights*, 1981.
Islamophobia, Runnymede Trust, 1997.
Ismail, Rose (ed.), *Hudud in Malaysia: the issues at stake*, SIS Forum, 1995.
Israeli, Raphael, *Palestinian women and children in the throes of Islamikaze terrorism*, Ariel Center for Policy Research, 2002.
Istiadah, *Muslim women in contemporary Indonesia: investigating paths to resist the patriarchal system*, Centre of Southeast Asian Studies, Monash University, 1995.

Jacobson, Jessica, *Islam in transition*, Taylor & Francis, 1998.
Jahan, Roushan, 'Hidden wounds, visible scars: violence against women in Bangladesh', in Bina Agarwal (ed.), *Structures of patriarchy: state, community and household in modernizing Asia*, Zed Books, 1988..
Jahan, Roushan, & Mahmuda Islam (eds.), *Violence against women in Bangladesh: analysis and action*, Women for Women and South Asian Association for Women Studies, 1997.
Jameelah, Maryam, *Islam and the Muslim woman today: the Muslim woman and her role in society, duties of the Muslim mother*, Mohammad Yusuf Khan, 1976.
Jaschok, Maria, & Shui Jingjun, *The history of women's mosques in Chinese Islam: a mosque of their own*, Curzon, 2000.
Jawad, Haifaa, *The rights of women in Islam: an authentic approach*, Palgrave Macmillan, 1998.
Jawadi, Sayyid Zeeshan Haider, *Woman and shari'at (divine law): complete rules regarding women in Islam*, Idarah Islam Shinasi, 1999.
Jeffery, Patricia, *Frogs in a well: Indian women in purdah*, Manohar, 2000.
Jeffery, Patricia, & Amrita Basu (eds.), *Appropriating gender: women's activism and politicized religion in South Asia*, Routledge, 1997.
Jenkins, Everett, *The Muslim Diaspora: a comprehensive reference to the spread of Islam in Asia, Africa, Europe and the Americas*, McFarland & Co, 1999.
Jennings, A., *The Nubians of West Aswan: village women in the midst of change*, Lynne Rienner, 1995.
Joheir, Hussein Moussa, *Polygamie et condition de la femme dans l'Islam*, Nouvelles Editions Africaines, 1983.
Johnston, James (ed.), *Report of the centenary conference on the Protestant missions of the world, held in Exeter Hall (June 9th-19th), London, 1888*, James Nisbet, 1888.
Joseph, Suad, & Susan Slyomovics, *Women and power in the Middle East: 17 essays*, University of Pennsylvania Press, 2000.

Juynboll, G. H. A., *Muslim tradition: studies in chronology, provenance and authorship of early Hadith*, Cambridge University Press, 1983.

Kabeer, Naila, *The quest for national identity: women, Islam, and the state in Bangladesh*, Institute of Development Studies, University of Sussex, 1989.

Kabbani, S. M. H., & Laleh Bakhtiar, *Encyclopedia of Muhammad's (PBUH) Women Companions and the traditions they related*, ABC International, 1998.

Kamali, M., *Freedom of expression in Islam*, Islamic Texts Society, 1997.

Kamali, M., *Principles of Islamic jurisprudence*, Islamic Texts Society, 2003.

Kamalkhani, Zehra, *Women's Islam: religious practice among women in today's Iran*, Kegan Paul International, 1998.

Kamaruddin, Zaleha, et. al. (eds.), *Women's issues: women's perspectives*, Women's Affairs Secretariat IIUM, 1995.

Kanaaneh, Rhoda Ann, *Birthing the nation: strategies of Palestinian women in Israel*, University of California Press, 2002.

Kandiyoti, Deniz (ed.), *Women, Islam and the state*, Temple University Press, 1991.

Kandiyoti, Deniz (ed.), *Gendering the Middle East: emerging perspectives*, Syracuse University Press, 1996.

Kandiyoti, Deniz, & Ayse Saktanber (eds.), *Fragments of culture: the everyday of modern Turkey*, I. B. Tauris, 2003.

Kapteÿns, Lidwien, with Mariam Omar Ali Sittaat, *Somali women's songs for 'the mothers of the believers'*, Heinemann, 1995.

Karam, Azza M., *Women, islamisms and the state: contemporary feminisms in Egypt*, Macmillan, 1998.

Karim, Wazir-Jahan Begum, *Women and culture: between Malay adat and Islam*, Westview Press, 1992.

Karl, David J., 'Islamic law in Saudi Arabia: what foreign attorneys should know', *George Washington Journal of International Law and Economics*, 113, 1991.

Karmi, G., 'Women, Islam and patriarchalism', in M. Yamani (ed.), *Feminism and Islam*, Garnet, 1996.

Kausar, Zinat, *Muslim women in Medieval India*, Janaki Prakashan, 1992.

Kawar, A., *Daughters of Palestine: leading women of the Palestinian national movement*, State University of New York Press, 1996.

Al-Kaysi, M., *Morals and manners in Islam: a guide to Islamic adab*, Islamic Foundation, 1986.

Kazi, Seema, *Muslim women in India*, Minority Rights Group, 1999.

Keddie, Nikki, *Scholars, saints and Sufis: Muslim religious institutions in the Middle East since 1500*, University of California Press, 1972.

Keddie, Nikki, & Beth Baron (eds.), *Women in Middle Eastern history: shifting boundaries in sex and gender*, Yale University Press, 1991.

Kelly, Michael, & Lynn M. Messina, *Religion in politics and society*, H. W. Wilson, 2002.

Kepel, Gilles (ed.), *Allah in the West*, Blackwell, 1997.

Kerr, Malcolm H., *Islamic reform: the political and legal theories of Muhammad 'Abduh and Rashid Rida*, University of California Press, 1966.

Khadduri, M., *Islamic jurisprudence: Shafi's 'Risala'*, Baltimore, 1961.

Khan, Ghulam, *Personal hygiene in Islam*, Ta-Ha, 1982.

Khan, H., *Marriage: a booklet on sexual health from an Islamic perspective*, Cycle of Life, 1997.

Khan, H., *Women: a booklet on sexual health from an Islamic perspective*, Cycle of Life, 1997.
Khan, M. M. A., *Muslim women in the Soviet Union,* Centre for the Study of Islam and Christian-Muslim Relations, 1987.
Khan, Maulana Wahiduddin (trans. Farida Khanam), *Women between Islam and Western society*, Goodword, 2000.
Khan, Maulana Wahiduddin, *Woman in Islamic Shari'ah*, Goodword, 2001.
Khan, Mazhar Ul Haq, *Purdah and polygamy: a study in the social pathology of the Muslim society*, Harman, 1983.
Khan, Mohammad Shabbir, *Status of women in Islam*, South Asia Books, 1996.
Khan, Muniza Rafiq, *Socio-legal status of Muslim women,* Radiant, 1993.
Khan, Nighat Said (ed.), *Voices within: dialogues with women on Islam*, ASR, 1992.
Khan, Qamaruddin, *Status of women in Islam*, Islamic Book Foundation, 1988.
Khan, Salim, 'Pakistanis in the Western United States', *Journal of Muslim Minority Affairs*, 5:1, 1983-84.
Khan, Salma, et al. (eds.), *Inventory for women's organizations in Bangladesh*, Women's Development Unit, UNICEF, 1981.
Khan, Shaharyar, *The Begums of Bhopal: a dynasty of women rulers in Raj India*, I. B. Tauris, 2000.
Khan, Shahnaz, *Muslim women crafting a North American identity*, University Press of Florida, 2000.
Khan, Vahiduddin, *Women in Islamic shari'ah,* Al-Risala Books, 1995.
Khan, Wahiduddin, *Woman between Islam and western society*, Islamic Centre, 1995.
Khare, R., *Islamic law, justice, and society: interdisciplinary issues and perspectives*, Rowman & Littlefield, 1999.
Khattab, Hind A. S, *The silent endurance: social conditions of women's reproductive health in rural Egypt*, UNICEF, 1992.
Khattab, Huda, *The Muslim woman's handbook*, Ta-Ha, 1993.
Al-Khattab, Huda, *Bent rib: a journey through women's issues in Islam*, Ta-Ha, 1997.
Khoury, Ran, *Palestinian Women and the Intifada,* International Centre of Bethlehem, 1995.
Kidwai, Shaikh M. H. Gadia, *Woman under different social and religious laws, Buddhism, Judaism, Christianity, Islam*, Seema Publications, 1976.
Kimball, Michelle R., & Barbara R. von Schlegell, *Muslim women throughout the world: a bibliography*, Lynne Rienner, 1997.
Knieps, Claudia, *Geschichte der Verschleierung der Frau im Islam,* Ergon, 1993.
Knowing our rights, Kali/Zubaan, 2003.
Kohlberg, E., *Belief and law in Imami Shi'ism*, Gower, 1991.
Koning, Juliette, et al. (eds.), *Women and households in Indonesia: cultural notions and social practices*, Curzon, 1999.
Krämer, Annette, *Geistliche Autorität und islamische Gesellschaft im Wandel: Studien über Frauenälteste (otin und xalfa) im unabhängigen Usbekistan*, Klaus Schwartz, 2002.
Kucukcan, Talip, *Politics of ethnicity, identity and religion*, Ashgate, 1999.
Kumar, Ann, *The diary of a Javanese Muslim: religion, politics and the pesantren 1883-1886,* Faculty of Asian Studies Monographs, 1985.
Kumar, Hajira (ed.), *Status of Muslim women in India*, Akkar Books, 2002.
Küng, Hans, & Josef van Ess, *Christentum und Weltreligionen: Islam*, Piper, 2003.
Künzler, Eva, *Zum westlichen Frauenbild von Musliminnen*, Ergon, 1993.

Küper-Basgöl, Sabine, *Frauen in der Türkei zwischen Feminismus und Reislamisierung*, Lit, 1992.
Kurzman, Charles (ed.), *Liberal Islam: a sourcebook*, Oxford University Press, 1998.
Kusha, Hamid R., *The sacred law of Islam: a case study of women's treatment in the Islamic Republic of Iran's justice system*, Ashgate, 2002.
Kvam, K., et al., *Eve and Adam: Jewish, Christian and Muslim readings on Genesis and gender*, Indiana University Press, 1998.

La femme musulmane: ses droits et ses devoirs, Carthage, 1966.
Laffin, John, *Dagger of Islam*, Sphere, 1978.
Laghzaoui, Latifa, *Women and shrines in urban Morocco: the case of the patron-saint of Salé*, thesis, SOAS, 1992.
Lai Olurode, Surulere, *Reproductive health within the context of Islam*, Islamic Women, Youth Centre, Anwar-ul Islam Movement of Nigeria, 2000.
Lamloum, Olfa, & Bernard Ravenel, *Femmes et islamisme*, L'Harmattan, 1998.
Lampe, Gerald E. (ed.), *Justice and human rights in Islamic Law*, ILI, 1997.
Lamsa, George M., *The secret of the Near East: slavery of women: social, religious and economic life in the Near East*, Ideal Press, 1923.
Lapidus, Ira, *A history of Islamic societies*, Cambridge, 1988.
Larguèche, Abdelhamid, & Dalenda Larguèche, *Marginales en terre d'Islam*, Cerès, 2000.
Lassner, Jacob, *Demonizing the Queen of Sheba: boundaries of gender and culture in postbiblical Judaism and medieval Islam*, University of Chicago Press, 1993.
Lateef, Shahida, *Muslim women in India: political and private realities 1890s-1980s*, ZedBooks, 1990.
Latifa, *My forbidden face: growing up under the Taliban: a young woman's story*, Virago, 2002.
Lazreg, Marnia, *The eloquence of silence: Algerian women in question*, Routledge, 1994.
LeBor, Adam, *A heart turned east*, Time Warner, 1998.
Lee, Martha F., *The Nation of Islam: an American millenerian movement*, Syracuse University Press, 1996.
Leites, Justin, 'Modernist jurisprudence as a vehicle for gender role reform in the Islamic world', *Columbia Human Rights Law Review*, 251, 1991.
Lemu, B. Aisha, & Fatima Heeren, *Woman in Islam*, Islamic Foundation, 1978.
Leonetti, Isabel Taboada (ed.), *Les femmes et l'islam: entre modernité et intégrisme*, L'Harmattan, 2004.
Lerner, Gerda, *The creation of patriarchy*, vol. I in the two-volume series *Women and history*, Oxford University Press, 1986.
Lewis, Bernard, *The Middle East: a brief history of the last 2,000 years*, Scribner, 1995.
Lewis, Bernard, & D. Schnapper (eds.), *Muslims in Europe*, Pinter, 1994.
Lewis, Franklin, & Farzin Yazdanfar (trans.), *In a voice of their own: a collection of stories by Iranian women*, Mazda, 1996.
Lewis, Philip, *Islamic Britain*, I. B. Tauris, 1994.
Lewis, Reina, & Sara Mills, *Feminist postcolonial theory: a reader*, Routledge, 2003.
Lewis, Reina, *Rethinking orientalism: women, travel and the Ottoman harem*, I. B. Tauris, 2004.
Liebesny, Herbert J., *The law of the Near and Middle East: readings, cases and materials*, Albany, 1975.
Linant de Bellefonds, Y., 'kanun', *Encyclopedia of Islam*, 2nd edition.
Lincoln, C. Eric. *The Black Muslims in America*, The Beacon Press, 1961.

Lings, Martin, *Muhammad: his life based on the earliest sources*, Islamic Texts Society, 1993.
Lippman, Matthew, Sean McConville & Mordechai Yerushalmi, *Islamic criminal law and procedure*, Praeger, 1988.
Lippman, Thomas W., *Understanding Islam: an introduction to the Muslim world*, Penguin, 1995.
Lobban, Richard (ed.), *Middle Eastern women and the invisible economy*, University of Florida Press, 1998.
Lochon, Christian, et al. (eds.), *Femmes et Islam: actes du colloque, rôle et statut des femmes dans les sociétés contemporaines de tradition musulmane, Paris, CHEAM, 15-16 décembre 1999*, Centre des Hautes Études sur l'Afrique et l'Asie Modernes, 2000.
Logan, Harriet, *Unveiled: voices of women in Afghanistan*, Regan, 2002.
Lucas, Marie-Aimee Helie, & Harsh Kapoor (eds.), *Fatwas against women in Bangladesh*, Women Living Under Muslim Laws, 1996.

Mack, Beverly B., & Jean Boyd, *One woman's jihad: Nana Asma'u, scholar and scribe*, Indiana University Press, 2000.
MacLeod, Arlene, *Accommodating protest: working women, the new veiling, and change in Cairo*, Columbia University Press, 1993.
Madani, S. M., *The family of the Holy Prophet*, Adam Publishers, n.d.
Mahdari, Shireen, 'The position of women in Shi'a Iran: views of the Ulama', in Elizabeth Warnock Fernea (ed.), *Women and the Family in the Middle East: new voices of change*, University of Texas, 1985.
Mahdavi-Khazeni, Shireen, *Women, the 'Ulama, and the state in Iran: a study in Shi'i ideology*, thesis), University of Utah, 1982.
Mahmood, T., 'Law in the Qur'an, a draft code', *Islamic and Comparative Law Quarterly*, 7, 1987.
Makowski, Samsam Renate, & Stefan Makowski, *Sufismus für Frauen: Zugänge zur islamischen Mystik*, Benziger, 1996.
Malcolm X, *Malcolm X speaks*, Grove Press, 1965.
Malik, Fida Hussain, *Wives of the Prophet (peace be upon him)*, Sh. Muhammad Ashraf, 1979.
Mallat, Chibli, & Jane Connors (eds.), *Islamic family law*, Graham & Trotman, 1990.
Mallat, Chibli, 'shari'a', *Oxford companion to world politics*, Oxford University Press, 1993.
Mallon, Elias, *Neighbors: Muslims in North America*, Friendship Press, 1989.
Malmassari, Jean, *De l'avortement chez la femme indigène musulmane, principalement en Algérie*, S. Crescenzo, 1934 .
Malti-Douglas, Fedwa, *Woman's body, woman's word: gender and discourse in Arabo-Islamic writing*, Princeton University Press, 1991.
Malti-Douglas, Fedwa, *Medicines of the soul: female bodies and sacred geographies in a transnational Islam*, University of California Press, 2001.
Mamiya, L.H., 'The Black Muslims as a new religious movement: their evolution and implications for the study of religion in a pluralistic society', in *Conflict and co-operation between contemporary religious groups*, Chuo Academic Research Institute, 1988, pp 201-227.
Mandaville, Peter G., *Transnational muslim politics: reimagining the Umma*, Routledge, 2003.
Manji, Irshad, *The trouble with Islam: a Muslim's call for reform in her faith*, Random House, 2003.
Maqsood, R., *The Muslim marriage guide*, Amana, 2000.

Marcus, Julie, *A world of difference: Islam and gender hierarchy in Turkey*, Zed Books, 1992.
Margoliouth, D. S., *The early development of Mohammedanism*, Williams & Norgate, 1914.
Marsh, Clifton E., *From Black Muslims to Muslims: the transition from separatism to Islam, 1930-1980*, Scarecrow Publishers, 1984.
Al-Marzouqi, I., *Human rights in Islamic law*, International Specialized Book Services, 2000.
Maududi, Sayyid Abul A'la, *Human rights in Islam*, Islamic Publications, 1980.
Maududi, Sayyid Abul A'la, *Purdah and the status of women in Islam*, Markazi Maktaba Islami, 1995.
Maulana, Ashraf Ali, & Barbara Daly Metcalf, *'Perfecting Women': a partial translation of 'Bihishti Zewar'*, Oxford University Press, 2002.
Mauloodi, Maulana Abul Aala, *The laws of marriage and divorce in Islam*, Islamic Book Publishers, 1993.
Mawdudi, A., *Human rights in Islam*, Islamic Publications, 1977.
Mawdudi, A., *The laws of marriage and divorce in Islam*, Islamic Book Publishers, 1983.
Mayer, Ann Elizabeth, 'Law and religion in the Muslim Middle East', *American Journal of Comparative Law*, 126, 1987.
Mayer, Ann Elizabeth, 'Universal versus Islamic human rights: a clash of cultures or a clash with a construct?', *Michigan Journal of International Law*, 307, 1994.
Mayer, Ann Elizabeth, *Islam and human rights: tradition and politics*, Westview Press, 1999.
Mayer, Tamar (ed.), *Women and the Israeli occupation: the politics of change*, Routledge, 1994.
Mbacké, Khadim, *Le Coran et la femme: mariage, divorce, viduit, allaitement et garde des enfants, succession*, K. Mbacké, 1991.
McAllister, Carol Lynn, *Matriliny, Islam and capitalism: combined and uneven development in the lives of Negeri Sembilan women*, thesis, University of Pittsburgh, 1987.
McCloud, Aminah Beverly, *African American Islam*, Routledge, 1995.
McDermott, Mustafa Yusuf, & Muhammad Manazir Ahsan, *The Muslim guide*, The Islamic Foundation, 1993.
McNee, Lisa, *Selfish gifts: Senegalese women's autobiographical discourses*, State University of New York Press, 2000.
Mehdi, Beverlee Turner (ed.), *The Arabs in America, 1492-1977: a chronology and fact book*, Oceana Publications, 1978.
Meissa, M. S., *La femme musulmane*, Vigie Marocaine, 1928.
Mercier, Ernest, *La condition de la femme musulmane dans l'Afrique septentrionale*, A. Jourdon, 1895.
Meriwether, Margaret L., Judith E. Tucker (eds.), *A social history of women and gender in the modern Middle East*, Westview Press, 1999.
Mernissi, Fatima, *Beyond the veil: male-female dynamics in modern Muslim society*, Indiana University Press/Al Saqi, 1985.
Mernissi, Fatima, *Women in Moslem paradise*, Kali for Women, 1986.
Mernissi, Fatima, *Le harem politique: le prophète et les femmes*, A. Michel, 1987.
Mernissi, Fatima, *Doing daily battle: interviews with Moroccan women*, Rutgers, 1989.
Mernissi, Fatima, *Can we women head a Muslim state?*, Simorgh, Women's Resource and Publications Centre, 1991.
Mernissi, Fatima (trans. Mary Jo Lakeland), *The veil and the male elite: a feminist interpretation of women's rights in Islam*, Addison Wesley, 1991.
Mernissi, Fatima, *Dreams of trespass: tales of a harem childhood*, Addison Wesley, 1995.

Mernissi, Fatima, *Women's rebellion and Islamic memory*, Zed Books, 1996.
Mernissi, Fatima, *The forgotten queens of Islam,* University of Minnesota Press, 1997.
Mernissi, Fatima, *Scheherazade goes west: different cultures, different harems*, Washington Square Press, 2001.
Mernissi, Fatima, *Women and Islam: a historical and theological inquiry*, Kali/Women Unlimited, 2002.
Mernissi, Fatima (trans. Mary Jo Lakeland), *Islam and democracy: fear of the modern world,* Perseus Books, 2002.
Mesbah, Muhammad Taqi, Muhammad Jawal Bahonar, & Lois Lamya al-Faruqi, *Status of women in Islam*, Sangam Books, 1990.
Messaoudi, Khalida (with Elisabeth Schemla; trans. Anne C. Vila), *Unbowed: an Algerian woman confronts Islamic fundamentalism*, University of Pennsylvania Press, 1998.
Meyerson, Mark D., & Edward D. English (eds.), *Christians, Muslims, and Jews in medieval and early modern Spain: interaction and cultural change*, University of Notre Dame Press, 2000.
Mikhail, Mona, *Images of Arab women: fact and fiction: essays*, Three Continents Press, 1979.
Milani, Farzaneh, *Veils and words: the emerging voices of Iranian women writers*, I. B. Tauris, 1992.
Minai, Naila, *Women in Islam: tradition and transition in the Middle East*, Seaview Books, 1981.
Minai, Naila, *Schwestern unterm Halbmond: Muslimische Frauen zwischen Tradition und Emanzipation*, DVT, 1990.
Minas, Juliette (trans. Michael Pallis), *The house of obedience: women in Arab society*, Zed Books, 1989.
Minault, Gail, *Secluded scholars: women's education and Muslim social reform in colonial India*, Oxford University Press, 1998.
Minces, Juliette, *La femme voilé,* Pluriel, 1990.
Minces, Juliette, *Veiled: women in Islam*, Blue Crane Books, 1994.
Minces, Juliette, *Le Coran et les femmes,* Hachette, 1996.
Mir-Hosseini, Ziba, *Islam and gender: the religious debate in contemporary Iran*, I. B. Tauris, 1999.
Mir-Hosseini, Ziba, *Marriage on trial: Islamic family law in Iran and Morocco*, I. B. Tauris, 2000.
Mirza, Jasmin, *Between chaddor and the market: female office workers in Lahore*, Oxford University Press, 2002.
Misbah, Muhammad Taqi, *Status of women in Islam,* Islamic Propagation Organization, 1985.
Mishriky, Salwa Elias, *Sans voix ou sans moi: Islam et islamisme*, P. Lang, 2001.
Mitchell, Ruth, 'Family law in Algeria before and after the 1404/1984 Family Code', in R. Gleave & E. Kermeli (eds.), *Islamic law: theory and practice*, I. B. Tauris, 1997.
Mogannam, Matiel, *The Arab woman and the Palestine problem*, Herbert Joseph, 1937.
Moghadam, Valentine M., *Modernizing women: gender and social change in the Middle East*, Lynne Rienner, 1993.
Moghadam, Valentine M., *Women, work and economic reform in the Middle East and North Africa*, Lynne Rienner, 1998.
Moghadam, Valentine M. (ed.), *Gender and national identity: women and politics in Muslim societies*, Zed Books for United Nations University, 1994.

Moghissi Haideh, *Feminism and Islamic fundamentalism: the limits of postmodern analysis*, Zed Books, 1999.

Moghissi, Haideh, *Populism and feminism in Iran: women's struggle in a male-defined revolutionary movement*, St Martin's Press, 1994.

Mohammad, Noor (ed.), *Indian Muslims: precepts and practices*, Rawat, 1999.

Mohammad, Warith Deen, *An African American Genesis*, MACA Publications, 1986.

Moin, Mumtaz, *Umm al Mu'minin, A'ishah Siddiqah: life and works*, Taj, 1982.

Moinuddin, S. A. H., *Divorce and Muslim women*, Rawat, 2000.

Mojab, Shahrzad, 'Women and the Gulf War: a critique of feminist responses', in T. Denean Sharpley-Whiting (ed.), *Spoils of war: women of color, cultures and revolutions*, Rowman & Littlefield, 1997.

Mojab, Shahrzad, *Women of a non-state nation: the Kurds*, Mazda Publishers, 2001.

Moors, Annelies, *Women, property and Islam: Palestinian experiences, 1920-1990*, Cambridge University Press, 1995.

Moqsood, Ruqayyah, *The Muslim marriage guide*, Quilliam Press, 1995.

el-Morr, Awad, 'The Supreme Constitutional Court of Egypt and the protection of human and political rights', in Chibli Mallat (ed.), *Islam and public law*, Graham & Trotman, 1993.

Mortley, Raoul, *Womanhood: the feminine in ancient Hellenism, Gnosticism, Christianity, and Islam*, Delacroix Press, 1981.

Mroudjae, Said Islam Moinaecha, *Rapport final du Projet COI/86/007/W01: Centre de recherche sur le statut et la situation de la femme*, PNUD/UNIFEM, 1991.

Mughni, Haya, *Women in Kuwait: the politics of gender*, Al Saqi, 2001.

Muhammad, Ava, *The myths and misconceptions of the role of women in Islam*, Uprising Communications, 1996.

Muhammad, Uma, *The marriage procedure in Islam*, Abul-Qasim, 2000.

Muhammad: encyclopedia of Seerah (Sunnah, da'wah & Islam), Seerah Foundation, 1987.

Mukherjee, Sooma, Royal Mughal ladies and their contribution, Gyan, 2001.

Mumtaz, Khawar, & Farida Shaheed, *Women of Pakistan: two steps forward, one step back?*, Zed Books, 1987.

Mundi, Martha, 'The family, inheritance and Islam: a re-examination of the sociology of Fara'id law', in Aziz Al-Azmeh (ed.), *Islamic law: social and historical contexts*, Routledge, 1988.

Munoz, Gema Martin (ed.), *Islam, modernism and the West*, I. B. Tauris, 1998.

Murata, Sachiko, *The Tao of Islam: a sourcebook on gender relationships in Islamic thought*, State University of New York Press, 1992.

Musallam, Basim, *Sex and society in Islam*, Cambridge University Press, 1983.

The Muslim family, Islam and world peace, Fons Vitae, 2003.

Mutahhari, Murtaza, *The rights of women in Islam*, World Organisation for Islamic services, 1981.

Mutahhari, Murtaza, *The Islamic modest dress*, Kazi, 1992.

Mutahhery, Murtaza, *Woman and her rights*, Islamic Seminary, 1982.

Nadvi, M., et al., *Biographies of the Women Companions of the Holy Prophet (PBUH) and the ways of their sacred lives*, Darul Ishaat, 1995.

Naff, Alixa, *Becoming American: the early Arab immigrant experience*, Southern Illinois University Press, 1985.

Nafisi, Azar, *Reading Lolita in Tehran: a memoir in books*, Random House, 2003.
Nahla Abdo-Zubi, *Family, women and social change in the Middle East: the Palestinian case*, Canadian Scholars Press, 1987.
An-Na'im, Abdullahi, 'Human rights in the Muslim world: socio-political conditions and scriptural imperatives', *Harvard Human Rights Journal*, vol 3, 1990.
An-Na'im, Abdullahi, *Towards an Islamic reformation: civil liberties, human rights, and international law*, Syracuse University Press, 1996.
Najjar, Orayb Akef, & Kitty Warnock, *Portraits of Palestinian women*, University of Utah Press, 1992.
Najmabadi, Afsaneh, *The story of the Daughters of Quchan: gender and national memory in Iranian history*, Syracuse University Press, 1998.
Najmabadi, Afsaneh, 'Crafting an educated housewife in Iran', in Lila Abu-Lughod (ed.), *Remaking women: feminism and modernity in the Middle East*, Princeton Unversity Press, 1998.
Naseef, Fatima Umar (trans. Saleha Mahmood Abedin), *Women in Islam: a discourse in rights and obligations*, International Islamic Committee for Woman & Child, 1999.
Nashat, Guity, & Judith Tucker, *Women in the Middle East and North Africa*, Indiana University Press, 1998.
Nasir, Jamil J., *The Islamic law of personal status*, Graham & Trotman, 1990.
Nasir, Jamal J., *The status of women under Islamic law and under modern Islamic legislation*, Graham & Trotman, 1994.
Nath, Renuka, *Notable Mughal and Hindu women in the 16th and 17th centuries A.D.*, South Asia Books, 1990.
National Seminar on the Status of Woman in Islam: 18th & 19th July 1983, organised by Bait-al-Hikmat (Academy of Rationalism), Bait-al-Hikmat, 1983.
Nawal, Yasmina, *Les femmes dans l'islam*, La Brèche, 1980.
Nazlee, Sajda (ed. Huda Khattab), *Feminism and Muslim women*, Ta-Ha, 1996.
Nelson, Cynthia, *Doria Shafik, Egyptian feminist: a woman apart*, University Press of Florida, 1996.
Nelson, Cynthia, & Shahnaz Rouse (eds.), *Situating globalization: views from Egypt*, Transcript, 2000.
Nielsen, J.S., *Towards a European Islam*, Palgrave Macmillan, 1999.
Nielsen, Jorgen, *Muslims in Western Europe*, Edinburgh University Press, 1992.
El Nimr, R., 'Women in Islamic law', in Mai Yamani (ed.), *Islam and feminism*, Garnet, 1995.
Nivedita, Sister (Margaret E. Noble), *The web of Indian life*, William Heinemann, 1904.
Noor, Queen, *Leap of faith; memoirs of an unexpected life*, Miramax, 2003.
Noor, Shahnaz, *Law relating to conversion in Islam towards harmony of conflicting matrimonial laws in India*, Kitab Bhavan, 2003.
Northrop, Douglas, *Veiled empire: gender and power in Stalinist Central Asia*, Cornell University Press, 2004.
Nu'man, Fareed H., *The Muslim population in the United States*, The American Muslim Council, 1992.
Nurbakhsh, Javad, *Sufi women*, Khaniqahi-Nimatullahi, 1983.

Öbilgin, Mustafa, & Diana Woodward, *Banking and gender: sex equality in the financial services in Britain and Turkey*, I. B. Tauris, 2003.

OIC, *Cairo Declaration on Human Rights in Islam*, 1990.
OIC, *Dhaka Declaration on Human Rights in Islam*, 1983.
Ong, Aihwa, *Spirits of resistance and capitalist discipline: factory women in Malaysia*, State University of New York Press, 1987.
Orlando, Valarie, 'Women, war, autobiography, and the historiographic metafictional text: unveiling the veiled in Assia Djebar's *L'amour, la fantasia*', in T. Denean Sharpley-Whiting (ed.), *Spoils of war: women of color, cultures and revolutions*, Rowman & Littlefield, 1997.
Othman, Haji Faisal bin Haji, *Women, Islam and nation building*, Berita, 1993.
Özdalga, Elisabeth, *The veiling issue, official secularism and popular Islam in modern Turkey*, Curzon, 1998.

Paidar, Parvin, *Women and the political process in twentieth-century Iran*, Cambridge University Press, 1997.
Paret, Rudi, *Zur Frauenfrage in der arabisch-islamischen Welt*, W. Kohlhammer, 1934 (& in Rudi Paret [ed. Josef van Ess], *Schriften zum Islam; Volksroman-Frauenfrage-Bilderverbot*, W. Kohlhammer, 1981).
Patel, Ismail Adam, *Islam: the choice of thinking women*, Ta-Ha, 1997.
Pedersen, Lars, *Newer Islamic movements in Western Europe*, Ashgate, 1999.
Peirce, Leslie P., *The imperial harem: women and sovereignty in the Ottoman Empire*, Oxford University Press, 1993.
Pesle, Octave, *La femme musulmane dans le droit, la religion, et les moeurs*, Éditions la Porte, 1946.
Peteet, Julie, *Gender in crisis: women and the Palestinian resistance movement*, Columbia University Press, 1991.
Phipps, William E., *Muhammad and Jesus: a comparison of the Prophets and their teachings*, Cassell, 1999.
Pickthall, Marmaduke (trans.), *The meaning of the Glorious Qur'an*, Everyman's Library, 1992.
Poole, Elizabeth, *Reporting Islam: media representations and British Muslims*, I. B. Tauris, 2002.
Pour nous-mêmes: des femmes lisent le Coran, Women Living Under Muslim Laws, 1998.
Powers, David S., *Studies in Qur'an and Hadith*, University of CaliforniaPress, 1986.
Powers, David S., 'On Judicial Review in Islamic Law', *Law and Society Review*, 313, 1992.
Poya, Maryam, *Women, work and Islamism: ideology and resistance in Iran*, Zed Books, 1999.
Présence de femmes collectif: Alger, mars 1984, Office des Publications Universitaires, 1987.
Price, Daniel E., *Islamic political culture, democracy and human rights: a comparative study*, Praeger, 1999.
Pruthi, Raj, & Bela Rani Sharma, *Islam and women*, Anmol, 1995.

Qadir, Sayeda Rowshan, & Mahmuda Islam, *Women representatives at the union level as change agent of development*, Women for Women, Research and Study Group, 1987.
Al-Qaradawi, Yusuf, *The lawful and the prohibited in Islam (Al-Halal Wal Haram Fil Islam)*, American Trust Publications, n.d..
Qasmi, Mufti Abdul Jaleel, *The complete system of divorce (talaaq)*, Adam, 2003.
Qutb, Sayyid (trans. J. Hardie), *Social justice in Islam*, Islamic Publications International, 2000.

Rafiq, Bashir Ahmad, *The status of women in Islam*, London Mosque, 1965.

Rahman, Afzalur, *The role of Muslim women in society*, Seerah Foundation, 1986.

Rahman, Falzur, *Major themes of the Quran*, Bibliotheca Islamica, 1989.

Rahman, Fazlur, 'Islamic modernism: its scope, method and alternatives', in *The International Journal of Middle East Studies*, 1, 1970, pp 317-333.

Rahman, Fazlur, *Islam*, University of Chicago Press, 1979.

Rahman, Fazlur, *Islam and modernity: transformation of an intellectual tradition*, University of Chicago Press, 1984.

Ramadan, Tariq, *Islam, the West and the challenges of modernity*, The Islamic Foundation, 2001.

Ramazani, Nesta, 'Women in Iran: the revolutionary ebb and flow', *Middle East Journal*, 409, 1993.

Raudvere, Catharina, *The book and the roses: Sufi women, visibility and zikir in contemporary Istanbul*, I. B. Tauris, 2003.

Rausch, Margaret, *Bodies, boundaries and spirit possession: Moroccan women and the revision of tradition*, Transcript, 2001.

Raza, Mohammad S., *Islam in Britain: past, present and future*, Volcano Press, 1993.

Razzaq, AAbu Bakr Abdu'r- (trans. Aisha Bewley), *Circumcision in Islam*, Dar Al Taqwa, 1998.

Reconstructing fundamentalism and feminism: the dynamics of change in Iran, Women Living Under Muslim Laws, 1995.

Reed, Betsy (ed.), *Nothing sacred: women respond to religious fundamentalism and terror*, Nation, 2003.

Reeves, Minou, *Female warriors of Allah: women and the Islamic revolution*, Dutton, 1989.

Regis, Helen A., *Fulbe voices: marriage, Islam and medicine in Northern Cameroon*, Louisiana State University Press, 2003.

Richter-Dridi, Irmhild, *Frauenbefreiung in einem islamischen Land: ein Widerspruch?*, Fischer, 1981.

Rippin, A., *Approaches to the history of the interpretation of the Qur'an*, Oxford University Press, 1988.

Rispler-Chaim, Vardit, *Islamic medical ethics in the twentieth century*, E. J. Brill, 1993.

Roald, Anne Sofie, *Women in Islam: the Western experience*, Routledge, 2001.

Robinson, Francis (ed.), *The Cambridge illustrated history of the Islamic world*, Cambridge University Press, 1996.

Robinson, Kathryn, & Sharon Bessell (ed.), *Women in Indonesia: gender, equity and development*, ISEAS, 2002.

Robinson, Neil, *Christ in Islam and Christianity*, Palgrave Macmillan, 1990.

Roded, Ruth, *Women in Islamic biographical collections: from Ibn Sa'd to Who's Who,* Lynne Rienner, 1994.

Roded, Ruth (ed.), *Women in Islam and the Middle East: a reader*, I. B. Tauris, 1999.

Rouach, David, *Imma: ou rites, coutumes et croyances chez la femme juive en Afrique du Nord,* Maisonneuve & Larose, 1990.

Roy, Shibani, *Status of Muslim women in North India*, B. R. Publishing Corporation, 1979.

Rugh, Andrea B., *Reveal and conceal: dress in contemporary Egypt*, Syracuse University Press, 1986.

Ruhela, Satya Pal, *Empowerment of the Indian Muslim women*, M. D. Publications, 1998.

Ruud, Inger Marie, *Women's status in the Muslim world: a bibliographical survey*, Indica et Tibetica, 1981.

El Saadawi, Nawal, *The hidden face of Eve: women in the Arab world*, Beacon Press 1980.
El Saadawi, Nawal (trans. Sherif Hetata), *Woman at point zero*, Zed Books, 1983.
El Saadawi, Nawal, *Memoirs from the women's prison*, Women's Press, 1994.
El Saadawi, Nawal, *The Nawal El Saadawi reader*, Zed Books, 1997.
Sabbagh, Suha (ed.), *Palestinian women of Gaza and the West Bank*, Indiana University Press, 1998.
Sabbagh, Suha (ed.), *Arab women: between defiance and restraint*, Interlink, 2002.
Sabbagh, Suha, & Ghada Talhami, *Images and reality: Palestinian women under occupation and in the diaspora*, The Institute for Arab Women's Studies, 1990.
Sabbah, Fatna A. (trans. Mary Jo Lakeland), *Woman in the Muslim unconscious*, Pergamon Press, 1984.
Sabiruddin, *A Muslim husband and wife: rights and duties*, Kitab Bhavan, 2000.
Sa'd, Ibn (trans. A. Bewley), *The women of Madina*, Ta-Ha, 1995.
Sadeghi, Zohreh, *Fatima von Qum: ein Beispiel für die Verehrung heiliger Frauen im Volksglauben der Zwölfer-Schia*, Klaus Schwarz, 1996.
al-Sadr, M. Baqir, *The principles of Islamic jurisprudence according to Shi'i law*, Al Saqi, 2004.
Safi, Omid (ed.), *Progressive Muslims: on justice, gender and pluralism*, Oneworld, 2003.
Sahebjam, Freidoune, *La femme lapidée*, Grasset, 1990.
Said, Edward W., *Orientalism*, Vintage, 1979.
Said, Edward W., *Covering Islam*, Vintage, 1997.
Saiyid, Dushka, *Muslim women of the British Punjab: from seclusion to politics*, Macmillan, 1998.
El Sakakini, W. (trans. trans. Nabil Safwat; introduction by Doris Lessing), *First among Sufis: the life and thought of Rabia al-Adawiyya*, Octagon, 1982.
Saktanber, Ayse, *Living Islam: women, religion and the politicization of culture in Turkey*, I. B. Tauris, 2003.
Saliba, Therese, Carolyn Allen & Judith A. Howard (eds.), *Gender, politics, and Islam*, Orient Longman, 2005.
Salme, Sayyida (Emily Ruete), *An Arabian princess between two worlds; memoirs, letters home, sequels to the memoirs, Syrian customs and usages*, E. J. Brill, 1993.
Al-Saltana, Taj, *Crowning anguish: memoirs of a Persian princess from the harem to modernity, 1884-1914*, Mage, 1993.
Samiuddin, Abida, et al. (eds.), *Muslim feminism and feminist movement: Africa*, Global Vision, 2002.
Samiuddin, Abida, et al. (eds.), *Muslim Feminism and Feminist Movement: Central Asia*, Global Vision, 2002.
Samiuddin, Abida, et al. (eds.), *Muslim Feminism and Feminist Movement: Middle-East Asia*, Global Vision, 2002.
Samiuddin, Abida, et al. (eds.), *Muslim Feminism and Feminist Movement: South Asia*, Global Vision, 2002.
Samiuddin, Abida, et al. (eds.), *Muslim feminism and feminist movement: South-East Asia*, (3 vols: India, Pakistan, Bangladesh), Global Vision, 2002.
Santen, José C.M. van, *They leave their jars behind: the conversion of Mafa women to Islam (North Cameroon) = Zij laten hun kruiken achter: de bekering van Mafa vrouwen tot de Islam (Noord Kameroen)*, Centrum Vrouwen en Autonomie (VENA), 1993.
Saunders, Paula, Nikki Keddie & Beth Baron (eds.), 'Gendering the Ungendered-in Women', in *Middle Eastern history*, Yale University Press, 1991, pp 74-95.

Sasson, Jean, *Mayada, daughter of Iraq: one woman's survival under Saddam Hussein*, Dutton Juvenile, 2003.
Sasson, Jean, *Princess: a true story of life behind the veil in Saudi Arabia*, Windsor-Brooke Books, 2001.
Sayyid, Bobby, *A fundamental fear*, Zed Books, 1997.
al-Sayyid-Marsot, A. L. (ed.), *Society and the sexes in medieval Islam*, Undena, 1979.
Scarce, J., *Women's costume of the Near and Middle East*, Unwin Hyman, 1997.
Scarce, J., *Domestic culture in the Middle East: an exploration of the household interior*, National Museums of Scotland, 1996.
Schacht, Joseph, *The origins of Muhammadan jurisprudence*, Oxford University Press, 1950.
Schacht, Joseph, *Introduction to Islamic law*, Oxford University Press, 1964.
Schacht, Joseph, 'fikh', *Encyclopedia of Islam*, 2nd edition.
Schimmel, Annemarie (trans. Susan H. Ray), *My soul is a woman: the feminine in Islam*, Continuum, 1997.
Schirilla, Nausikaa, *Die Frau, das Andere der Vernunft?: Frauenbilder in der arabisch-islamischen und europäischen Philosophie*, IKO-Verlag für Interkulturelle Kommunikation, 1996.
Schleifer, Aliah, *Motherhood in Islam*, Fons Vitae, 1996.
Schleifer, Aliah, *Mary, the Blessed Virgin of Islam*, Fons Vitae, 1998.
Schöning-Kalender, Claudia, Aylâ Neusel & Mechtild M. Jansen (eds.), *Feminismus, Islam, Nation: Frauenbewegungen im Maghreb, in Zentralasien und in der Türkei*, Campus, 1997.
Scott, Joan Wallach, *Gender and the politics of history*, Columbia University Press, 1988.
De Seife, R., *The Shari'a: an introduction to the law of Islam*, Austin & Winfield, 1993.
Seikaly, May, 'Women and social change in Bahrain', in *The International Journal of Middle East Studies*, 26, no. 3, pp 415-426.
Sells, Michael (trans.), *Approaching the Qur'an: the early revelations*, White Cloud Press, 1999.
Seteney, Shami, et al, *Women, work and social position in Arab society: case studies from Egypt, Jordan and Sudan*, UNESCO, 1990.
Shaaban, Bouthaina (ed.), *Both right and left handed: Arab women talk about their lives*, Indiana University Press, 1991.
Shaarawi, Huda (ed. Margot Badran), *Feminists, Islam, and nation: gender and the making of modern Egypt*, Princeton University Press 1995.
Shadid, W. A. R., & P. S. van Koningsveld (eds.), *Political participation and identities of Muslims in non-Muslim states*, Kok Pharos, 1997.
Shafik, Doria, *Egyptian feminist: a woman apart*, American University in Cairo Press, 1996.
Shah, Nik Noriani Nik Badli, *Women as judges*, Sisters in Islam, 2002.
Shah, Saira, *The storyteller's daughter*, Anchor, 2004.
Shaham, R., *Family and the courts in modern Egypt: a study based on decisions by the Shari'a courts, 1900-1955*, E. J. Brill, 1997.
Shahidian, Hammed, 'The Iranian Left and the "Woman Question" in the Revolution of 1978-79', in *The International Journal of Middle East Studies*, vol. 26, no. 2, pp 223-247.
Shahidian, Hammed, *Women in Iran*, Greenwood Press, 2002.
Shakir, Evelyn, *Bint Arab: Arab and Arab American women in the United States*, Praeger, 1997.
Shamy, H., *Tales Arab women tell and the behavioral patterns they portray*, Indiana University Press, 1999.

Sharma, Arvind (ed.), *Today's woman in world religions*, State University of New York Press, 1994.

Sharma, S. Ram, *Women's education in the Ancient and Muslim period*, Discovery, 1996.

Sharoni, Simona, *Gender and the Israeli-Palestinian conflict: the politics of women's resistance*, Syracuse University Press, 1995.

al-Shati, Bint, *Wives of the Prophet*, Muhammad Ashraf, 1971.

Shehab, Rafi Ullah, *Rights of women in Islamic shariah*, Indus, 1986.

Shehadeh, Lamia Rustum, *The idea of women in fundamentalist Islam*, University Press of Florida, 2003.

Sheikh, N. M., *Woman in Muslim society*, International Islamic Publishers, 1987.

Shell-Duncan, Bettina, & Ylva Hernlund (eds.), *Female 'circumcision' in Africa: culture, controversy and change*, Lynne Rienner, 2000.

Shukri, S., *Social changes and women in the Middle East: state policy, education, economics and development*, Ashgate, 1999.

Siapno, Jacqueline Aquino, *Gender, Islam, nationalism and the state in Aceh: the paradox of power, co-optation and resistance*, Curzon, 2002.

Siddiqi, M.Z., *Hadith literature: its origin, development, special features and criticism*, Islamic Texts Society, 1993.

Siddiqi, Mohammad Mazheruddin, *Women in Islam*, Institute of Islamic Culture, 1992.

Siddiqi, Muhammad Saeed, *The modest status of women in Islam*, Kazi, 1991.

Siddique, Kaukab, *Liberation of women through Islam*, American Society for Education and Religion, 1990.

Siddiqui, Ataullah, *Christian-Muslim dialogue in the twentieth century*, Palgrave Macmillan, 1997.

Siddiqui, K., *The struggle of Muslim women*, American Society for Education and Religion, 1985.

Siddiqui, M. S., *The blessed women of Islam*, Kazi, 1982.

Siddiqui, Muhammad Iqbal, *Islam forbids free mixing of men and women*, Kazi, 1990.

Siddiqui, Muhammad Iqbal, *Marriage and family life in Islam*, Bilal Books, 1996.

Sikri, Rehana, *Women in Islamic culture and society: a study of family, feminism and franchise*, Kanishka, 1999.

Singh, Alka, *Women in Muslim personal law*, Rawat, 1992.

Skaine, Rosemary, *The women of Afghanistan under the Taliban*, McFarland, 2002.

Small, A. H., *Islam in India*, 1888.

Smith, Margaret, *Muslim women mystics: the life and work of Rábi'a and other women mystics in Islám*, Oneworld, 2001.

Snouck Hurgronje, Christian, *Selected works*, E. J. Brill, 1957.

Snouck Hurgronje, Christiaan, *Bijdragen tot de taal- en volkenkunde van Nederlandsch-India*, Bonn-Leipzig, 1923.

El-Solh, Camillia Fawzi, & Judy Mabro (eds.), *Muslim women's choices: religious belief and social reality*, Berg, 1994.

Sonbol, Amira El-Azhary (ed.), *Women, the family, and divorce laws in Islamic history*, Syracuse University Press, 1996.

Sonbol, Amira El-Azhary, *Women of Jordan: Islam, labor and the law*, Syracuse University Press, 2003.

Soorma, C. A., *Status of woman in world religions and civilizations*, Dar-ul-Isha'at-Kutub-e-Islamia, 1996.

Souad, *Burned alive; a victim of the law of men*, Warner, 2004.
de Souza, Eunice, *Purdah: an anthology*, Oxford University Press, 2004.
Special bulletin on fundamentalism and secularism in South Asia, Women Living Under Muslim Laws: Shirkat Gah, 1992.
Spellberg, D. A., *Politics, gender, and the Islamic past: the legacy of 'A'isha Bint Abi Bakr*, Columbia University Press, 1994.
Stowasser, Barbara Freyer, *Women in the Qur'an, traditions, and interpretation,* Oxford University Press, 1994.
Stowasser, Barbara Freyer, 'Women and citizenship in the Qur'an', in Amira El-Azhary Sonbol (ed.), *Women, the family and divorce laws in Islamic history*, 1996.
Stowasser, Barbara Freyer, *Women in the Qur'an: traditions, and interpretation*, Oxford University Press, 1996.
Strawson, John, *Encountering Islamic law*, University of East London Law Department, Research Publication Series, 1996.
Strum, Phillipa, *The women are marching: the second sex and the Palestinian revolution*, Lawrence Hill Books, New York, 1992.
Subbamma, Malladi (trans. M. V. Ramamurty), *Islam and women*, Sterling Publishers, 1988.
Swarup, Ram, *Woman in Islam*, Voice of India, 2000.
Sweetman, Caroline (ed.), *Gender, religion and spirituality*, Oxfam, 1999.
Swisher, Clarice (ed.), *The spread of Islam*, Greenhaven Press, 1999.
Syed, Mohammad Ali, *The position of women in Islam: a progressive view*, State University of New York Press, 2004.

Tabari, Azar, & Nahid Yeganeh, *In the shadow of Islam: the women's movement in Iran*, Zed Books, 1982.
Tabataba'i, Hossein Modarressi, *An introduction to Shi'i law: a bibliographical study*, Ithaca, 1984.
Tahar, Mansouri, 'Byzantine women in the Muslim world: an onomastic study', *Journal of Oriental and African Studies*, 11, Athens, 2000.
Talatoff, Kamran, 'Iranian women's literature: from pre-revolutionary social discourse to post-revolutionary feminism', in *International Journal of Middle East Studies*, vol. 29, no. 4, pp 531-558.
Talatoff, Kamran, *Contemporary debates in Islam*, Palgrave Macmillan, 1999.
Teaching about Islam and Muslims in the public school classroom: a handbook for educators, Council on Islamic Education, 1995.
Tekeli, Sirin (ed.), *Women in modern Turkish society: a reader*, Zed Books, 1995.
Thomson, Ahmad, *The wives of the Prophet Muhammad*, Ta-Ha, 1993.
Thompson, Elizabeth, *Colonial citizens: republican rights, paternal privilege, and gender in French Syria and Lebanon*, History and Society of the Modern Middle East series, Columbia University Press, 2000.
Thornhill, Teresa, *Making women talk: the interrogation of Palestinian detainees by the Israeli general security services*, Lawyers for Palestinian Human Rights, London, 1992.
Tjomsland, Marit, *The educated way of thinking: individualisation and Islamism in Tunisia*, DERAP, Chr. Michelsen Institute, 1993.
Tokhtakhodjaeva, Marfua (trans. Sufian Aslam), *Between the slogans of communism and the laws of Islam*, Women Living Under Muslim Laws, 1995.

Training the women [sic] *to know her place*, (sound recording), Pacifica Radio Archive, 1983.

Tucker, Judith, *Women in nineteenth century Egypt*, Cambridge University Press, 1985.

Tucker, Judith (ed.), *Arab Women: Old Boundaries, New Frontiers*, Indiana University Press, 1993.

Tucker, Judith, *In the house of the law: gender and islamic law in Ottoman Syria and Palestine*, University of California Press, 1998.

Turabi, Hasan, *Women in Islam and Muslim society*, Milestones Publications, London, 1991.

Turner, Bryan S., *Orientalism, postmodernism and globalism*, Routledge, 1994.

Tuwayjiri, Abd al-Aziz ibn Uthman, *Women in Islam and their status in the islamic society = L'Islam et le statut de la femme et sa place dans la société*, ISESCO, 1993.

Umri, Sayed Jalaluddin, *The rights of Muslim women: an appraisal*, Kitab Bhavan, n.d.

Understanding Islam and the Muslims, Embassy of Saudi Arabia, Washington DC, 1989.

Uthman, S., *The laws of marriage in Islam*, Dar Al Taqwa, 1995.

Varoqua, Khair-Eddin, *Islam revisited*, Vantage Press, 2001.

Venkatraman, Bharathi Anandhi, 'Islamic states and the United Nations convention on the elimination of all forms of discrimination against women', *American University Law Review*, 1988 (1995).

Vertovec, Steven, & Ceri Peach (eds.), *Islam in Europe*, Palgrave Macmillan, 1997.

Vertovec, Steven, & Alisdair Rogers (eds.), *Muslim European youth*, Ashgate, 1998.

Vesey-Fitzgerald, Seymour, *Muhammadan law: an abridgement according to its various schools*, Oxford University Press, 1931.

Vesey-Fitzgerald, Seymour, 'The alleged debt of Islamic to Roman law', *Law Quarterly Review*, 67, 1951, pp 81–102.

Visram, R., *Women in India and Pakistan: the struggle for independence from British rule*, Cambridge University Press, 1997.

de Vitray-Meyerovitch, Eva, *Towards the heart of Islam: a woman's approach*, Fons Vitae, 2002.

Vogel, F., *Islamic law and legal system: studies of Saudi Arabia*, E. J. Brill, 2000.

Vreede-de Stuers, Cora, *Parda: a study of Muslim women's life in northern India*, Humanities Press, 1968.

Waddy, Charis, *Women in Muslim history*, Longmans, 1980.

Wadud, Amina, *Qur'an and woman: rereading the sacred text from a woman's perspective*, Oxford University Press, 1999.

Walbridge, Linda, 'Sex and the single Shi'ite: mut'a marriage in an American Lebanese Shi'ite community', in Aswad, Barbara, & Barbara Bilge (eds.), *Family and gender among American Muslims: issues facing Middle Eastern immigrants and their descendants*, Temple University, 1996.

Walther, Wiebke, *Women in Islam*, M. Wiener, 1993.

Wani, M.A., *Maintenance rights of Muslim women: principles*, Precedents & Trends, 1987.

Wansbrough, J., *Qur'anic studies: sources and methods of scriptural interpretation*, Cambridge University Press, 1977.

Warnock, Kitty, 'Land before honor: Palestinian women in the occupied territories', *Monthly Review Press*, 1990.

Watt, W. Montgomery, *Bell's introduction to the Qur'an*, Edinburgh University Press, 1970.
Watt, W. Montgomery, *Muhammad: Prophet and statesman*, Oxford University Press, 1974.
Watt, W. Montgomery, *Muhammad at Medina*, Oxford University Press, 1988.
Waugh, Earle H., 'The imam in the new world: models and modifications', in F. E. Reynolds (ed.), *Transitions and transformations in the history of religions*, E. J. Brill, 1980.
Waugh, Earle W., et al (eds.), *The Muslim community in North America*, University of Alberta Press, Edmonton, 1983.
Waugh, Earle W., & R. B. Quereshi (eds.), *Muslim families in North America*, University of Alberta Press, 1991.
Webb, Gisela (ed.), *Windows of faith: Muslim women scholar-activists in North America*, Syracuse University Press, 2000.
Weiss, Bernard G., *The spirit of Islamic law*, University of Georgia Press, 1998.
Weiss, Walter M., *Islam: an illustrated historical overview*, Barron's, 2000.
Wheeler, Brannon M. (ed.), *Teaching Islam*, Oxford University Press, 2003.
White, Jenny B., *Money makes us relatives: women's labor in urban Turkey*, University of Texas Press, 1994.
Wieringa, Saskia, *Sexual politics in Indonesia*, Palgrave, 2002.
Wilcox, Lynn, *Women and the Holy Quran: a Sufi perspective,* M.T.O. Shahmaghsoudi, 1998.
Winters, Paul A. (ed.), *Islam: opposing viewpoints*, Greenhaven Press, 1995.
Wolfe, Michael, *One Thousand Roads to Mecca*, Grove Press, 2000.
Women and Islam in Muslim societies, Ministry of Foreign Affairs, Development Cooperation Information Dept., The Hague, Netherlands, 1994.
Women in musaajid and Islam, Mujlisul-Ulema/Young Men's Muslim Association, 1988.
Women in society according to Islam and Christianity: acts of a Muslim-Christian colloquium organized jointly by the Pontifical Council for Interreligious Dialogue (Vatican City) and the Royal Academy for Islamic Civilization Research Al Albait Foundation (Amman) 24-26 June 1992, Rome, 1992.
Women in the villages, men in the towns, UNESCO, 1984.
Women, Islam and equality, The National Council of Resistance of Iran, 1995.
Wood, M. M., *In desert and town: life in Moslem lands*, United Council for Missionary Education, 1925.
Woodsmall, Ruth Frances, *Women in the changing Islamic system*, Bimla Publishing House, 1983.

Yacoob, May, *Ahmadiyya and urbanization: migrant women in Abidjan,* African Studies Center, Boston University, 1983.
Yamani, Mai (ed.), *Feminism and Islam: legal and literary perspectives*, Ithaca Press, 1996.
Yasgur, Batya Swift, *Behind the burqa: our life in Afghanistan and how we escaped to freedom*, Wiley, 2002.
Yazdi, Misbah, *Status of women in Islam*, Islamic Propagation Organization, 1985.
Young, Elise G., *Keepers of the history: Women and the Israeli-Palestinian conflict*, NYC, Teachers College Press, 1992.
Young, Katherine K., & Arvind Sharma, *Images of the feminine — mythic, philosophic and human — in the Buddhist, Hindu, and Islamic traditions: a bibliography of women in India*, New Horizons Press, 1974.

Zaidi, Syed M. H., *Position of woman under Islam: being an exhaustive survey of the position of woman under Islam in every walk of life based on the Holy Quoran, tradition, history, and other records*, Premier Book House, 1978.

Zakaria, Rafiq, et al., *The trial of Benazir Bhutto: an insight into the status of women in Islam*, Pelanduk Publications, 1990.

Al-Zayat, Faruk Muhammad, *Mutter der Glaubigen*, Munich, n.d.

Zebiri, Kate, *Muslims and Christians face to face*, Oneworld, 1997.

Zeghidour, Slimane, *Le voile et la bannière*, Hachette, 1994.

Zia, Afiya Shehrbano, *Sex crime in the Islamic context: rape, class and gender in Pakistan*, ASR, 1994.

Ziadeh, F. J., 'usul al-fiqh', *Oxford encyclopedia of the modern Islamic world*, Oxford, 1995.

Zilfi, Madeline C., *Women in the Ottoman Empire: Middle Eastern women in the early modern era*, E. J. Brill, 1997.

Zolan, Alexandra J., 'The effect of Islamization on the legal and social status of women in Iran', *Third World Law Journal*, 183, 1987.

Zomeno, Amalia, 'Kafa'a in the Maliki School: a fatwa from fifteenth century Fez', in R. Gleave & E. Kermeli (eds.), *Islamic law: theory and practice*, I. B. Tauris, 1997.

Zouilai, Kaddour, *Des voiles et des serrures: de la fermeture en Islam*, L'Harmattan, 1990.

Zoya, Hasan, & Ritu Menon, *Unequal citizens: a study of Muslim women in India*, Oxford University Press, 2004.

Zoya, John Follain, & Rita Cristofari, *Zoya's story: an Afghan woman's struggle for freedom*, William Morrow, 2002.

Al-Zwaini, Laila, & Rudolph Peters, *A bibliography of Islamic law, 1980-1993*, E. J. Brill, 1994.

Zweigert, K., & H. Kotz, 'Islamic Law', in *An introduction to comparative law*, Oxford, 1987.

Zwemer, Samuel M., & Annie Van Sommer, *Our Moslem sisters: a cry from lands of darkness interpreted by those who heard it*, Fleming H. Revell, 1907.

Zwemer, Samuel M., *Islam: a challenge to faith*, Student Volunteer Movement, 1908.

Zwemer, Dr. & Mrs. Samuel M., *Moslem women*, Central Committee on the United Study of Foreign Missions, 1926.

Index

INDEX

al-Ḥarra 189
Ḥārūn, sister of *see* Mary
Ḥasan 172
hate 36, 54, 66
Hawā *see* Eve 165
head(s): of the Prophet 97; shaving of 32; exposing 48; raised during prayer 72; washing 120
healing effects of kohl 179
heart 136, 132, 60; diseased 153; covered up 125
heathen woman 109
heaven 35-7, 109, 148-3, 180, 186
heir(s) 104-6; of father 17; of the Prophet 105; destitute 106; wealthy 106
hell 35-7, 148-52, 180, 202; envoys of 33; fires of 121-2; inhabitants of 35-7, 91
helmet, broken 140
Helpers 171
helpless, care for 109-10
hereditary feature 134
heretic 72
hiding: at night 118; from God 125; oneself 125
hijra 38, 157, 171, 181
Hilāl ibn ᶜUmayya 15, 80; wife of 15, 80
Hind bint ᶜUtba 110
hirer of asses 40-1
hiring of employee 92
Hishām ibn al-Mughīra: tribe of 121; tribe of, daughter of 121
Holy Spirit 203
holy war 180
homage: of women believers 128; to the Prophet 29; verbal 128
home, house(s) 153; of dead husband 148; right to stay in 148; of the Prophet 155; of the Prophet's wives 153; of ᶜĀ'isha 132; of Ḥafṣa 132; of Umm Salama 135; providing 67; cast from 23
homosexual affair 62
homosexuals 202
honeymoon 184
honour: perverted sense of 197; sleight on 19
hooves 131
horn of Satan 132, 200
horse(s): cavalry 111; evil omen 92; of pedigree 100
houris 36, 180, 202
house(s): of ᶜĀ'isha 114-5, 200; of Ḥafṣa 132; of wife 194; of husband 107; of the Prophet 126; of the Prophet's wives 66, 131; enclosure of the Prophet's 132; entering of 110; food from 125; mourning in 27
household 186; duties 186; of nobleman 169; member of 168; members of the Prophet's 153
Ḥubaira, son of 92
Ḥudaibiya 27, 192; terms of 87
Hudhail, tribe of 41
human beings 98, 198-9
hunger 119
Ḥusain 172
husband 12, 15-16, 18, 23, 25-7, 30, 36, 46, 49, 51, 54, 59, 61, 68, 95, 113, 167-8 177-80, 189, 206; of Christian woman 51; property of 143; consent of 96; possessions of 110; responsibility of 107; return to wife after absence 103; sister of 117; betrayal from wife 140; calling wife to bed 84; dead 28, 31; demand for dowry 114; gift to wife 114; jealous 92; killed 85; miserly 110; possessive 92; sons of 46; ingratitude to 91; describing a woman to 118; feelings for wives 204; children of 183; absent 186; acting like a fool 178; coming at night to family 195; death of 147-8; divorcing wife 177; incompetent 178; obligation of 204; proving false to 202; *and see* spouses, men
husband-to-be 70
hygiene 11-3
hypocrite 139, 149, 161

Ibn ᶜAbbās 12, 48, 51, 54, 59-61, 75, 113, 125, 134, 140
Ibnat Abū Ṣabra 29, 180
Ibn Hishām 98, 172
Ibn Juraij 52
Ibn Kaᶜb ibn Mālik 143
Ibn Masᶜūd 30, 100, 172, 175
Ibn Shihāb 16, 82
Ibn Sīrīn 11, 54, 61, 172
Ibn ᶜUmar 23, 24, 84
Ibn ᶜUmar ibn al-Khaṭṭāb 19, 172
Ibrāhim 11, 46, 54, 112, 114; son of the Prophet 10; *and see* Abraham
Ibrāhim al-Sā'igh 51
ignorance 33, 163
ill luck 193
illness 55, 89, 104-5, 110, 120, 156, 193; of the Prophet 114, 131, 141
ill-treatment of wife 15, 26
ill will of women 158
imam, reponsibility of 107
immoral: acts 123, 52-3, 61, 158; conduct of wife 204
impious people 88
impotence 26, 134
imprisonment of cat 37
impurity, ritual 94, 187, 201
ᶜImrān 143; daughter of 144; line of 141
in-laws, woman's male 118
incompetence 113
indemnity 181
infancy, children died in 122
infection, eye 27
ingratitude to husbands 91
inhabitants: of hell 37; of Medina 101; of Paradise 101
inheritance 57, 104-6, 159; rights of 16; against wives' will 158
injured party 41, 181
injustice, witness to 115
innocence 169
insanity 78
insults 157
intelligence, woman's lack in 91
intention 38
interest *see* loans
interruption in prayer 127
invention against God 162-3
invitation 70, 155
iron ring 63; as dowry 185
irrevocable *see* divorce
Īsā *see* Jesus
Ishmael, mother of 201
Islam 170-5, 180, 197; coming of 68; champions of 137
Islamic women 200
Israelites 12, 44, 83, 140, 201; women of 50; *and see* Jews
istibḍāᶜ 186

Jābir 104, 189
Jābir ibn ᶜAbdullāh 53, 62, 75
Jābir ibn Zaid 61, 81, 172
Jaᶜfar 29

INDEX

62; respect for 206; name used as abuse 101; vow to do the *ḥājj* 76; best of companionship 88; death in childbirth 121; divorced 18; sex with 62; marriage of own 61; forbidden in marriage 60; over-angry 122; of children died in infancy 122; nursing 148; body of 160, 163; wombs of 205; rightful 186; the Prophet's wives as 160; of the Faithful 76, 88, 90, 98, 203; *and see* foster-, milk-, parents
mourner, wages of 112;
mourning 27-9, 31-2, 179
moustache 126, 198
mouth 160, 198; of wife 106
Mu'tamar, father of 11
Muʿādh 180
Muʿāwiya 88, 137
Muʿāwiya ibn Abū Sufyān 50
al-Mughīra 41
Mughīth 54
Muḥammad *see* Prophet Muḥammad
Muḥammad ibn ʿAbād ibn Jaʿfar 125
Muḥammad ibn Maslama 96
muḥarrama 17, 177
Mujāhid 24, 52
murder *see* killing
Mūsā *see* Moses
musk 13; sweating 35
Muslim, compiler of ḥadīths 173
Muslim(s) 7, 40, 52, 70, 75, 87, 90, 105, 109, 111, 128, 154, 170-5, 183, 157, 203-4, *passim*; women 16, 86, 118, 136-4; slaves/freemen 99; warriors 157; leaders 76, 191, 200; true 198; community 75; state 174; becoming 51; Shīʿi 184-5, 200, 205
al-Mustaʿliq, tribe of 10, 83
mutʿa 183, 185
mysteries 154

al-Naḍir 111; clan of 111
al-Nadr, daughter of 41
Nāfiʿ 41
nag 167
name(s) 136; of mother as abuse 101; of fathers 160
nature, call of 118, 125, 132, 156, 157
neck 111
neighbour 100; gift of 118
nephew 109
New Testament 202
Next World 85-6, 136, 142
niece *see* daughter
night 35, 80, 166; going out at 118; going to mosques at 91; *and see* turn
nightfall 80
Noah 141; wife of 167, 202; ark 205
noble: descent, of woman 64; person of Israelites 44; woman of beauty 133
nobleman 169
nomads 54
non-Arabs 182
non-virgin slave girl 39
nose, blowing of 35
nose-rein 28
Nūḥ *see* Noah
al-Nuʿmān ibn Bashīr 115; parents of 115
nursing mother 148
nursing the sick 117

oath: of allegiance 164; of divorce 20-1, 177, 190; of friendship 64; to God 20
obeying: by women 158; God 136; ʿĀ'isha 136
obligation 77; of husband 204
occupants of hell 36
offal 139
offer of betrothal 147
offspring 18; of Maryam 142; of slaves 55; of noble blood 69; of God 205; attributed to God 163; of believers 150
old age 77
old women 152
onagers 184
opinion: of the Prophet 109; legal 77
opponents of the Prophet 198
oppressed person 15
oppression of wives 158
oppressive circumstances 130
oppressor 15
option of divorce 21, 54
orchard 25
organ, sexual 157
ornaments 46
orphan 57; female 58, 184; estate of 86; unattractive 58; slave girl 197
outbidding 54
owner: of slave 82; of female slave 30, 40, 84, 94, 99
oxen, acquisition of 111

pact 87; with the Prophet 51
pact-polytheists 52
pagan 143, 197; Arabs 198
pain, labour 17, 160, 166
palm: tree(s) 111-2; trunk 166; grove 192
pantheon 198, 205
parable 143, 202
Paradise 11, 35, 85, 138, 148-9; people of 36, 48, 101, 141; original inhabitants of 201; maidens of 36, 180
parents 17, 57, 160; of ʿĀ'isha 22; treating respectfully 160; consultation with 14; cursing 88; as only heirs 104-5
parting, after temporary marriage 62
partner in marriage 25
passion 167-2
paternal aunts 60, 65, 154
paternal foster-uncle 132
paternal relatives 61
paternal uncles 154
paternity: denied 177; doubted 133
path of righteousness 61
patronage 99, 113
pavilion of jewels 138
payer of women behind men 197
payment: of bequests 104-5; of debts 104-5; of slave girl's value 40; to departed wives 164; for conjugal rights 177
peace 149, 151, 159; settlement 52; offering 193
pearl-barley 87
pearls 150-1
penalty 80, 189-90; for unlawful sex 191; fixed 39; for immoral conduct 61; legal 44; retaliatory 41
penance 130
penetration, sexual 74, 188-9
Peoples of the Book 94, 152-7
perfection, attaining 144
perfume 31, 116, 124
period 176, 192, 11; of pregnancy 17; of swearing off one's wives 24; mourning 27; *and see* menstrual period

Index of Qur'ānic Selections